Alexandra Cotofana, James M. Nyce (eds.)

RELIGION AND MAGIC IN SOCIALIST AND POST-SOCIALIST CONTEXTS I

Historic and Ethnographic Case Studies of Orthodoxy, Heterodoxy, and Alternative Spirituality

With a foreword by Patrick Lally Michelson

ibidem-Verlag
Stuttgart

Bibliografische Information der Deutschen Nationalbibliothek
Die Deutsche Nationalbibliothek verzeichnet diese Publikation in der Deutschen Nationalbibliografie; detaillierte bibliografische Daten sind im Internet über http://dnb.d-nb.de abrufbar.

Bibliographic information published by the Deutsche Nationalbibliothek
Die Deutsche Nationalbibliothek lists this publication in the Deutsche Nationalbibliografie; detailed bibliographic data are available in the Internet at http://dnb.d-nb.de.

Cover picture: © Aziz Fatnassi. Reprint with kind permission.

∞

Gedruckt auf alterungsbeständigem, säurefreien Papier
Printed on acid-free paper

ISSN: 1614-3515

ISBN-13: 978-3-8382-0989-0

© *ibidem*-Verlag

Stuttgart 2017

Alle Rechte vorbehalten

Das Werk einschließlich aller seiner Teile ist urheberrechtlich geschützt. Jede Verwertung außerhalb der engen Grenzen des Urheberrechtsgesetzes ist ohne Zustimmung des Verlages unzulässig und strafbar. Dies gilt insbesondere für Vervielfältigungen, Übersetzungen, Mikroverfilmungen und elektronische Speicherformen sowie die Einspeicherung und Verarbeitung in elektronischen Systemen.

All rights reserved. No part of this publication may be reproduced, stored in or introduced into a retrieval system, or transmitted, in any form, or by any means (electronic, mechanical, photocopying, recording or otherwise) without the prior written permission of the publisher. Any person who does any unauthorized act in relation to this publication may be liable to criminal prosecution and civil claims for damages.

Printed in the EU

Soviet and Post-Soviet Politics and Society (SPPS) Vol. 163
ISSN 1614-3515

General Editor: Andreas Umland,
Institute for Euro-Atlantic Cooperation, Kyiv, umland@stanfordalumni.org

Commissioning Editor: Max Jakob Horstmann,
London, mjh@ibidem.eu

EDITORIAL COMMITTEE*

DOMESTIC & COMPARATIVE POLITICS
Prof. **Ellen Bos**, *Andrássy University of Budapest*
Dr. **Ingmar Bredies**, *FH Bund, Brühl*
Dr. **Andrey Kazantsev**, *MGIMO (U) MID RF, Moscow*
Prof. **Heiko Pleines**, *University of Bremen*
Prof. **Richard Sakwa**, *University of Kent at Canterbury*
Dr. **Sarah Whitmore**, *Oxford Brookes University*
Dr. **Harald Wydra**, *University of Cambridge*

SOCIETY, CLASS & ETHNICITY
Col. **David Glantz**, *"Journal of Slavic Military Studies"*
Dr. **Marlène Laruelle**, *George Washington University*
Dr. **Stephen Shulman**, *Southern Illinois University*
Prof. **Stefan Troebst**, *University of Leipzig*

POLITICAL ECONOMY & PUBLIC POLICY
Prof. em. **Marshall Goldman**, *Wellesley College, Mass.*
Dr. **Andreas Goldthau**, *Central European University*
Dr. **Robert Kravchuk**, *University of North Carolina*
Dr. **David Lane**, *University of Cambridge*
Dr. **Carol Leonard**, *Higher School of Economics, Moscow*
Dr. **Maria Popova**, *McGill University, Montreal*

FOREIGN POLICY & INTERNATIONAL AFFAIRS
Dr. **Peter Duncan**, *University College London*
Prof. **Andreas Heinemann-Grüder**, *University of Bonn*
Dr. **Taras Kuzio**, *Johns Hopkins University*
Prof. **Gerhard Mangott**, *University of Innsbruck*
Dr. **Diana Schmidt-Pfister**, *University of Konstanz*
Dr. **Lisbeth Tarlow**, *Harvard University, Cambridge*
Dr. **Christian Wipperfürth**, *N-Ost Network, Berlin*
Dr. **William Zimmerman**, *University of Michigan*

HISTORY, CULTURE & THOUGHT
Dr. **Catherine Andreyev**, *University of Oxford*
Prof. **Mark Bassin**, *Södertörn University*
Prof. **Karsten Brüggemann**, *Tallinn University*
Dr. **Alexander Etkind**, *University of Cambridge*
Dr. **Gasan Gusejnov**, *Moscow State University*
Prof. em. **Walter Laqueur**, *Georgetown University*
Prof. **Leonid Luks**, *Catholic University of Eichstaett*
Dr. **Olga Malinova**, *Russian Academy of Sciences*
Prof. **Andrei Rogatchevski**, *University of Tromsø*
Dr. **Mark Tauger**, *West Virginia University*

ADVISORY BOARD*
Prof. **Dominique Arel**, *University of Ottawa*
Prof. **Jörg Baberowski**, *Humboldt University of Berlin*
Prof. **Margarita Balmaceda**, *Seton Hall University*
Dr. **John Barber**, *University of Cambridge*
Prof. **Timm Beichelt**, *European University Viadrina*
Dr. **Katrin Boeckh**, *University of Munich*
Prof. em. **Archie Brown**, *University of Oxford*
Dr. **Vyacheslav Bryukhovetsky**, *Kyiv-Mohyla Academy*
Prof. **Timothy Colton**, *Harvard University, Cambridge*
Prof. **Paul D'Anieri**, *University of Florida*
Dr. **Heike Dörrenbächer**, *Friedrich Naumann Foundation*
Dr. **John Dunlop**, *Hoover Institution, Stanford, California*
Dr. **Sabine Fischer**, *SWP, Berlin*
Dr. **Geir Flikke**, *NUPI, Oslo*
Prof. **David Galbreath**, *University of Aberdeen*
Prof. **Alexander Galkin**, *Russian Academy of Sciences*
Prof. **Frank Golczewski**, *University of Hamburg*
Dr. **Nikolas Gvosdev**, *Naval War College, Newport, RI*
Prof. **Mark von Hagen**, *Arizona State University*
Dr. **Guido Hausmann**, *University of Munich*
Prof. **Dale Herspring**, *Kansas State University*
Dr. **Stefani Hoffman**, *Hebrew University of Jerusalem*
Prof. **Mikhail Ilyin**, *MGIMO (U) MID RF, Moscow*
Prof. **Vladimir Kantor**, *Higher School of Economics*
Dr. **Ivan Katchanovski**, *University of Ottawa*
Prof. em. **Andrzej Korbonski**, *University of California*
Dr. **Iris Kempe**, *"Caucasus Analytical Digest"*
Prof. **Herbert Küpper**, *Institut für Ostrecht Regensburg*
Dr. **Rainer Lindner**, *CEEER, Berlin*
Dr. **Vladimir Malakhov**, *Russian Academy of Sciences*

Dr. **Luke March**, *University of Edinburgh*
Prof. **Michael McFaul**, *Stanford University, Palo Alto*
Prof. **Birgit Menzel**, *University of Mainz-Germersheim*
Prof. **Valery Mikhailenko**, *The Urals State University*
Prof. **Emil Pain**, *Higher School of Economics, Moscow*
Dr. **Oleg Podvintsev**, *Russian Academy of Sciences*
Prof. **Olga Popova**, *St. Petersburg State University*
Dr. **Alex Pravda**, *University of Oxford*
Dr. **Erik van Ree**, *University of Amsterdam*
Dr. **Joachim Rogall**, *Robert Bosch Foundation Stuttgart*
Prof. **Peter Rutland**, *Wesleyan University, Middletown*
Prof. **Marat Salikov**, *The Urals State Law Academy*
Dr. **Gwendolyn Sasse**, *University of Oxford*
Prof. **Jutta Scherrer**, *EHESS, Paris*
Prof. **Robert Service**, *University of Oxford*
Mr. **James Sherr**, *RIIA Chatham House London*
Dr. **Oxana Shevel**, *Tufts University, Medford*
Prof. **Eberhard Schneider**, *University of Siegen*
Prof. **Olexander Shnyrkov**, *Shevchenko University, Kyiv*
Prof. **Hans-Henning Schröder**, *SWP, Berlin*
Prof. **Yuri Shapoval**, *Ukrainian Academy of Sciences*
Prof. **Viktor Shnirelman**, *Russian Academy of Sciences*
Dr. **Lisa Sundstrom**, *University of British Columbia*
Dr. **Philip Walters**, *"Religion, State and Society"*, *Oxford*
Prof. **Zenon Wasyliw**, *Ithaca College, New York State*
Dr. **Lucan Way**, *University of Toronto*
Dr. **Markus Wehner**, *"Frankfurter Allgemeine Zeitung"*
Dr. **Andrew Wilson**, *University College London*
Prof. **Jan Zielonka**, *University of Oxford*
Prof. **Andrei Zorin**, *University of Oxford*

* While the Editorial Committee and Advisory Board support the General Editor in the choice and improvement of manuscripts for publication, responsibility for remaining errors and misinterpretations in the series' volumes lies with the books' authors.

Soviet and Post-Soviet Politics and Society (SPPS)
ISSN 1614-3515

Founded in 2004 and refereed since 2007, SPPS makes available affordable English-, German-, and Russian-language studies on the history of the countries of the former Soviet bloc from the late Tsarist period to today. It publishes between 5 and 20 volumes per year and focuses on issues in transitions to and from democracy such as economic crisis, identity formation, civil society development, and constitutional reform in CEE and the NIS. SPPS also aims to highlight so far understudied themes in East European studies such as right-wing radicalism, religious life, higher education, or human rights protection. The authors and titles of all previously published volumes are listed at the end of this book. For a full description of the series and reviews of its books, see www.ibidem-verlag.de/red/spps.

Editorial correspondence & manuscripts should be sent to: Dr. Andreas Umland, Institute for Euro-Atlantic Cooperation, vul. Volodymyrska 42, off. 21, UA-01030 Kyiv, Ukraine

Business correspondence & review copy requests should be sent to: *ibidem* Press, Leuschnerstr. 40, 30457 Hannover, Germany; tel.: +49 511 2622200; fax: +49 511 2622201; spps@ibidem.eu.

Authors, reviewers, referees, and editors for (as well as all other persons sympathetic to) SPPS are invited to join its networks at www.facebook.com/group.php?gid=52638198614 www.linkedin.com/groups?about=&gid=103012 www.xing.com/net/spps-ibidem-verlag/

Recent Volumes

162 *Natalya Ryabinska*
Ukraine's Post-Communist Mass Media
Between Capture and Commercialization
With a foreword by Marta Dyczok
ISBN 978-3-8382-1011-7

163 *Alexandra Cotofana, James M. Nyce (eds.)*
Religion and Magic in Socialist and Post-Socialist Contexts I
Historic and Ethnographic Case Studies of Orthodoxy, Heterodoxy, and Alternative Spirituality
With a foreword by Patrick L. Michelson
ISBN 978-3-8382-0989-0

164 *Nozima Akhrarkhodjaeva*
The Instrumentalisation of Mass Media in Electoral Authoritarian Regimes
Evidence from Russia's Presidential Election Campaigns of 2000 and 2008
ISBN 978-3-8382-1013-1

165 *Yulia Krasheninnikova*
Informal Healthcare in Contemporary Russia
Sociographic Essays on the Post-Soviet Infrastructure for Alternative Healing Practices
ISBN 978-3-8382-0970-8

166 *Peter Kaiser*
Das Schachbrett der Macht
Die Handlungsspielräume eines sowjetischen Funktionärs unter Stalin am Beispiel des Generalsekretärs des Komsomol Aleksandr Kosarev (1929-1938)
Mit einem Vorwort von Dietmar Neutatz
ISBN 978-3-8382-1052-0

167 *Oksana Kim*
The Effects and Implications of Kazakhstan's Adoption of International Financial Reporting Standards
A Resource Dependence Perspective
With a foreword by Svetlana Vlady
ISBN 978-3-8382-0987-6

168 *Anna Sanina*
Patriotic Education in Contemporary Russia
Sociological Studies in the Making of the Post-Soviet Citizen
ISBN 978-3-8382-0993-7

Contents

Patrick Lally Michelson
Foreword 7

Alexandra Coţofană and James M. Nyce
Introduction 17

Tatiana Bužeková
Common Work on the Future: Concept of Healing in Neo-Shamanism 33

Ekaterina Grishaeva, Valeria Shumkova
What Does It Mean to Be a True Orthodox in Post-Secular Russia: Attitude Toward Magic Among Orthodox Believers in the Middle Ural 51

Victor Shnirelman
How to Become the "Slavic-Aryans": The Founders of the Russian Neo-Paganism and Their Ambitions 75

Alexandra Coţofană
The Curse Prayers of Saint Vasile or How to "Declare War to the Devil" 99

Dzvenyslava Hanus
Maternity Rituals in the Soviet Western Ukrainian Borderland ... 119

Tatiana Khoruzhenko
"Media Witches" in the 21st-Century Russia 141

Sarah Rafailjović
(Un)orthodox Practice: Magic and Retraditionalization in Post-Socialist Serbia 157

Anna Ozhiganova
Health Magic in Russian New Age 175

List of Contributors 175

Foreword

The chapters collected in *Religion and Magic in Socialist and Post-Socialist Contexts* are informed by two political events of the recent past: the fall of the Berlin Wall in 1989 and the dissolution of the Soviet Union in 1991. Without those events and the sociocultural dislocations that ensued, interest in religion and magic in Eastern Europe very likely would have remained displaced by the more familiar stories, at least among Anglo-Saxon scholars of secularization and disenchantment. Instead, the upheaval of those years helped reveal an array of transnational, national, and regional cultures in Eastern Europe that, like cultures around the globe, are permeated by religion and magic. In turn, this resiliency of religion and magic in the broad geography of Eastern Europe has brought a new set of questions about the region to the fore of scholarship, including the chapters collected in this volume. What roles, for example, have religion and magic played in the formation of cultural norms and the social psychology in Eastern Europe after the discourses and practices of state socialism broke down? How did religion and magic preserve aspects of popular culture for successive generations, despite concerted efforts by atheistic states to lead their citizens beyond practices and epistemologies deemed superstitious, bourgeois, and reactionary? Do religion and magic transgress sociocultural and political boundaries in Eastern Europe, or do they help reify those boundaries? Are popular and elite cultures cleaved by competing notions of religion and magic, or do shared practices across that divide blur the analytical binary of the popular and elite? How might religion and magic constitute forms of resistance to cultural, institutional, and political power, or, conversely, how do religion and magic reinforce those very same power structures in acts of accommodation, legitimization, and privileging?

In the most immediate sense, the questions asked in this volume help reinforce a two-track shift in anthropological and ethnographic studies about Eastern Europe. The former took shape in the late Soviet period and has since claimed a leading place in contemporary scholarship about Russia and Eurasia but has come late, or not yet, to studies of

Eastern Europe. Starting in the 1980s and finding sustained academic interest in the early 2000s, this return to anthropology and ethnography has sought, among other things, to account for regional and historical variety among the many peoples who inhabit the post-Soviet space and its peripheries; situate local practices and traditions in the larger frame of comparative politics; and track alterations and continuities in culture following the political, socioeconomic, and ideological ruptures of 1989–1991 (Mühlfried and Sokolovskiy 2011). "Religion," "morality," and "community" are key categories to these studies and have been used by historians and social scientists to study how ethnic Russians and other citizens of the Russian Federation have reconfigured traditional modes of social and cultural practice, sometimes even generating new forms of practice, so as to "give" meaning to their post-Soviet experiences, thereby generating a sense of belonging in an age of uncertainty (Steinberg and Wanner 2008; Zigon 2011). At the same time that religion has come to the fore of anthropological and ethnographic studies of postsocialist Russia and Eurasia, so too has disciplinary self-consciousness. As anthropologists and ethnographers of religion, morality, and magic expanded their studies into Eastern Europe, they also began to interrogate the intellectual and institutional histories of their own discipline. The result has not just been renewed interest in religion. Scholars now focus on the ways in which anthropology, including the anthropology of religion, has long been implicated in the ideologies and practices of power, knowledge, and empire maintenance (Cvetkovski and Hofmeister 2014), including the modes of linguistic and ethnic analysis first established in the 19th century by Russian Orthodox missionaries as they appropriated "locally generated" categories of distinction (Graber and Murray 2015).

The fact that religion and magic now resonate in anthropological and ethnographic studies of Eastern Europe is reminiscent of the so-called religious turn in the study of modern Russia, which began in the 1990s as part of an academic response to the collapse of the Soviet Union. Whereas *Religion and Magic in Socialist and Post-Socialist Contexts* largely concentrate on the post-history of state socialism's demise in Eastern Europe, the religious turn in Russian studies is mainly interested in the prehistory of a different chronological marker: the Bolshevik Revolution of 1917. As the consequences of communist revolution in Russia seemed to come to a close nearly seventy-five years after its triumph, historians in North America, Europe, and Russia became more liberated from émigré and Cold War narratives about the course of Russian history. In the wake of this reconsideration about the meaning of 1917, scholars began to rediscover that the Russian Empire was a variegated religious habitus, that is, a multivalent cultural topography populated by an array of religious modalities, identities, and cosmologies. Orthodox Christianity, Roman Catholicism, Protestantism, Islam, Judaism, and Buddhism, as well as the many other faiths and religions have been practiced in the empire and its peripheries. These then often became analytical categories through which historians would explore Russia's imperial space. Almost a decade after the collapse of the Soviet Union, lived religion, especially lived Orthodoxy, assumed a central place in scholarship about Russian history. These studies explained that the discrete cultures of Russia's Orthodox heartland, as well as Russia's imperial borderlands, were thoroughly religious, in the sense that religious experiences, practices, and attitudes shaped behavior, psychology, and perception at both the individual and societal levels, and that Orthodoxy simultaneously constituted a source of cohesion and a source of disruption. Religion, in other words, informed the prosaics of everyday life, providing a seemingly fixed and culturally acceptable way to act in and make sense of the world, while at the same time calling into question the sociopolitical structures that underlay local and imperial communities (Worobec 2006; Werth 2011).

One result of this historiographical development has been to make religion a key to understanding and narrating the course of Russian history. Scholars of Orthodox Christianity in the late imperial period have shown how an imperative to recover what was imagined to be authentic Orthodoxy eventually became an ideological competition over tradition, practice, and authority within the Russian Church, gradually fracturing that institution into an array of antagonistic groups, each of which laid claim to representing and embodying "right belief." What was intended to generate unity and community among the Orthodox faithful, imagined by its advocates as the pillar of some sociocultural Russian Orthodox order, lead to fragmentation and cacophony (Shevzov 2004; Dixon 2006). Historians of Muscovite and imperial Russia have similarly turned to the study of magic, witchcraft, sorcery, and folk medicine to explore how historical actors responded to and tried to make sense of daily hardships; to bring into relief the opaque contours of a mostly oral culture; and to elucidate modes of resistance to patriarchy, patronage, and serfdom (Ryan 1999; Worobec 1999; Smilianskaia 2003; Kivelson 2013). These studies similarly cast a light on the everyday lives of the Orthodox faithful, whose experiences and interpretations of the world were deeply shaped by a non-canonical sense of enchantment, while also demonstrating how attempts by church and state to regulate or eradicate such practices played a role in reconfiguring, but not eliminating, magic as practice and experience (Lavrov 2000). Collectively, these studies have helped blunt the precision by which historians had used political chronology to demarcate historical change in Russia and have helped situate Russian culture in a pan-European context, thereby bringing previously ignored currents of Russian history into the frame of comparative analysis.

This digression into the particulars of religion and magic in the study of Russian history illuminates a central feature of this volume. The anthropological study of religion and magic in contemporary Eastern Europe does more than recover cultures theoretically long neglected and illuminate societies in transition. In giving a voice to "native ethnographers" and in focusing on the "native subjectivity" of those who live religion and magic at the local level, *Religion and Magic in Socialist and Post-Socialist Contexts* is participating in the decolonization of historiography. It reveals, for example, the resilience of the idea of backwardness in academic and journalistic accounts of Eastern Europe, which frequently use such categories of "interpretation" to rank, evaluate, and plot the course of Eastern Europe; and these findings demonstrate that sociocultural trends in Eastern Europe still largely remain "under Western eyes" (Malia 1999), an interpretative gaze that, for more than two centuries, has premised Western Europe's pride of place in schemes of enlightenment and civilization on the assumption that the oriental other occupies lower rungs of those schemes (Wolff 1994; Todorova 1997). Read in conjunction with anthropological, sociological, and psychological accounts of religion and magic in Western Europe and North America (de Blécourt, Hutton, and La Fontaine 1999; Orsi 2005; Urban 2015), this volume demonstrates that such practices do not make Eastern Europe exotic or primitive, but rather part of a practical and epistemological continuum that stretches well across the hermeneutic divide of East and West. More broadly, *Religion and Magic in Socialist and Post-Socialist Contexts* challenges the ways in which scholars and commentators have commonly read sociocultural change in Eastern Europe as a move toward "post-socialism," a seemingly 19th-century trajectory broadly dependent on political events that did not always substantially alter local society and culture, as partly evidenced by continuities in the practice of religion and magic in Eastern Europe before and after 1989–1991.

This awareness of the ways in which Eurocentric, often Protestant, categories shape the study of religion and magic (Fitzgerald 2000; Styers 2004; Masuzawa 2005; Keane 2007), not to mention how those categories inform the study of non-Western cultures and societies, draws our attention not only to the subject matter examined in this volume, but also to the nativist framing devices used here. As this volume directs the study of religion and magic in Eastern Europe to beyond the contours of Western scholarship, it implicitly raises the following question: Why other narratives such as "post-secular" offer a more meaningful description of contemporary Eastern Europe? Many of the chapters, for example, suggest that 20th-century Eastern Europe was far from a secular habitus, that the practice of religion and magic was a cultural constant in the years prior to the fall of the Berlin Wall. So why should any political event like the demise of the Soviet Union be considered the start of a post-secular moment in Eastern Europe? Is it because religion and magic have now become mainstream after decades of state-sponsored censure? Is it because the state and other institutions of power have appropriated religious rituals and practices in the symbols and ceremonies of officialdom? But why should the shift from private, often clandestine, practice to public performance determine claims that a previous moment in historical time was secular and the present moment is post-secular? To raise questions about academic narratives previously ascribed to the historical trajectory of Eastern Europe is also to raise fundamental questions about such narratives.

Similarly, claims that Orthodox Christianity constitutes a type of religion that generates cultures and societies distinct from those generated by Roman Catholicism and Protestantism are largely the result of earlier attempts to make the dominant confessional religion of Eastern Europe into some kind of discrete, determinative force, an argument that appears not only in the work of Western European thinkers seeking to distinguish West from East or Central European thinkers hoping to lay claim to belonging to the West, but also in the work of East European thinkers who sought to rank their own cultural geography over that of the West. This particular conceptualization (the last) of Orthodox Christianity is especially evident in the privileging of native modalities and "popular belief" in ideological struggles against cultural imperialism from the West. Such privileging initially found discursive viability during the reign of Nicholas I (1825–1855), when a small number of educated Russians, most notably the Moscow Slavophiles, responded to the assertion that Russia was a backward culture that resided in the philosophically moribund East and/or that it resided outside the flow of historical time altogether, with counterclaims that Russian Orthodox culture was both distinct from and superior to Western culture. These counterclaims soon gained credence in capital-city society and in institutions of higher education, as the cultural and epistemological integrity of the Russian people (*russkii narod*) was increasingly perceived to be under threat from the West (Gerasimov, Glebov, and Mogilner 2013), a concern that was exacerbated by Russia's disastrous campaign in the Crimean War (1853–1856). The result was the formation of a new discourse among educated Russians organized around the advantages of backwardness, the vitality of native culture, and the centrality of folk Orthodoxy (*narodnoe pravoslavie*) in understanding Russian culture.

The paradox then, as it is now, resides in the fact that this invitation to reconsider the idea of backwardness and the invitation to study native culture and popular belief are indebted to categories and narratives largely derived from the West. Among the Slavophiles, whose theories once again resonate in Russia, this new narrative entailed the inversion of philosophical, theological, and historical trajectories first articulated in Germany and France, whereby Russia succeeded Europe as the vanguard of history (or an agent of Providence), and the East was to triumph over the West in the study of national and civilizational cultures (Michelson 2010). To be both the other and to reclaim interpretative authority regarding local culture meant, in this context, relying onto plot devices inherited from ostensibly alien cultures and confessions. Virtually all attempts to decolonize methodology, historiography, and narration both in the past and in the present are thus almost always wedded to the imperialist, rationalist, world-historical, and Western categories they seek to displace, including the very notion of decolonization (Shepard 2006). What this volume helps reveal is scholarship's long reliance on Western or Protestant modes of analysis and narration when it comes to magic and religion; the necessity to challenge those modes of interpretation by drawing on countervailing theories and by turning to native sources, and to acknowledge the likelihood that such shifts in scholarship and hermeneutics almost always subvert the epistemologies that they seek to overcome.

Patrick Lally Michelson
January 2017

Bibliography

Willem de Blécourt, Ronald Hutton, and Jean La Fontaine, eds., *Witchcraft and Magic in Europe: The Twentieth Century* (London: Athlone Press, 1999).

Roland Cvetkovski and Alexis Hofmeister, eds., *An Empire of Others: Creating Ethnographic Knowledge in Imperial Russia and the USSR* (Budapest: CEU Press, 2014).

Simon Dixon, "The Russian Orthodox Church in Imperial Russia 1721–1917," in Michael Angold (ed.). *Eastern Christianity, Vol. 5 of The Cambridge History of Christianity*, 325–347 (Cambridge: Cambridge University Press, 2006).

Timothy Fitzgerald, *The Ideology of Religious Studies* (Oxford: Oxford Univeristy Press, 2000).

Ilya Gerasimov, Sergey Glebov, and Marina Mogilner, "The Postimperial Meets the Postcolonial: Russian Historical Experience and the Postcolonial Moment," in *Ab Imperio*, no. 2 (2013), pp. 97–135.

Kathyn Graber and Jesse Murray, "The Local History of an Imperial Category: Language and Religion in Russia's Eastern Borderlands, 1860s–1930s," in *Slavic Review*, vol. 74, no. 1 (2015), pp. 127–152.

Leonid Heretz, *Russia on the Eve of Modernity: Popular Religion and Traditional Culture Under the Last Tsars* (Cambridge: Cambridge University Press, 2008).

Webb Keane, *Christian Moderns: Freedom and Fetish in the Mission Encounter* (Los Angeles: University of California Press, 2007).

Valerie Kivelson, *Desperate Magic: The Moral Economy of Witchcraft in Seventeenth-Century Russia* (Ithaca, NY: Cornell University Press, 2013).

Aleksandr Sergeevich Lavrov, *Koldovstvo i religiia v Rossii, 1700–1740 gg.* (Moscow: Drevlekhranilishche, 2000).

Martin Malia, *Russia Under Western Eyes: From the Bronze Horseman to the Lenin Mausoleum* (Cambridge: Harvard University Press, 1999).

Laurie Manchester, *Holy Fathers, Secular Sons: Clergy, Intelligentsia, and the Modern Self in Revolutionary Russia* (DeKalb: Northern Illinois University Press, 2008).

Tomoko Masuzawa, *The Invention of World Religions* (Chicago: University of Chicago Press, 2005).

Patrick Laly Michelson, "Slavophile Religious Thought and the Dilemma of Russian Modernity, 1830–1860," in *Modern Intellectual History*, vol. 7, no. 2 (2010), pp. 239–267.

Florian Mühlfried and Sergey Sokolovskiy, eds., *Exploring the Edge of Empire: Soviet Era Anthropology in the Caucasus and Central Asia* (Berlin: LIT Verlag, 2011).

Robert Orsi, *Between Heaven and Earth: The Religious Worlds People Make and the Scholars Who Study Them* (Princeton, NJ: Princeton University Press, 2005).

Will F. Ryan, *The Bathhouse at Midnight: A Historical Survey of Magic and Divination in Russia* (University Park: The Pennsylvania State University, 1999).

Todd Shepard, *The Invention of Decolonization: The Algerian War and the Remaking of France* (Ithaca, NY: Cornell University Press, 2006).

Vera Shevzov, *Russian Orthodoxy on the Eve of Revolution* (Oxford: Oxford University Press, 2004).

Elena B. Smilianskaia, *Volshebniki, bogokhul'niki, eretiki: Narodnaia religioznost' i "dukhovnye prestupleniia" v Rossii XVIII v.* (Moscow: indrik, 2003).

Randall Styers, *Making Magic: Religion, Magic, and Science in the Modern World* (Oxford: Oxford Univeristy Press, 2004).

Maria Todorova, *Imagining the Balkans* (Oxford: Oxford Univeristy Press, 1997).

Hugh B. Urban, *New Age, Neopagan, and New Religious Movements: Alternative Spirituality in Contemporary America* (Los Angeles: University of California Press, 2015).

Christine Worobec, *Possessed: Women: Witches, and Demons in Imperial Russia* (DeKalb: Northern Illinois University Press, 1999).

Christine Worobec, "Lived Orthodoxy in Imperial Russia," in *Kritika: Explorations in Russian and Eurasian History*, vol. 7, no. 2 (Spring 2006), pp. 329–350.

Paul W. Werth, "Lived Orthodoxy and Confessional Diversity: The Last Decade on Religion in Modern Russia," in *Kritika: Explorations in Russian and Eurasian History*, vol. 12, no. 4 (Fall 2011), pp. 849–865.

Larry Wolff, *Inventing Eastern Europe: The Map of Civilization on the Mind of the Enlightenment* (Stanford, CA: Stanford University Press, 1994).

Jarrett Zigon, Multiple Moralities and Religions in Post-Soviet Russia (New York: Berghahn Books, 2011).

Introduction

Alexandra Coțofană and James M. Nyce

As the first of two volumes, this collection is intended to fill some of the theoretical and ethnographic gaps in the study of religion and magic in socialist and post-socialist Europe and its peripheries. Although we use the word "socialist" throughout the two volumes, we understand the biases (empirical and ideological) inherent in this term, and invite further research to expand on (and critique) the problems of using this term to represent such an intricate and complex cultural space as the one investigated by these volumes. Given this, we invite readers to consider these chapters not just as individual examples of Eastern European entanglements of the state, society, and the occult, but also to consider how the meanings ascribed to East and West work in the communities presented.

Wolff (1994) has argued that Eastern Europe is more or less an intellectual convention of the Enlightenment movement, a geographical and ideological shift from the previously accepted North/South axis. This East-West binary was created by 19th-century scholars (although the legacy predates this), who saw Paris as the center of Europe, and served a larger project of constructing Eastern Europe as a space of backwardness, in order to affirm the progress of the West. Superstition, "extreme" religiosity, and irrationality are essential to the definition of this space, opposed to the West, which in part explains the fascination of 19th-century Anglo-Saxon scholars with Eastern folklore, tradition, and belief (Buchowski 2004). However, the chapters in this volume, their literature reviews, and bibliographies will provide readers some sense of what the local literature and native scholars have had to say on subjects related to religion and traditional belief.

In the 1950s, the Cold War led scholars once again to ask questions about the origin and nature of the state. At that time, Eastern Europe and the Soviet Union, given their postwar conditions, were taken by Anglo-Saxon scholars to be something like natural laboratories in which the social anthropology of the state could be observed (Ssorin-Chiakov

2003; Shafir 2008). Perhaps the first of these anthropologists was Sanders who published *Balkan Village* in 1949 (Cole 1977; Sanders 1949). An earlier noteworthy text comes from Ruth Benedict, who wrote on Romania as part of the war effort, and then worked on Romania, Poland, and Czechoslovakia postwar (Benedict 1949; Mead and Métraux 1957). Joel Halpern is well known for his fieldwork in Serbia in 1953 (Halpern 1958) and later turned his attention to the rest of Eastern Europe. Given their theoretical interests, prior ideological commitments, and mentors (Halpern's advisors included Mead, Conrad Arensberg, and Philip Mosely who had done field research in Romania). It is not surprising that these researchers were less concerned with religious belief than with the local operations of socialism and Marxism (Mintz 1974; Kideckel 1977). Still, village ritual was covered in some of these studies, which paved the way for later ethnographies on the role ritual had in the post-socialist state (Agadjanian 2001; Bernstein 2013; Buyandelger 2014). Given early researchers' interests and theoretical commitment, it is not surprising that in their studies of religious ideology and practice, what can be called *native subjectivity* received little attention. This did not change much after 1989, when researchers focused mostly on how the Eastern regimes failed as modernist projects and the resultant consequences of these failures. Materialistic exchanges and material culture, a consistent theme in this region's Anglo-Saxon ethnology, continue to be an important research topic (Sampson 1984; Ledeneva 1998; Chelcea 2002). As for popular belief, not ritual, the cupboard remained more or less bare.

Since the late 1980s revolutions, there has been more scholarly interest in religion in the former Eastern bloc, especially in the role religion plays in post-socialist transformations (Lindquist 2000, 2005, 2006; Knox 2005; Kivelson and Shaheen 2011; Kizenko 2013; Naumescu 2008; Wanner 2008). The number of Western ethnographers visiting Eastern European countries before 1991 was not very large (Romania was the only exception, as will be discussed subsequently). Even so, the topic of religion was mostly neglected, except through the study of ritual (Kligman 1981), and the links that this body of work had to state policies.

One major concern of researchers looking at the Soviet bloc and its zones of influence, when it came to religion, was the relationship between religion and the attempts of socialist states to build modernity (Chirot 1978; Leuștean 2007). This is often looked at through the study of ethnic and national identity (Hann 1988; Kligman 1988; Dorondel 2002; Deletant 2012). Anthropologists were also concerned with rituals of burial as a means to explore the place socialism and religion had in everyday life (Balzer 1980, 1981; Verdery 1999). In scholarship focused on Eastern Europe, the study of ritual became legitimatized, as means, through a Durkheimian lens of analyzing religion as an institutional and personal expression. While this gave anthropologists access to people's everyday experiences of belief and practice, little on the topic has been published. From several years of fieldwork in Romania, we have evidence of complicity between magical figures and the elite under communism, but few other scholars so far have paid much attention to this issue.

For Anglo-Saxon anthropological scholarship after the 1980s, Romanian fieldwork is foundational not only to how we see Eastern Europe as a research area but to how we define most state formations which claim adherence to Marxist principles in the region. Katherine Verdery's term "post-socialism" has become universally employed and it has mostly been spared the kind of scrutiny most of the anthropological lexicon has received. All one has to do is think of the attention given to other terms in the discipline, like *totemism, mana,* or *religion* itself. We tend to give the term "post-socialism" its credibility and seldom question its authority, primarily because it came from researchers working in centers of political, academic, and economic power. The question then is: After the "post-socialisms" of various Anglo-Saxon anthropologists, what is left for the native ethnographer to theorize, and how and when do we get to hear native voices—both of local scholars and those of the community itself (Buchowski 2004)? Tismăneanu (2003) offers "Stalinism" as an alternative to "socialism," since Stalinism provided the model for state policies in some of Eastern European countries. However, other scholars argue that some of the Eastern European national and political autarchic impulses make the term "Stalinism" less tenable, and that we should use the term "communism" instead, especially since this was the term more commonly used by political elites of Eastern Europe in their quest for hegemony (Skalnik 2000; Buchowski 2004).

The issues with Anglo-Saxon terminology do not end here. The post-appellation in social science and area studies is very much a case of relabeling/recategorizing the native subjective in broad Western terms. By calling certain post-revolutionary countries post-socialist/post-colonial, foreign scholarship and policies manage to limit both analytic freedom, inside and outside these countries, and the local forms of development. The social analysis these terms permit, and the fact that such analysis often happened very quickly after the collapse of the Soviet Union and neighboring regimes, means these terms often have had an interventionist quality to them that intended to legitimize Western voices, while silencing native voices and the alternatives and critiques they might be put into press. Furthermore, as we have seen, certain disciplinary terminology used in reference to both Eastern Europe and Russia has seldom been critically deconstructed. One consequence of this is that some of the widely used "post-" appellations do not fit the lived experience of people or local, national, inter-state political realities. Further, the notion of post-socialism often sounds triumphal and like some kind of Western victory over other, more local possibilities. It can be argued that these terms and attendant models obscure the interworking of global, regional, and national economies and set up an artificial, ideological binary of "Us" against "Them."

On the ground, in Eastern European nation-states, the notion of post-socialism does not always resonate with lived experiences before or after 1989. In fact, onsite, as the chapters in this volume show, one can often find far more continuities than the discontinuities pre- or post-socialism assumes. This suggests that other analytic and interpretive motifs and terminologies should be inserted into the debate about what life was "really like" in Eastern Europe and Russia under a variety of regimes. By working solely within terms of pre- or post-socialism, the implication is that there was some arbitrary point in time when a socialist society became capitalist. However, on the ground, and in people's experience, socialism and capitalism often seem to work together. This alludes to the issue of whether both modernity and its endpoints have to follow the same single path. Collier (2011) challenges this idea and further argues that, unlike in the 1990s, Russia is no longer a failed neoliberal state, but can, instead, represent an example of sustainable social modernity. Tangentially, a fair number of chapters in this volume look at the connection religion and traditional belief have in this Russian modernity.

Recent studies have dismantled some of the pre- or post-dichotomies. Chioni (2001) suggests that the term "postcolonial" can be reasonably applied to former Soviet spaces and argues that other related concepts such as "resistance," "liberation," and "hangover" can be employed as well. Chioni believes that the postcolonial condition is as fundamental to the world's cultures as *race*, *gender*, and *age*. We would add to this list *class* and note that Chioni's arguments have much to offer us. Furthermore, his argument is enforced by the fact that the Eastern European countries were not colonies per se. Such arguments seem to rest on very narrow definitions of these two terms, and exempt Eastern European states from the important roles they played across history as both colonized and colonizers.

On the issue of colonizers and the colonized, the discipline of anthropology has its own fault line. Anthropology is not solely based on some "pure" logic or science. Rather, it is informed by colonial politics and ideology (Weber 1930; Girard 1987; Ferguson 1999; Habermas and Mendieta 2002; Collier 2011; Harvey 2011). The early beginnings of anthropology defined the territorial and cultural *other* along lines that were as much aesthetic and ideological as scientific, that is, by absence or presence of reason (Husserl 1988; Abu-Lughod 1990; Hornborg 2011).

Reason was seen as a characteristic of the Western metropole, while unreason defined the colonies. Slowly, it became evident that the discursive separation between what is Western and what is non-Western is thus not just about geography, but represents an epistemic difference related to the colonial history of anthropology (Harvey 2005; Sharma and Gupta 2006; Ferguson 2010). From a different point of view, we could say that the local often seems exotic, simply because it is described from the perspective of another, culturally different local. For example, the occult was an easy target to paint as discursively opposed to reason. However, what is defined as reason is the product of a very long historically contingent debate about how the world works, and consequently about how it should be understood. In brief, the Western fascination with its own magic (and that of others) has helped establish what we see today as "reasonable," and to link this to what we call today post-Enlightenment secularism (Kapferer 2002).

As anthropologists have already noted, there is a need for decolonizing the discipline—in other words, to give equal space to native anthropology and voices in the kinds of analysis we do, as well as in what we advocate for on the basis of this knowledge. In short, this requires not only an epistemological and methodological turn, but also the consideration of where and how we historically produce knowledge. It also involves an ideological and political turn, which both acknowledges and works to dismantle dismissive and colonial hierarchies of taste and production. Anthropology's historically complicated relationship with magic is perhaps the best example of how the decolonizing of the discipline has not yet occurred, and that the modern opposition of science versus nonscience sets up the divide between Western models modernity and those of Others.

Fundamentally, this divide also impinges on how reality is both defined and thought to be capable of manipulation. As such, if one is to understand power and how it both disappears and reappears, one can better understand how science establishes an a priori discontinuity with magic, religion, and ideology. This discontinuity helps conceal the workings of (social) reality and at the same time helps mystify almost all forms of hierarchy, and supports the legitimization of inequity found in every society. To turn the table around, this volume has several studies by Eastern ethnographers who describe how magic and religion in local communities can redefine, resist, and accommodate the power of the state and society.

Hanus (see "Maternity Rituals in the Soviet Western Ukrainian Borderland") discusses her fieldwork in rural Ukrainian communities. She investigates how the state, prior to democracy, has intervened in one set of beliefs and practices, those related to maternity, and the effects this has had on various social groups along the unstable Ukrainian-Polish border. Many of the rituals that once had magic and religious meaning in these communities have become Soviet rituals and have thus gained new meanings. It is this impingement of the secular that has led to the reinvention of tradition and ritual that interests the author, as Hanus shows how the secular and the Soviet entered very intimate aspects of personal and family life along the Polish-Ukrainian border.

Similarly, Shnirelman's study ("How to Become the 'Slavic-Aryans': The Founders of the Russian Neo-Paganism and Their Ambitions") reveals how the Russian occult corpus is being used today, how these beliefs and practices have been reinvented in different esoteric communities, and the role these beliefs have come to play in modern political and social discourse. Shnirelman presents magic as a common form of resistance in the last decades of the 20th century, one that he links to the context of the many reinventions of self, which ex-Soviet citizens are presently undergoing. How do we conceptualize the notions of Russian and Soviet in relationship with each other? Shnirelman's investigation addresses the anthropological and historical aspects of this question.

Using the idea of Neo-shamanism, Grishaeva, Farkhitdinova, Khaziev, and Shumkova's chapter ("What Does It Mean to Be a True Orthodox in Post-Secular Russia: Attitude Toward Magic Among Orthodox Believers in the Middle Ural") picks up on Shnirelman's question about identity, but turns it in a different direction. Here, the question becomes: What does it mean to be Orthodox in post-secular Russia? Their analysis focuses on the important role that Christian Orthodoxy as an institution has played in the Russian state-making after 1991, and, given this, how faith can be defined in Russia. The chapter raises awareness about the many Orthodoxies present in Christianity and how neoliberalism can help build religious identity in a post-Soviet/post-secular world.

Ozhiganova's chapter ("Health Magic in Russian New Age") also has much in common with Shnirelman's chapter, but here the author looks at two New Age communities (with quite different demographics) to phase out the role "pagan" survivals play in these groups' appeal to

Russians. Furthermore, Ozhiganova explains facets of Neo-paganism and magic in Russia that, when added to Shnirelman analysis, make clear why seemingly countercultural beliefs and aspirations can have very significant roles in today's mainstream Russian society.

In another ethnographic study ("Common Work on the Future: Concept of Healing in Neo-Shamanism"), Bužeková shows how, using the term Neo-shamanism, long-standing Slovak positions regarding religion and healing are modified and continue to be important in everyday life. The author finds that individuals can be both shamans and urbanites in post-socialist Central Europe. In other words, neoliberalism here provides opportunities for the reinvention of magic and tradition, which in turn can create contexts for discussing democracy, civil society, and equality.

Taken together, these chapters remind us of how little we know about how religious and magical belief and practice differ community by community, border to border, and under the various political regimes linked, in one way or another, to Marxist ideology.

This raises another issue that we were largely unable to address in this volume. This is the effect that the growth of Protestant fundamentalism has had not just on religious life, but also on the social institutions and discourses that inform private and public life in Eastern Europe today.

There is little on this here, but Hanus discusses Soviet responses to religion and traditional belief in the Ukraine. The anthropological literature has also seldom focused on the Soviet atheist or secularization programs, how they differed from nation to nation, and how their message was diffused throughout the society (also see Luehrmann 2011). Neither did we know much about what these programs were contesting under communism nor did we know what the points of resistance to these programs might have been.

As for Christian Orthodoxy, once we turn away from church-state issues, like property restitution, there is little available in English other than confessional accounts. Even more problematic, these accounts give little analytic insight into the faith, especially its felt and communal dimensions, and how they differ from the various forms of Western Christianity.

This is an issue because Christian Orthodoxy helps define some important domains—among them, experiential, aesthetic, and doctrinal ones—in ways often quite different than Western variants of Christianity. The next volume, like this one, will also be a collection of ethnographies. It will take up and expand some of the issues above as they play out in countries and cultures where religion has played important sociopolitical roles throughout history. However, it will introduce some cultures where Orthodoxy does not play a role as important as it does in the ethnographies here (Bužeková being the only exception in our first volume).

The importance of the Orthodox Church as an institution in many of these state-religion-magic relationships is large. If ignored, there is a good chance we will think about sociocultural institutions in Russia and Eastern European in biased terms, regardless of the time period the author is writing about. In fact, most discussions of the transition in Eastern Europe, from "communism" to "democracy," suffer from having too much of a resemblance to the transitions between barbarism, savagery, and civilization/Christianity, popular in 19th-century Anglo-Saxon anthropology. Discussions of social life and sociopolitical institutions in Eastern Europe suffer even more when magical and religious belief and the role both have in the Orthodox Church and faith are ignored or treated tangentially.

For example, it is not possible to understand such a modern phenomenon as Khoruzhenko's Russian Media Witches ("'Media Witches' in the 21st-Century Russia") unless one takes, as she does, Orthodoxy into account. She shows the role the media and advertisements have played in on the professionalization of witchcraft in Christian Orthodox Russia today, and she demonstrates how the media helps define expertise and provides competition and legitimacy to Media Witches. This, in turn, helps fuel the ongoing debate in contemporary Russia about the utility and reality of magic itself.

Rafajlović ("(Un)orthodox Practice: Magic and Retraditionalization in Post-Socialist Serbia"), like Khoruzhenko, centers on traditional and popular healers, but this time in Serbia. Rafajlović's ethnography presents witchcraft in relation to a kind of putative ahistoricity, in which neither past nor present regimes or ideologies have managed to convince

Serbians of witchcraft's illegitimacy. One irony is that the modernity Rafajlović presents seems to encourage "traditional" witchcraft practices, especially among urbanites who wish to know what the future holds and/or gain wealth for themselves.

The traditional and the urban are not new themes in the anthropology of Eastern Europe. Katherine Verdery (1999) has provided anthropology with a cartography of Romania which, because of Verdery's extensive work and prestige, is often mistaken for Romania itself. However, almost none of her work refers to the church, except for burials, or to any belief or practice other than the secular or the "rational." The result is a geography of Romania in which central features of the cultural landscape either do not appear or whose scale (significance) is often misrepresented.

To see the kinds of issues this raises for making sense of social life in Romania, let us take just one example. As the faith of an overwhelming majority of Romanians, "Orthodox religion in Romanian society [...] accepts magical aggression as a valid diagnosis for unhappiness" (Tătăran 2016: 83). Most Anglo-Saxon denominations today would not explain misfortune this way. Nor would most Roman Catholic or Protestant clergy use binding or unbinding from magic to help laity for any reason. Nor would many of Western clergy see, as in Orthodoxy, that the church's rituals are a legitimate therapy for witchcraft and misfortune (Tătăran 2016: 123). However, in Romania today, as Tătăran (2016) points out, the issue is still not whether or not Orthodox priests can bind or unbind. Instead, the issue is: What is this one priest doing at this point in time and how does this affect myself and my family?

Coțofană ("The Curse Prayers of Saint Vasile or How to "Declare War to the Devil) raises the analytic stakes here. She suggests the line, the firm line, between good and evil, Western Christians like to believe in, can lead us astray when it comes to both religion and social life in Romania. The issue is not if good and evil are at work in Romania. The problem is that what operates in the world is not entirely subject to this binary. One way to solve this dilemma is to appeal to something like the *amoral familism*, that Banfield (1958) said he found in southern Italy. It may be instead that the logics inherent in Western Christianity are in themselves too finite, perhaps even too dogmatic and "empirical" to be put to the test in Romania. While Romanian Orthodoxy shares much the same pantheon of devils and angels with Western Christianity, this does not necessarily mean that the place or order they have (and the work they do) is the same for these faiths. In other words, there is something more (and different) at work in Romania.

It can be argued that the rhetoric and models used in the anthropological literature on Eastern Europe have reduced religion and popular belief to its materialist "traces." This in turn has tended to reduce (or dismiss) the place belief, tradition, and conventions associated with them have had in the lives of our informants, a point Steinberg and Wanner (2008) have made in their discussion of Eastern European faith communities. While theoretical materialism is not congruent with informant experience, it does mirror the standard ideological position of the communist parties in Eastern Europe, and the former USSR.

This raises the question of analytic and ideological complicity and may help explain why the positions regarding religion and magic have been so weakly developed by Anglo-Saxon anthropologists. The focus thus turns on questions about the conditions and understandings under which anthropological fieldwork has been carried out in this part of the world. In other words, the devaluation and disappearance of faith, magic and religion from the postwar Anglo-Saxon anthropological record raises the question of ideological/political commitment either prior to (or derived from) their research in Eastern Europe itself.

It is a truism that anthropologists often portray themselves as the most self-critical of the social scientists. However, when it comes to Eastern Europe, we have yet to ask ourselves what have we gained and lost when we have neglected often central elements of our informants' world, like magic, religion, and popular belief in our analysis of the Soviet and socialist world, as well as their legacies. Perhaps one merit of this volume lies in that it will help raise an important question: What is going on here? And this will help us turn the mirror, once again, on ourselves.

Bibliography

Lila Abu-Lughod, "The Romance of Resistance: Tracing Transformations of Power Through Bedouin Women," in *American Ethnologist*, vol. 17, no. 1 (1990), pp. 41–55.

Alexander Agadjanian, "Revising Pandora's Gifts: Religious and National Identity in the Post-Soviet Societal Fabric," in *Europe-Asia Studies*, vol. 53, no. 3 (May 2001), pp. 473–488.

Marjorie Mandelstam Balzer, "Rituals of Gender Identity: Markers of Siberian Khanty Ethnicity, Status and Belief," in *American Anthropologist*, vol. 83, no. 4 (1981), pp. 850–867.

Marjorie Mandelstam Balzer,"Route to Eternity: Cultural Persistence and Change in Siberian Khanty Burial Ritual," in *Arctic Anthropology*, vol. 17, no.1 (1980), pp. 77–90.

Edward C. Banfield, *The Moral Basis of a Backward Society* (Glencoe, IL: The Free Press, 1958).

Ruth Benedict, *Rumanian Culture and Behavior, Issue 1 of Occasional Papers in Anthropology* (Fort Collins: Colorado State University, 1949).

Anya Bernstein, *Religious Bodies Politic: Rituals of Sovereignty in Buryat Buddhism* (Chicago: University of Chicago Press, 2013).

Michael Buchowski, "Hierarchies of Knowledge in Central-Eastern European Anthropology", in *Anthropology of East Europe Review*, vol. 22, no. 2 (2004), pp. 5–14.

Manduhai Buyandelger, *Tragic Spirits: Shamanism, Memory, and Gender in Contemporary Mongolia* (Chicago: University of Chicago Press, 2014).

Liviu Chelcea, "The Culture of Shortage During Socialism: Goods, Strategies and Consumption Practices in a Romanian Village," in *Cultural Studies*, vol. 16, no. 1 (2002), pp. 16–43.

David Chioni, "Is the Post in Postcolonial the Post in Post-Soviet? Notes Toward a Global Postcolonial Critique," in *PMLA, Special Issue on Globalizing Literary Studies*, vol. 116, no. 1 (January 2001), pp. 111–128.

Daniel Chirot, "Social Change in Communist Romania," in *Social Forces*, vol. 52, no. 2 (1978), pp. 457–497.

John Cole, "Anthropology Comes Part-Way Home: Community Studies in Europe," in *Annual Review of Anthropology*, vol. 6 (October 1977), pp. 349–378.

INTRODUCTION 29

Stephen J. Collier, *Post-Soviet Social: Neoliberalism, Social Modernity, Biopolitics* (Princeton, NJ: Princeton University Press, 2011).

Dennis Deletant, "Nationalism as Unification. Some Considerations on the Role of the Historian as Nation-Builder," in Adriano Roccucci (ed.). *La Costruzione dello Stato-nazione in Italia*, 25–38 (Rome: Viella, 2012).

Stefan Dorondel, "Orthodoxy, Nationalism and Local Identity: A Romanian Case Study," in *Ethnologia Balkanica*, vol. VI (2002), pp. 117–144.

James Ferguson, *Expectations of Modernity: Myths and Meanings of Urban Life on the Zambian Copperbelt* (Chicago: University of Chicago Press, 1999).

James Ferguson, "The Uses of Neoliberalism," in *Antipode*, vol. 41, no. 1 (2010), pp. 166–184.

Rene Girard, *Things Hidden Since the Foundation of the World* (Stanford: Stanford University Press, 1987).

Jurgen Habermas and Eduardo Mendieta, *Religion and Rationality: Essays on Reason, God, and Modernity* (Cambridge: MIT Press, 2002).

Joel Martin Halpern, *A Serbian Village* (NYC: Columbia University Press, 1958).

Chris Hann, "Christianity's Internal Frontier: Uniates in South-East Poland," in *Anthropology Today*, vol. 4, no. 3 (1988), pp. 9–13.

David Harvey, *A Brief History of Neoliberalism* (Oxford: Oxford University Press, 2005).

David Harvey, *Spaces of Capital: Towards a Critical Geography* (New York: Routledge, 2011)

Alf Hornborg, "Rethinking the Industrial Revolution and the Rise of the West: Historical Contingencies and the Global Prerequisites of Modern Technology," in Hans Ruin and Andrus Ers (eds.). *Rethinking Time: Essays on Historical Consciousness, Memory and Representation*, vol. 9, 267–275 (Södertörn Philosophical Studies, 2011).

Edmund Husserl, *Cartesian Meditations: An Introduction to Phenomenology* (Dordrecht: Kluwer Academic Publishers, 1988).

Bruce Kapferer, "Introduction: Outside All Reason: Magic, Sorcery and Epistemology in Anthropology," in *Social Analysis: The International Journal of Social and Cultural Practice, Beyond Rationalism: Rethinking Magic, Witchcraft and Sorcery*, vol. 46, no. 3 (Fall 2002), pp. 1–30.

David A. Kideckel, "The Dialectic of Rural Development: Cooperative Farm Goals and Family Strategies in a Romanian Commune," in *Journal of Rural Cooperation*, vol. 5, no. 1 (1977), pp. 43–62.

Valerie Kivelson and J. Shaheen, "Prosaic Witchcraft and Semiotic Totalitarianism: Muscovite Magic Reconsidered," in *Slavic Review*, vol. 70, no. 1 (Spring 2011), pp. 23–44.

Nadieszda Kizenko, "Feminized Patriarchy? Orthodoxy and Gender in Post-Soviet Russia," in *Signs*, vol. 38, no. 3 (Spring 2013), pp. 595–621.

Gail Kligman, *The Wedding of the Dead: Ritual, Poetics, and Popular Culture in Transylvania* (Berkeley: University of California Press, 1988).

Zoe Knox, *Russian Society and the Orthodox Church Religion in Russia After Communism* (New York: BASEES/Routledge Curzon Series on Russian and East European Studies, 2005).

Alena Ledeneva, *Russia's Economy of Favours* (Cambridge: Cambridge University Press, 1998).

Lucian N. Leuștean, "Constructing Communism in the Romanian People's Republic. Orthodoxy and State, 1948–49", in *Europe-Asia Studies,* vol. 59, no. 2 (March 2007), pp. 303–329.

Lucian N. Leuștean, *Introduction in Religion, Politics and Law in the European Union* (co-ed. with John Madeley) (New York: Routledge, 2010).

Galina Lindquist, *Conjuring Hope: Magic and Healing In Contemporary Russia* (Epistemologies of Healing) (New York: Berghahn Books, 2005).

Galina Lindquist, "Ethnic Identity and Religious Competition: Buddhism and Shamanism in Southern Siberia," in Galina Lindquist† and Don Handelman (eds.). *Religion, Politics, and Globalization Anthropological Approaches*. (New York: Berghahn Books, 2006).

Galina Lindquist, "In Search of the Magic Flow: Magic and Market in Contemporary Russia," in *Urban Anthropology*, vol. 29, no. 4 (2000), p. 315.

Sonja Luehrmann, *Secularism Soviet Style* (Bloomington: Indiana University Press, 2011).

Margaret Mead and Rhoda Métraux, eds., *The Study of Culture at a Distance* (Chicago: University of Chicago Press, 1957).

Sidney Mintz, "The Rural Proletariat and the Problem of Rural Proletariat Consciousness," in *Journal of Peasant Studies*, vol. 1 (1974), pp. 290–325.

Vlad Naumescu, *Modes of Religiosity in Eastern Christianity: Religious Process and Social Change in Ukraine* (Halle Studies in the Anthropology of Eurasia, Berlin: Lit Verlag, 2008).

Steven L. Sampson, *National Integration Through Socialist Planning: An Anthropological Study of a Romanian New Town* (Boulder, CO: East European Monographs, 1984).

Irwin T. Sanders, *Balkan Village* (Lexington: University of Kentucky Press, 1949).

Michael Shafir, "From Historical to „Dialectical" Populism: The Case of Post-Communist Romania," *Canadian Slavonic Papers* I.3–4 (September–December 2008): 425–470.

Aradhana Sharma and Akhil Gupta, eds., *The Anthropology of the State: A Reader* (Oxford: Blackwell, 2006).

Nikolai Ssorin-Chiakov, *The Social Life of the State in Subarctic Siberia* (Stanford: Stanford University Press, 2003).

Peter Skalnik, ed., *Sociocultural Anthropology at the Turn of the Century: Voices from the Periphery* (Prague: Set Out, 2000).

Alexandra Tătăran, *Contemporary Life and Witchcraft: Magic, Divination, and Religious Ritual in Europe* (Stuttgart: Ibidem Verlag, 2016).

Vladimir Tismăneanu, *Stalinism for all Seasons: A Political History of Romanian Communism* (Los Angeles: University of California Press, 2003).

Katherine Verdery, *The Political Lives of Dead Bodies: Reburial and Post-socialist Change* (New York: Columbia University Press, 1999).

Mark D. Steinberg and Catherine Wanner, eds. *Religion, Morality and Community in Post-Soviet Societies* (Bloomington: Indiana University Press, 2008).

Max Weber, *The Protestant Ethic and the Spirit of Capitalism* (London and Boston: Unwin Hyman, 1930).

Larry Wolff, *Inventing Eastern Europe* (Stanford: Stanford University Press, 1994).

Common Work on the Future: Concept of Healing in Neo-Shamanism

Tatiana Bužeková

Abstract

The chapter focuses on the concept of healing as it is represented by Neo-shamanic practitioners in Slovakia: healing is synonymous to shamanic work that requires the use of ritual magic. On the other side, healing is linked to shamans' political values and social background. The chapter is based on the results of ethnographic research under the auspices of the Foundation for Shamanic Studies, conducted on a group of Neo-shamans practicing in Bratislava. The urban shamans' position in Slovakian society is marginal. The shamans are perceived in a negative way in the dominant Catholic discourse, as evildoers, who conjure demons and the souls of dead through magical means. The shamans' themselves on the other hand see magic practices as natural instruments for healing, a long-forgotten knowledge they have revived. Healing is perceived as work on both an individual and a global level: being a shaman is considered helpful to the general transformation that should result in the creation of a healthier and happier world.

Keywords: Neo-shamanism, Slovakia, magic practices, healing

Introduction

At the beginning of the 1990s, with the fall of the communist regime, multiple systems of beliefs started to circulate in Slovakia. Religious and spiritual themes became part of television and radio broadcasting; books on spiritual matters and magic practices flooded bookshops; and with the advent of the Internet, people gained access to diverse spiritual traditions, in particular ideas about the New Age movement. The atmosphere in Slovak cities after the change of the political regime was quite favorable to such teachings, offering paths to spiritual growth that had earlier on the situation. I am an accountant, so if I make mistakes, they have consequences, and there is nothing else, no powers behind. But sometimes I help myself [by shamanism] to make things better.

Yet diseases are an important factor in practicing shamanism. Most of my respondents came to shamanism because of their own serious biomedical health problems. Initially, most of them were skeptical and cautious about magic practices, but eventually most began to perceive shamanism as complementary to biomedicine. Their initial motivation—allopathic health—was replaced by a focus on the spiritual dimension and a holistic view of personality. Elena's story offers an example of this:

> Diana, I don't know if you know her, she had a center in Ružinov [a city quarter in Bratislava—the author's note]. I was going to a bellydance course at this center, and she organized some lectures there—so-called *babince* ["women's parties"—the author's note]. I don't know, I never liked this word, babinec [singular of *babince*—the author's note]. But one day the topic was shamanism. I told myself—it is crazy, I have to try it. So I attended the lecture, and you know how persuasive Alena is. Alena delivered a lecture there, and then she was not teaching any seminars yet; I believe it was before the seminars started. I checked up on Alena at my job—my colleague Alex attended a Rogerian training course with Alena—because I was afraid: shamanism was associated with craziness. Besides, I heard that if people have some potential illnesses, shamanism might trigger it. Then I got ill and Alena helped me a lot. And I attended the FSS seminar; it was the second seminar. It was the basic one, and then I attended all of them. She treated me many times. For instance, I had two surgeries and she always prepared me for the surgery because it was difficult for me. For example, the second time... she was very confused and told me that something very unpleasant would happen, not related to illness, but to some approach... And alas, it happened like that. A doctor who treated me had a wife who died of the same illness, and he did not manage to heal her. So his behavior was excessive sometimes... well, you know, surgeons are not psychologists. They would come to you and tell you that you will die in a week. And that he did—well, not precisely, but he frightened me needlessly. And then Alena treated me and I overcame it easier. Then I attended the seminars and I practiced by myself.

In the Neo-shamanic discourse, biomedical explanations of diseases are not discarded, but rather elaborated on a physiological disorder is considered to be the result of spiritual unbalance. Specific physiological symptoms are explained by means of certain Neo-shamanic concepts:

Common Work on the Future: Concept of Healing in Neo-Shamanism

Tatiana Bužeková

Abstract

The chapter focuses on the concept of healing as it is represented by Neo-shamanic practitioners in Slovakia: healing is synonymous to shamanic work that requires the use of ritual magic. On the other side, healing is linked to shamans' political values and social background. The chapter is based on the results of ethnographic research under the auspices of the Foundation for Shamanic Studies, conducted on a group of Neo-shamans practicing in Bratislava. The urban shamans' position in Slovakian society is marginal. The shamans are perceived in a negative way in the dominant Catholic discourse, as evildoers, who conjure demons and the souls of dead through magical means. The shamans' themselves on the other hand see magic practices as natural instruments for healing, a long-forgotten knowledge they have revived. Healing is perceived as work on both an individual and a global level: being a shaman is considered helpful to the general transformation that should result in the creation of a healthier and happier world.

Keywords: Neo-shamanism, Slovakia, magic practices, healing

Introduction

At the beginning of the 1990s, with the fall of the communist regime, multiple systems of beliefs started to circulate in Slovakia. Religious and spiritual themes became part of television and radio broadcasting; books on spiritual matters and magic practices flooded bookshops; and with the advent of the Internet, people gained access to diverse spiritual traditions, in particular ideas about the New Age movement. The atmosphere in Slovak cities after the change of the political regime was quite favorable to such teachings, offering paths to spiritual growth that had earlier been discouraged or even suppressed by communist institutions. At the same time, these ideas were presented as an alternative to Christianity and were particularly attractive to young people seeking spirituality.

Neo-shamanism or urban shamanism belonged to these new trends, as part of a larger discourse on nature-based spirituality. They shared with the New Age movement the belief that people are living in times of radical social change and are approaching a new era. According to this view, individuals, as well as society as a whole, are undergoing a significant transformation. This transformation is not understood only as a spiritual issue: it is a transformation of the body as well as the soul.[1] Magic healing practices are essential in many New Age activities; in Neo-shamanism this importance is further strengthened by the common definition of the shaman as a magical healer.

Neo-shamanic groups began to form in Slovakia and in the Czech Republic in the 1990s, immediately after the fall of communism, for the most part due to the activities of the Foundation for Shamanic Studies (hereinafter referred to as the FSS), in particular, the FSS Europe in Vienna. The main purpose of this organization has been passing on the long-forgotten knowledge—the core shamanism, which for FSS refers to the "essence" of various spiritual traditions, to the "universal principles and practices not bound to any specific cultural group or perspective."[2] The primary activity of the FSS was teaching core shamanism at workshops and training courses all over the world. The teaching programs were specifically aimed at people in the West who wanted to acquire access to their rightful spiritual heritage, and thus to facilitate the transformation of the world.

I have conducted research on Neo-shamanic beliefs and practices in Bratislava between 2009 and 2013. However, I have known many shamans since 2004, when I first participated in the Neo-shamanic seminar as a translator. During my research, I have not only been in contact mainly with the FSS groups but also with an independent group that was

---

[1] Lužný 1995: 177–178.
[2] "What is core shamanism?" *Shamanism in Europe. The Foundation for Shamanic Studies Europe*, accessed December 12, 2015, http://www.shamanicstudies.net/Page/ID/94?Language=English

formed around a spiritual teacher who had a private practice. In this chapter, I will mainly consider the FSS, its practices and beliefs. My respondents were middle-aged people (35–58), although I have met many younger participants during the Neo-shamanic seminars. Most of them were women. It is not an exceptional phenomenon: Neo-shamanic groups in Western societies consist mostly of women this age as well.[3]

The common concept of the Neo-shamanic discourse is *work*. My respondents used this term to describe various aspects of shamanic activities: various magic practices, healing techniques, drumming meetings, contacts with the world of spirits, individual meditation, reading, or improving economic conditions. This notion is embedded in the worldview that cannot be understood without looking at the specific conditions of the life of Slovak Neo-shamans. In the first part of the chapter, I investigate my respondents' political values and the influence of shamanism on their life trajectories. In the second part, I consider shamanic healing and argue that it is related to complementary and alternative medicine. The third part will be dedicated to the uneasy relationship of Neo-shamanism and Christianity in Slovakia.

Civil discourse

The social background of the Neo-shamans is determined first of all by their economic situation: although the FSS is defined as a nonprofit organization, every workshop and course costs money. Another important factor is the intellectual side of shamanic teaching, attracting people who are interested in spiritual growth. Thus, the FSS version of Neo-shamanism primarily addresses a particular social category—educated people with access to certain ideas from the literature or other media and who have the money to follow their spiritual interests. The political values of my respondents, on the other side, are oriented toward liberal thinking and democracy. This orientation corresponds to the holistic and "egalitarian" shamanic worldview: human beings participate in the functioning

---

[3] Lindquist 2001a: 3, 2001b: 24. I considered gender stratification of the shamanic groups in Slovakia elsewhere (Bužeková 2012b).

of the universal cobweb as one of the forms of existence. Galina Lindquist argued that this idea demonstrates a "democratic" dimension of Neo-shamanism: everything in the world is equal; and people are not superior to other living beings.[4]

On the other side, human beings have more opportunities to influence the world and therefore their duty is to protect and heal weaker beings. The shamanic mission is to heal the environment, the community, and individual bodies, thereby maintaining balance in the world. Lindquist assumes that the idea of common work and general balance is linked to the political ideals of the urban shamans: egalitarian social order, citizens' engagement, ecological lifestyle, individualism, free choice, and gender equality.[5] I observed similar attitudes during my research. Ecologism, for instance, is characteristic of the Slovak shamans' worldview, as well as the ideas of interconnectedness, coming back to nature and healing the Earth. Kornélia,[6] one of my respondents, says:

> I think everything that happens on Earth has a cause. Water and Mother Earth show us that nature is stronger than we imagine, and we are not the masters: the natural elements demonstrate what they can do. But it is just a delicate reminder. And I think that when in some area, the natural elements behave in a certain way, it means that that area is not tuned to the universe and people are not wholly loyal to the world. Either they plunder or they do something that does not correspond to God's plans or ecology. Thus I think that [...] all those tsunamis and all those problems that appeared during recent years are a reminder for us. I am just frozen and shocked when I think about the mere possibility of these events... But I've realized that they occurred in certain areas and people there behaved in a certain way. They cannot just take things from the sea; they have to learn how to create things, to breed, to cultivate. Life is about this: we start working. In the past there were fishermen who were catching fish. But the world has changed and developed and now there are fish factories breeding fish and people learn. ... They even place trout and, I don't know, salmon into rivers. Thus, there are people who do that and there are people who just take. It is impossible, just to take. I used to say: you will get what you give. It does not work the other way around, that is, if you take, you will get something. It does not work. The universe and the world do not work like that. The initiative must come from us. It means that if we will give something to a beggar, we will get something. It is simple—the initiative must be ours.

---

[4] Lindquist 2004: 87.
[5] Ibid.
[6] I changed the names of my respondents.

Most of my respondents try to follow ecological lifestyles and are engaged in public activities: some of them are volunteers; others are involved in social work. A shaman I call Milada started work on her bachelor's degree in social work when she was fifty-five; she successfully graduated and her intention for the present is to work with homeless people. She says:

> We belong to the sensational 5% of the planet's population who are millionaires: we have a home, a roof above our heads; we have heating, water, and a luxury life. But people here do not realize that millions do not have their own home. I think people should give, should support others, because for those who do not have anything this support means hope. But they should not do it out of pity. They have to create respect for people, to make them understand that this is normal work. ... I contribute a lot. I buy Nota Bene.[7] Now I am at the university, I am practicing; I try to understand why people are homeless, what is the cause. It is a global problem. I like to give, and I give a lot. I contribute to some organizations and I give what I can give, what I have.

Robert, a leader of one of the FSS groups in Bratislava, assumes that shamans can contribute to the society by applying their specific knowledge: This is their responsibility and their duty. He too emphasizes the social dimension of shamanic healing practices:

> I think any shaman is a healer, but he also undertakes a spiritual journey. His spirits keep him there; they give strength to him and show him things, thus they educate him. His basic activities, in my opinion, are his healing practices, his prophesies. He has to know how to speak to his people, as it was in the past. "Yes, now we will plant this, and there we will hunt, and then we have to do this or that; because otherwise we will be frozen and will not have food." [...] Thus he is integrated into common activities in the community; he is not exceptional, he does not have any specific position. He does not use his spirits to cultivate his own garden, no way. He serves the society, the community. I am certain of this.

Another important value connected with the notion of shamanic work is the freedom of choice. First of all, the set of practices is not restricted: in core shamanism: There are also no dogmas, no "right" choices, or "right" techniques: "The common approach here is if a spiritual technique works

---

[7] A magazine aimed to help homeless people, who sell the magazine on the streets and keep some of the money they make from sales. Thus, they can earn some money to start a new life.

for one person, it is acceptable."[8] Shamans also feel free to change their lives in terms of work or study. Milada, who I mentioned above, and another shaman, Elena, decided to start their shamanic study when they were middle aged. Robert left his previous work in a firm and started a new career as a masseur. Mirka left a bank where she had worked for a long time and began to paint.

A number of women associated their "shamanic" transformation with divorce. Some started practicing shamanism after their divorces and perceived magic practices as an instrument for improving their life conditions then. For others, divorce was a result of practicing shamanism— a change of behavior that their husbands were not willing to accept. For instance, Lydia was married to a famous musician and in the past had lived in her husband's shadow. She has always been inclined to spiritual beliefs, but at some crucial point, she started to actively work on her personal development, and eventually she divorced her husband who did not like the resulting transformation.

Independent decisions and resistance to social pressure correspond to the general position of urban shamanism towards individualism. The shamans in Slovakia, like their Western counterparts, emphasize an individualistic attitude, independence, and responsibility. But their individualism does not necessarily contradict the idea of collective work. Nina, Milada's close friend, says:

> There was a period of time when I ran an organization employing about 50 people who were doing marketing. Then I realized that I did not want to do it anymore, it was tiring. And I pleaded to the heavens: "I would like to meet people who would work independently, who would not be dependent on others who do not have to rely on others."... And this somehow brought me to shamanism. I realized that those people who got to know shamanism or started practicing shamanism were very independent, they were not reliant on others, and they were able to work independently. It does not matter to what degree they are involved. They do not rely on you, do not call you every day, do not ask you what to do or how to do it; they do not tell that they need something; they do not need a guru. These are independent people. And that suits me. I need to talk to them, and they need to talk to me, but we meet only when we want to meet; we do not push ourselves, and we do not stick to each other.

---

[8] Znamenski 2007: 251.

The shamans emphasized that independence is also important in the economic sphere, both at the individual and the social levels. Many of them have their own business (and use shamanic techniques in their businesses). At the same time, the world economic crisis has been an important part of their stories. Some of the shamanic meetings in which I participated were dedicated to this complex situation that was interpreted as an "illness"—the result of unbalanced social conditions—that had to be cured through common efforts. The bad economic conditions in Slovakia were sometimes discussed as the result of a general passive attitude of the Slovak people, in contrast to the active attitude of shamans. Mirka stated:

> To say more, this feature of Slovaks is deeply rooted: they always whine and cry; they always pity themselves. It is manifested in folk songs, in the whole tradition that is about 1500 years old. All of them just whined and cried; they were angry at their masters; it was better for them to rob, to take things. ... All of them worked hard, that is true, and I do not question it. But to rise, to start doing better, that was much harder. And most of us, who are here now, do not manage things. The master shaman manages at least the basic things. And money is the most basic: though we can do without them, we would be just pilgrims, the poor ones. Without money we can just go on a pilgrimage to Santiago de Compostela or somewhere else. ... Or we can try to do things in a different way—with money.

The economic crisis was in fact one of the main topics of discussion in a shamanic meeting I attended in the summer of 2010: It was dedicated to the creation of what is called a medicine wheel. The goal of the seminar was to solve participants' personal problems and improve their use of shamanic techniques. However, the meeting was also supposed to contribute to the cure of Slovakia, in particular to healing the area where the medicine wheel was constructed. Thus, in the discussions, the shamans often referred to the authentic Slovak tradition and the old Slavic deities.[9] Robert, for instance, is deeply interested in the reconstruction and revitalization of the old Slavic tradition: he claims that the Slavic deities could help cure Slovakia. According to him, the shamans should study the old Slavic healing practices and use them at present (see below).

---

[9] Bužeková 2011.

Shamanic healing

Shamanic work is synonymous to shamanic healing. The FSS courses are supposed to teach participants healing techniques that include various magic practices. People who complete the whole process of the shamanic education (that lasts at least three years) obtain the Certificate of Completion, which "is meant to publicly acknowledge the considerable time and effort invested by students in the completion of the Foundation's training programs in advanced shamanism and shamanic healing."[10] However, the FSS does not assume responsibility for the success of individual healers: "The Foundation cannot certify that a person is a shaman—it is successful results in shamanic healing that make a person recognized by his/her clients as a shaman or shamanic healer, and even that status can change at any time according to a practitioner's relationship with the helping spirits."[11]

Thus, unlike a biomedical diploma, the shamanic certificate does not automatically make one a trustworthy healer in other people's eyes. As any alternative healer, a certificated shaman can try to solve people's problems, including bodily illnesses, by magic practices, but the dominance of biomedicine and the legislation in Slovakia can pose severe restrictions to this. The laws do not permit a person to treat others unless they are biomedical doctors or have a legitimate license compatible with biomedical practices. Shamans can establish their own trade (*živnosť*) with the intention of solving people's problems, but they then have to have a license in counseling—a very broad category that does not refer to biomedicine.

Only three of my respondents have offered shamanic healing services. All three of them have been leaders of the particular groups and two of them have taught the courses on core shamanism. They have been considered to be authoritative healers by other shamans, but their authority has also been contested. There are many tensions between

---

[10] "Certificates of Completion," The Foundation for Shamanic Studies, accessed December 12, 2015, https://www.shamanism.org/workshops/certificates.html
[11] Ibid.

members of these groups. They have never admitted that those animosities might have been caused by competition for clients; they rather referred to the "improper" use of healing techniques. Even the whole system of core shamanism might have been questioned, in particular by the "independent" shaman who does not cooperate with the FSS.

In any case, the healers have attempted to legitimize their authority. Elsewhere[12] I demonstrated that the general strategy of leaders is to make reference to their superior knowledge of tradition/traditions. But the most effective approach is emphasizing a special inner gift. In some sense the FSS certificate is analogous to a medical diploma, but, very much like an ingenious doctor, an exceptionally skillful shaman is good not only because they have a certificate confirming his skills but also because they have extraordinary abilities.[13]

However, during my research, most of my respondents were still in the process of completing their education, and therefore did not have the certificate of completion. They did not consider themselves to be professional healers. For them, shamanic techniques were complementary to the biomedical model. They practiced mostly when they wanted to solve personal problems—to heal illnesses in the sense of unbalanced situations, not diseases in terms of biomedicine. Linda says:

> I drum alone, for instance, when I need something for myself. I do not work with clients, because I don't think that it is my way—to work with clients. I drum only for people from our circle or my friends. But I would not have the courage to work with a stranger, because it is a serious matter for me. I really believe that I would not be able to help people with certain problems, because I am not experienced enough. I use shamanism in a different way—when I don't know what to do, or when I want to help someone to decide. For instance, when my son was taking the admission exams, I was helping him a lot. I always ask [spirits] what is the best for me, but I leave my illnesses to an acupuncturist. I do not consider acupuncture as an alternative thing; it is a normal form of medicine, although a non-Western one. I think it is important for everybody to find something suitable for themselves—whether it is shamanism, or Silva's method, or an internist. When I am desperate, I even call the saints; when I am in the doctor's office, I call the archangel Raphael. It depends

---

[12] Bužeková 2011.
[13] Bužeková 2012b.

on the situation. I am an accountant, so if I make mistakes, they have consequences, and there is nothing else, no powers behind. But sometimes I help myself [by shamanism] to make things better.

Yet diseases are an important factor in practicing shamanism. Most of my respondents came to shamanism because of their own serious biomedical health problems. Initially, most of them were skeptical and cautious about magic practices, but eventually most began to perceive shamanism as complementary to biomedicine. Their initial motivation—allopathic health—was replaced by a focus on the spiritual dimension and a holistic view of personality. Elena's story offers an example of this:

> Diana, I don't know if you know her, she had a center in Ružinov [a city quarter in Bratislava—the author's note]. I was going to a bellydance course at this center, and she organized some lectures there—so-called *babince* ["women's parties"—the author's note]. I don't know, I never liked this word, babinec [singular of *babince*—the author's note]. But one day the topic was shamanism. I told myself—it is crazy, I have to try it. So I attended the lecture, and you know how persuasive Alena is. Alena delivered a lecture there, and then she was not teaching any seminars yet; I believe it was before the seminars started. I checked up on Alena at my job—my colleague Alex attended a Rogerian training course with Alena—because I was afraid: shamanism was associated with craziness. Besides, I heard that if people have some potential illnesses, shamanism might trigger it. Then I got ill and Alena helped me a lot. And I attended the FSS seminar; it was the second seminar. It was the basic one, and then I attended all of them. She treated me many times. For instance, I had two surgeries and she always prepared me for the surgery because it was difficult for me. For example, the second time... she was very confused and told me that something very unpleasant would happen, not related to illness, but to some approach... And alas, it happened like that. A doctor who treated me had a wife who died of the same illness, and he did not manage to heal her. So his behavior was excessive sometimes... well, you know, surgeons are not psychologists. They would come to you and tell you that you will die in a week. And that he did—well, not precisely, but he frightened me needlessly. And then Alena treated me and I overcame it easier. Then I attended the seminars and I practiced by myself.

In the Neo-shamanic discourse, biomedical explanations of diseases are not discarded, but rather elaborated on a physiological disorder is considered to be the result of spiritual unbalance. Specific physiological symptoms are explained by means of certain Neo-shamanic concepts:

soul loss, ignoring one's inner child, etc.[14] It does not mean, however, that biomedical healing is viewed as ineffective; it is just one part of the whole picture, and the magic techniques can also facilitate cure. In a broader sense, Neo-shamanic healing can be put in a category of the complementary and alternative medicine (hereinafter referred to as the CAM).

In Europe, North America, and Australia, the CAM therapies have had a relatively long history.[15] The popularity of the CAM depends on many factors, including one's values, the transformation of personal worldviews, dissatisfaction with biomedical healthcare and the nature of relationships, which exist between patients and medical workers. It is important to note that the CAM attracts more women than men. This tendency has been explained in various ways by social scientists. According to Nina Nissen, the use of the CAM therapies is linked to women's personal transformation and values. It also "contributes towards promoting and achieving social change through the changing of the customary social practices of biomedicine, the development of new epistemic paradigms, the shaping of new working practices, and the creation of alternative communities."[16]

Indeed, personal transformation is a motive my respondents linked to practicing shamanisms. As I mentioned above, two of them, both middle-aged women, were brave enough to begin university-level studies—which is still a rare phenomenon in Slovakia. Other women started their own businesses successfully, and they ascribe their success to their use of shamanic techniques. They emphasized that they could not have achieved such personal changes in the past during the socialist era, and they linked their personal transformation to the social change—not only to the change of political regime but also to growing religious tolerance.[17]

---

[14] Psychology, in particular psychoanalysis, plays an important role in this extrapolation. Its influence on the formation of core shamanism is described in detail in Znamenski 2007: 79–120.
[15] Harris and Rees 2000.
[16] Nissen 2011: 187.
[17] I stress that my respondents live in Bratislava and its vicinity; people's perception of social change in rural areas might be very different.

The shamans often change their lifestyle to a healthier one, some with becoming aware of one's nutrition (healthy food, diets). Many of them start practicing Eastern traditional techniques, such as yoga or Tai Chi, or even martial arts. Soňa, who suffers from sever visual impairment, says:

> Shamanism helped me connect with the Earth's energies and to recover, when I conducted shamanic journeys. I am an Air [an Air Sign in the Zodiac—the author's note], and thus I existentially need earth. I found out that 99.9 % of people are not grounded; they do not even know what that is. I have practiced Tai Chi and Qigong for two and half years; I studied I Ching, and all the time it turned out that I had to be grounded. And all those Eastern people talk about it: be grounded and relax! It means that when I am relaxed, I am not blocked, and when I am grounded, I see reality as it is, and that means that I do not have to see only positive things. It is just about this: I would not reject them and would not resist them and would not be blind. So my eyes have not seen reality, but now it is much better.

Several of my respondents even started their own businesses related to promoting a healthy lifestyle. For instance, Liza offers courses in power yoga; Milada teaches courses on spiritual painting on silk (which is supposed to heal the soul) and sells silk kerchiefs of her own production; Eva is running a teahouse where she mixes teas and herbal drinks in accordance with techniques borrowed from various cultures' traditions.[18] Simona created an Internet course on diets and healthy nutrition. She sees this interest in diet as something that offers an alternative to the existing biomedical healthcare model:

> I want to start courses for weight loss, for change of food or nutrition. I would open other motivational courses. I would open them on the internet, so that people would apply; a course would last several weeks, and I would use all my experience with diets and food. A couple of years ago I attended a lecture delivered by a Slovak doctor, which was dedicated to nutrition. I was shocked because he severely opposed diets. And I've tried perhaps all the diets I've heard about. The diets taught me to search, to observe myself in the slightest detail: if I have pimples or not; if I have inflammation; what secretions I have. And my shamanic search for myself started with nutrition. For me—and I think for any woman—diets are a blessing, because they make the woman focus on her inner state, instead of her appearance. Thus, I have an extremely positive attitude towards diets. I think I tried all of them,

---

[18] The subject of esoteric teahouses is complex and consists of many interesting sub-themes, for instance, competition and tensions similar to those in biomedical practices. However, I do not have space here to pay attention to this topic.

because I wanted to know how they work and if they work at all. I even fasted for thirteen days with my friend who had a tumor on her uterus. She did not want to undergo surgery, so she decided to fast and to drink only juices. She fasted for twenty-one days. I decided to try the same diet out of solidarity and I managed to do it for thirteen days. On the fifth day I thought I would die; but then it changed and I endured it for thirteen days. It was an incredible purification. Thus I began to be interested in purification, in why hunger is important and why cleansing is important. And my friend did not have to undergo surgery in the end: the tumor was just absorbed. It did not disappear, it was absorbed.

According to Sointu and Woodhead (2008), the increasing popularity of the CAM, especially among women, is related to trends in contemporary culture that involve conceptualizing the person "more" holistically. CAM and other "holistic spiritualities" aim toward "the attainment of wholeness and wellbeing of the body, mind and spirit."[19] These trends offer women, and some men, ways of negotiating contemporary dilemmas related to selfhood, "including the contradiction between 'living for others' and forging 'a life of one's own'."[20] Neo-shamanism resonates with such holistic perspectives, about the interconnection of individual and social dimensions of life.

Religious discourse

Neo-shamanism, like other spiritual New Age movements, criticizes monotheistic religions, especially Christianity, for dogmatic premises that do not allow the free development of individuals. On the other hand, Christianity rejects shamanism, specifically because of the magic practices that shamans use. In Slovakia, Christianity (in particular Catholicism) is the dominant religious system and therefore the position of urban shamans in society is uncertain. They are perceived as people doing bizarre things, even as crazy people, but most importantly as errant people. Christian authors in media (especially on the Internet) charge them for example with conjuring demons and the souls of the dead, allying with dark powers, serving Satan, etc. The argument in such attacks is quite

---

[19] Sointu and Woodhead 2008: 259.
[20] Ibid., 268.

simple. For instance, as an anonymous author explains it on the Christian web page "Pray," Christians must not practice shamanism; in shamanism, spirits replace God. Shamans evoke spirits, and a person practicing shamanism is mastered/possessed by them. It means doing evil' spirits are demons, and a shaman can harm others. Moreover, shamanic contacts with spirits take place with the help of drugs, and this t is a criminal act.[21]

The perception that Christian authors have of shamanism is the opposite of the shamans'. The shamans see this practice as an advanced universal spiritual knowledge leading to cure and well-being, while the Christian discourse emphasizes its backwardness, and considers it as a primitive pagan tradition whose practice leads to destruction and evil. Hence my informants' relatives, mostly Christians, typically are not open toward shamanism. To deal with this problem, some shamans conceal their activities. Others try to confront their relatives and end up having conflicts in their families.

I have also witnessed some public attacks on shamanic groups. For example, during one of the weekend meetings, we stayed at a guesthouse in the hills near Bratislava. Our neighbors were school children who intended to go on the tours. An Indian lecturer supervised the shamanic seminar. One day, children verbally attacked her; their teachers tried to control the, but the children continued their slurs. Another example of such hostility refers to the medicine wheel, which every year is to be rebuilt from scratch at the same place because people from the neighborhood destroy the "pagan" stones.

One of the strategies that shamans use to prevent such conflicts is to frequently assert that shamanism is not a religion. Although they use such terms as "God," "deity," "sacred," and "shrine," its practitioners typically claim to refer to a general spiritual dimension, not to religion itself. Furthermore, according to them, people may combine shamanism with any religious system—Christianity, Judaism, Buddhism, or any other.

---

[21] Temné témy. Mohli by ste nám povedať niečo o šamanizme a aký je postoj Cirkvi k nemu? [Dark themes. Can you tell us something about shamanism and the Church's attitude toward it?], *Modlitba* [Pray], accessed December 12, 2015, http://www.modli tba.sk/htm/okultizmus/temy/temy/saman.htm

However, most of my respondents stated that they were not religious in principle. They saw shamanism as a practical spiritual path that offered a specific way of healing through an altered state of consciousness achieved during the shamanic journey to a non-ordinary reality. This path was considered to be compatible with any religious system (if people wished to be religious). Spiritual leaders of various traditions have been sometimes represented in these debates as exemplary people engaged in work that also could change the world. For instance, for Milada they are prototypical social workers:

> Apart from tarot cards, I have cards with the saints. I greatly respect them because I think that the saints—we learned in school—were those people who started social work in human history. That was social work: it meant they made people understand that it was important to give. They were fantastic. Since my childhood I have had a profound respect for them and I am always touched... I love Mother Therese. I do not care if she is here or if she is a heavenly being—I love her. I respect her greatly and I know what her work means. It means five or six thousand shelters, it means helping people, the poorest ones, not to let them sink to the bottom.

Most of my informants are rather cautious about making their shamanic identity public. This is not problematic if one practices in a closed circle of friends. But it is not that easy when shamans want to attract clients and earn money. Those shamans will mainly rely on personal contacts. They also create web pages, like shamans from Western countries. The typical strategy to legitimize shamanic healing is to represent shamanism as the oldest universal spiritual tradition of humankind.[22] However, they often try to avoid the term "shamanism," because they are aware of the prejudices they would face from the majority of local people. Robert says:

> Several times people asked me for help via the internet: they could find those things there. But I think that this form of contact does not work properly, because many people do not know the real meaning of the word "shamanism." They often mistake it for something else and do not trust it. That's why I say to my clients that I use the old healing techniques. I know what I do, and I let people develop their own attitude; then I explain that we will work with this and that; now we will drum a little bit, we will do this, we will call spirits—but please, do not be afraid, the spirits are not souls of the deceased, they are compassionate spirits, our helpers. From the very beginning I explain things, not to make people feel that they are in danger. ... Then they

---

[22] I described this strategy in detail in Bužeková 2012a.

are satisfied. Some of them return to me; we consult about dreams, or some things about the future, or their relationships. Some people come, try, and leave—they do not manage. It is as everywhere I guess.

Yet Robert does not see this passive concealment of his shamanic identity to be entirely satisfactory. His preferred strategy is to actively legitimize shamanic practices by referring specifically to the Slavic tradition, to make shamanism at home in Slovakia. He described his vision of the Slavic deities to me, or, as he called it, his "awakening":

> I was awoken [by the Slavic deities] after Christmas. It was reproachful: they told me that they felt forgotten; that they have grieved because Slavic people have looked for models of behavior in Odin and the Norse gods, while the right models have always been here, in this land, but forgotten in the dust of time. When I journeyed for the first time to the Goddess and wanted to reach her, it was very difficult, because of her distrust and doubts about my intentions. ... No wonder. But I managed to come to her again and again and I received some answers. It is very important to me... I think of them and humbly summon them, and sometimes they come and tell me what I should do. It would be good to go by this road, not only for me, but for all of us here, to go to our Slovak or Slavic ancestors, to bring them again to their own land. We look elsewhere for the things that we have at home. We do not see them. For now on I intend to look for the old techniques, for instance, divination techniques that were once common here.

Robert is deeply interested in the history of Slovakia as well as in the ethnographic works on Slavic folklore and traditional healing. He is not an exception. I observed a general interest in local tradition(s), and a general tendency to conduct rituals at the historical sites or the places that have been significant in Slovakia's religious past. The shamans call these sites places of power inhabited by local spirits; some of those localities are Christian sites, others are pre-Christian. In any case, the shamans' usual strategy in facing the challenges posed by the society is legitimization by local tradition.

Conclusion

In my chapter, I argue that the participants of the FSS seminars consider shamanic work/healing as part of the general positive transformation of the world, on individual as well as global level. Most of them use shamanic techniques to solve their personal problems. Yet such instrumental tendency does not contradict a general vision of social change: healing at a personal level is perceived as part of healing the world. Practicing shamanism in Slovakia, however, is not easy: it fits neither the dominant Catholic worldview nor the biomedical model. Nonetheless, the shamans take view practicing as their responsibility and as way to bring about positive change in the world. They adjust their activities to the specific social context by various strategies. Among them, legitimization by Slovak history and Slavic tradition/folklore is essential. The past here becomes the main instrument in individual and collective shamanic work on the future.

Bibliography

Tatiana Bužeková, "Tradícia a experti. Legitimizácia neošamanskych praktík" [Traditions and experts: Legitimisation of neo-shamanic practices], in Tatiana Bužeková, Danijela Jerotijević, and Martin Kanovský (eds.). *Kognitívne vysvetlenie magických predstáv a praktík* [*Cognitive explanation of magic beliefs and practices*], 75–130 (Bratislava: Eterna Press, 2011).

Tatiana Bužeková, "Modern Faces of Ancient Wisdom," in Michaela Ferencová, Christian Jahoda, Helmut Lukas, and Gabriela Kiliánová (eds.). *Ritual, Conflict and Consensus: Case Studies from Asia and Europe*, 75–90 (Wien: Verlag der Österreichischen Akademie der Wissenschaften, 2012a).

Tatiana Bužeková, "Posvätná ženskosť a autorita: rodová stratifikácia neošamanských skupín" [Sacred femininity and authority: Gender stratification of neo-shamanic groups], in *Cargo*, vol. 1 (2012b), pp. 61–88.

Phillip Harris, Philip and Rebecca Rees, "The Prevalence of Complementary and Alternative Medicine Use Among the General Population: A Systematic Review of the Literature," in *Complementary Therapies in Medicine*, vol. 8 (2000), pp. 88–96.

Galina Lindquist, "The Culture of Charisma: Wielding Legitimacy in Contemporary Russian Healing," in *Anthropology Today*, vol. 17 (2001), pp. 3–8.

Galina Lindquist, "Wizards, Gurus, and Energy-Information Fields: Wielding Legitimacy in Contemporary Russian Healing," in *Anthropology of East Europe Review*, vol. 19 (2001a), pp. 16–28.

Galina Lindquist, "Meanings and Identities," in Andrei Znamenski (ed.). *Shamanism: Critical Concepts in Sociology (3rd volume)*, 86–114 (New York: Routledge Curzon, 2004).

Dušan Lužný, "Neošamanismus—postmoderní techniky extáze. K problematice náboženství v dnešní době" [Neo-shamanism as postomodern techniques of ecstasy. The problem of religion today], in *Religio: Revue pro religionistiku*, vol. 2 (1995), pp. 169–80.

Nina Nissen, "Challenging Perspectives: Women, Complementary and Alternative Medicine, and Social Change," in *Interface: A Journal for and About Social Movements*, vol. 3 (2011), pp. 187–212.

Eeva Sointu and Linda Woodhead, "Spirituality, Gender and Expressive Selfhood," in *Journal for the Scientific Study of Religion*, vol. 47 (2008), pp. 259–276.

Andrei Znamenski, *The Beauty of the Primitive: Shamanism and the Western Imagination*. New York: Oxford University Press, 2007.

What Does It Mean to Be a True Orthodox in Post-Secular Russia: Attitude Toward Magic Among Orthodox Believers in the Middle Ural

Ekaterina Grishaeva and Valeria Shumkova

Abstract

Researchers of Russian Orthodox Christianity emphasize the "paradox of religiosity." In short, while more than 60% of population consider themselves to be Orthodox believers, less than 11% follow religious guidelines and believe them to be obligatory. This could be explained through several overlapping factors. First, the post-Soviet lack of religious socialization and religious education lead to the emergence of great numbers of formal religious believers. Second, religious pluralism and individualism are factors that characterize post-secular societies, and influence the fact that some Orthodox believers incorporate magic ideas and practices in their Orthodox identity. We use the concept of *eclectic religiosity* as a combination of various non-Orthodox religious ideas and practices, which exist as vernacular interpretations of the Orthodox tradition for Orthodox believers. It has been argued that seldom practicing believers are more interested in magic than active practicing or formal believers: they produce vernacular interpretations, unconsciously combining Orthodox and non-Orthodox ideas, or providing Orthodoxy interpretations to practices of magic. Levels of urbanization, gender, age, and education do not make for a stable correlation with attitudes toward magic. The results of this chapter are based on a qualitative survey held in 2015 in Sverdlovskaya Oblast, the sample being 1,084 questionnaires.

Keywords: post-secular society, Orthodox Christianity, Russian Orthodox Church, post-Soviet society, religious pluralism, deinstitutionalization of religion, magic, eclectic religiosity, Ural region

Introduction

The last decade of the 20th century in Russia witnessed a change of position and role of religion in the public sphere. In a situation of political and economic instability, of moral disorientation and ideological vacuum, characteristic of the 1990s, Orthodoxy became a spiritual anchor for many people, a significant component of the national and cultural identity of citizens. National polls show high levels of approval for the Russian Orthodox Church (ROC) as a social institution.[1] Many people, who used to be atheists, were baptized; however, they have not become active practicing believers. The number of respondents who identify as Orthodox has witnessed a constant growth during the past decades. At the same time, researchers note so-called "paradoxes of religiosity": while more than 60% of population consider themselves Orthodox, less than 10% follow religious precepts and expect them to be obligatory.[2]

The Soviet past determines the present attitude toward Orthodoxy. The existence of religion as an outcast practice in Soviet society, the state-forced gaps in religious tradition, and the lack of religious socialization led to the current formal and cultural attitude to religion among new believers.[3] Despite the strong presence of the ROC in the public space, post-secular factors such as individualized religious choices, de-institutionalization of religion, and religious pluralism still influence Russian Christians. Believers strive to combine different Orthodox and non-Orthodox ideas and practices according to their lifestyles, spiritual, and practical ends. In our analysis, we use the term "eclectic religiosity" to designate this phenomenon—a combination of various non-Orthodox religious ideas and practices, which exists as vernacular interpretation of the Orthodox tradition for Orthodox believers. The eclecticism of the re-

---

[1] "Ratings of Social Institutions." Russian Public Opinion Research Center. Accessed March 15, 2016. http://www.wciom.com/index.php?id=123
[2] Roman Lunkin, "The Numbers of the Faith and Values: May 2012. Analytical Review from Research Service "Sreda" / Cifry o vere i cennostyah: May 2012. Analiticheskiy obzor ot Sluzhby "Sreda." *SREDA*. June 05, 2012. Accessed March 15, 2016. http://sreda.org/en/2012/tsifryi-o-vere-i-tsennostyah-may-2012-analiticheskiy-obzor-ot-sluzhbyi-sreda/5293#
[3] Grishaeva and Cherkasova 2013: 9–20.

ligious experience is more typical for believers who have formal confessional affiliation and who perceive religious tradition as a part of a national/ethnic culture. Depending on values, lifestyle, education, and previous religious preferences, believers combine Orthodox ideas with non-Orthodox concepts and practices.

While Thomas Luckmann[4] is one of the harshest critics of the secularization theory: he agrees that the crisis of institutionalized religion, and church-oriented religiosity contradict the principle of perfect competition in a society of goods and producers. Further he sees religiosity as an inherent part of human nature, and suggests that only its manifestations will undergo changes. The contemporary form of religion is a "private" religion that every person creates independently from religious ideas and cults in his/her disposition. Karel Dobbelaere points out that "the loss of church authority, a more pluralistic religious market, and growing individualization have led to religious bricolage, an individual patchwork or recomposition."[5]

The current discussion of the attitudes of Orthodox believers to non-Orthodox ideas is based on the results of quantitative surveys conducted in the Middle Ural in July 2015 to October 2015. The Ural is historically a strongly secular region: its population has been made up mainly of labors of large metallurgical factories ever since the 17th century. During the 17th century, thousands of Old Believers (*staroobrjadzy*) were deported in the Ural region because of their ideological conflict with the ROC. Well educated and hardworking, the Old Believers became influential as merchants and as high-level managers of factories. Their attitude toward the institution of the Orthodox Church was distrustful and skeptical.

In 1917, the Bolshevik political group received a great deal of support from the Ural workers who protested against social inequality. One immediate result was having the last Russian Emperor Nicolay II and his family exiled and then executed in Yekaterinburg, the capital of Middle

---

[4] Luckmann 1967.
[5] Dobbelaere 1999: 239.

Ural. The secular trend and skeptical attitude toward official religious institutions are still influential. Many inhabitants have a negative attitude toward the presence of Orthodoxy in the public sphere. For example, there were several rallies against rebuilding destroyed churches in downtown Yekaterinburg, while the cooperation between the government and the ROC is openly criticized. Only 34% of Orthodox believers actively participate in parish life and regularly consult with priests, others demonstrate a certain level of distrust toward the Orthodox clergy. Some believers replace institutionalized religious experiences with non-Orthodox ideas and practices, such as magic or New Age spirituality. Other believers combine Orthodox and non-Orthodox ideas to make institutionalized religion more suitable to their everyday needs.

This chapter addresses the following two main research questions:

1. Can we describe Orthodox Believers' attitudes toward magic in the Middle Ural region by distinguishing different religious behavior patterns?
2. How do different factors influence attitudes toward magic ideas and practices?

Here we explore factors such as ritual activity, involvement in parish life, religious literacy, urbanization, age, gender, and education level.

A fair number of sociologists of religion have conceptualized the phenomenon of eclectic religiosity. Danièle Hervieu-Léger believes that "religious modernity is individualism,"[6] and proposes the term "patchwork religiosity" to characterize individual religiosity. Patchwork religiosity appears as a result of a crisis of authority in traditional religious institutions, which allows for the legitimating of faith to be transferred to individuals. Belorussian Sociologists Irena Borowik[7] and Larisa Titarenko[8] use the term "eclectic religiosity" to describe the combination of various religious beliefs that are typical for West and East European societies. Nancy T.

---

[6] Hervieu-Léger 2015: 261.
[7] Borowik 2006: 267–278.
[8] Titarenko 2008: 237–254.

Ammerman[9] notes on the other hand that religious pluralism is not a distinctive feature of modernity: it existed, for instance, in medieval societies when people combined Christian faith with pagan practices.

Eclectic religiosity was initially studied mostly by folklorists and was defined as folk religion. The latter is formed on the basis of social relationships that exist within the community: it emerges as a result of interactions between local tradition and world religions.[10] Scholars usually approach folk religion by opposing it to official religion and making a distinction between religions of the majority and religions of the minority.

Researchers note that folk religion is heterogeneous: it involves the coexistence of magical, mythological, and folkloric beliefs and practices. Combining different academic approaches, Don Yoder insists on opposition to a final synthetically definition: "Folk religion is the totality of all those views and practices of religion that exist among the people apart from and alongside the strictly theological and liturgical forms of the official religion."[11]

Primiano argues that the word "folk" has a negative, derogatory connotation, because it implicitly compares collective, official, and unofficial, individual religiosity, belittling the value of individual religious experiences.[12] Primiano emphasizes that it is necessary to distinguish between official religion and personal religious experience, which is always vernacular, unique, and based on principles of creative and independent comprehension of religious tradition. Using the term "vernacular religion," Primiano insists on shifting the methodological perspective: from the group-oriented study to the study of individuals, from the confessional-based research to nondenominational and neutral factual research.

We use the concept of vernacular religion to avoid any denominational, theological, or slighting assessment of everyday religious views of Orthodox believers. We look at them as the expression of personal religious experience formed in a certain social, cultural, and historical con-

---

[9]   Ammerman 2007: 8.
[10] Schneider 1970: 73–74.
[11] Yoder 1974: 14.
[12] Primiano 1995: 45.

text; this eclectic combination is important in itself. In a post-secular society, eclectic religiosity gains a fundamentally different nature. The difference is determined by the availability of information on new religious and spiritual movements, by mass media covering news on the various religious and quasi-religious ideas, importance of individual religious choice in comparison to traditional authority of religious institutions.

Magic and New Age concepts

There is a long debate over the nature of magic and its demarcation from religion and science. Tylor[13] and Frazer[14] insisted that magic is a superstition, an evolutionarily early stage of science, inadequate and misleading, and it is in contradiction with the rational character of modernity. According to Styers,[15] the ambition to find notional differentiation is in itself characteristic to modernity,[16] and fits certain cultural attitudes in contemporary society.[17] Religion incorporates the elements of magic, and in practice it is difficult to make a clear distinction between the realms of magic and religion.

In their many conceptual attempts to distinguish magic from religion and science, scholars elaborated the main features of magic. As Durkheim noted, magic is not concerned with the meaning of the universe, but with "technical and utilitarian ends" and, hence, "it does not waste its time in speculation."[18] Wax and Wax support Durkheim's concept by stating that "magic is immoral and anti-social: where religion solidifies the group, magic is individualistic."[19] In this sense, some scholars agree that magic could not be institutionalized because there are no long lasting relationships between the practitioners of magic and people who act as clients.

---

[13] Tylor 1958.
[14] Frazer 1950.
[15] Styers 2004.
[16] Tylor 1958.
[17] Frazer 1950.
[18] Durkheim 1995: 52.
[19] Wax and Wax 1963: 503.

Similarly, Malinowski made a distinction between religion, concerned mainly with general, long-term goals, and magic, concerned with immediate and concrete goals.[20] He saw religion as based on the veneration of God or Gods, while magic as limited by impersonal conceptions of the supernatural. To go on, Middleton pointed out that magic is an effort to manipulate supernatural forces to gain a certain result without appealing to divine powers through sacrifice or prayer.[21] Stark synthesized the former concepts and definitions: "magic refers to all efforts to manipulate supernatural forces to gain rewards (or avoid costs) without reference to a God or Gods or to general explanations of existence."[22] Magic gives individuals supernatural instruments to achieve utilitarian goals without affiliation to religious institution and continuous participation in rituals. As a non-institutional activity, it can easily be combined with religion.

Because of New Age and the deinstitutionalization of religion, we can see post-Soviet trends in Orthodoxy, as well as new forms of magic that have appeared. Thus, the delimitations between magic and science or magic and religion are in the process of continuous changes. In contemporary, Russian society traditional manifestations of magic practitioners as wizards coexist with relatively new ones. In the early 1990s, a spiritual boom took place, and different New Age centers have emerged—they are still very active in most of the post-Soviet Republics. These New Age pseudoscientific concepts use cause-effect explanations similar to (traditional) magic. The explanations and use of concepts such as aura or horoscope are defined similarly to imitative magic, in that they use supernatural forces without appealing to divine beings accepted by institutionalized actors. This use of the supernatural is necessary for pursuing concrete utilitarian ends.

In this chapter, we treat magic, conceptually, as related to science; it became a separate phenomenon when modern science excluded the sympathetic principle ("like produces like") from its methodology. Today

---

[20] Malinowski 1992.
[21] Middleton 1967: ix.
[22] Stark 2001: 111.

the boundaries between magic, science, and religion are discursively unclear, while new concepts and ideas emerge often at their margins. For some believers, concerned only with utilitarian goals, Orthodox rituals are deprived of the sacred and of transcendence and are seen as magical rites. Such religious experiences (institutionalized or external to the institution) are very close to magic as strict sequences of operations, aimed to achieve certain goals.

In order to analyze the "New Age" (or eclectic) complex of magic, mantic (divination) pseudoscientific ideas and practices, it is important to note that these ideas coexist with traditional images of magic as witchcraft, sorcery, and spells. For example, the contemporary concept of the energy-informational properties of water can be considered as a kind of return to magical origins, to a sympathetic principle, with the retention of scientific-like language. According to the logic of this concept, the human body consists mostly of water; the positive energy or information influences the structure of water and has a healing effect on biological organisms. Here, we consider that the principle of belief in the power of words is at work to convey this magical concept to some social groups.

The sympathetic principle works similarly for the belief in horoscopes and astrology. The main idea of such beliefs is that there is an isomorphism between the sphere of macro objects (planets, stars) and the human world. To go on, the principle states that cosmic events influence the life of individuals or even entire nations. As an example, astrology (even in a "profane" form) has a special meaning and a particular cultural value in Russia: in some cases it maintains a strong pseudoscientific aspect, due to the philosophical ideas of Russian cosmists. This kind of turn to "science" happens often against Russia's strong Christian Orthodox identity.

The popularity of magic in Russia is connected, on the one hand, with the wide mass media coverage and uncritical attitude of its consumers; from the 1990s, the yellow press actively relayed problematic events and cases to magic. Some newspaper advertisements include information on services offered by magicians, clairvoyants, and healers. There are various films programs and TV broadcasts that imitate the structure of the scientific genre (Ren TV, TV3-mystic, etc.), and advertise magic. Equally, the popular literature (digests of folk superstitions and signs; books on magic of herbs and minerals, amulets and talismans; handbooks of witchcraft and magic, including various rituals and spells "*zagovory*" to gain love, success, wealth, healing, etc.) are constantly published, and always in bookstores. On the other hand, based on our survey data, the popularity of magic could have a psychological explanation an individual may consider magic as a last resort in desperate situations or in situations when no rational actions can affect the course of events.

In order to further analyze these issues, we are working with seven of the twelve non-Orthodox concepts/attitudes related to magic, that we identified in our survey. They are (1) a belief in magic and witchcraft; (2) a belief in the effects of talismans and amulets; (3) a willingness to consult with magicians; (4) an openness to consider Spiritism; (5) conceptualizing the aura as a special energy within and around the human body; (6) a belief in horoscopes and astrological predictions; and (7) a belief in the idea that water can transmit positive or negative emotions. The last three concepts are quasi-scientific and are close to magic because they are based on belief in controlling the supernatural or in foretelling natural events or forces, as well as on the principle of imitative magic. The concept of water having energetic and informational features is close to spells or incantations, in the sense that the words are believed to have an effect on the qualities of physical substances.

Methodology

The research is based on the results of a sociological survey that was conducted between July 2015 and October 2015 in three cities of Sverdlovskaya Oblast': Yekaterinburg (1.5 million inhabitants), Nizhny Tagil (350,000 inhabitants), and Kirovgrad (22,000 inhabitants). A total of 1,084 questionnaires were collected: 644 in Yekaterinburg, 320 in Nizhny Tagil, and 120 in Kirovgrad. Only respondents who identify as Christian Orthodox took part in the research. The survey was organized in fifteen parishes after the Sunday Eucharistic service (mass) as well as during working days, and during the evenings. We used the method of cluster analysis in data processing. In addition to quantitative methods, qualitative methods were also used, such as in-depth interviews with priests and semi-structured interviews with believers, where we focused on their attitude toward magic.

We turn to the concept of *religiousness* to indicate the level of religiosity held by Orthodox believers. Borrowing analytical tools from Charles Glock and, Rodney Stark,[23] Valentina Chesnokova,[24] Jlia Sinelina,[25] Sergey Lebedev and Vladimir Sukhorukov,[26] and Svetlana Karaseva and Elena Shkurova[27] we measured the level of *religiousness* in three dimensions namely, ritualistic, intellectual-ideological, and social. The questions focused on detecting involvement in religious rituals were modeled on Chesnokova's surveys. This part includes questions focused on the frequency of service attendance; participation in masses (Confession, Eucharist); frequency of reading prayers, Gospel, and texts of Sacrament Tradition; and frequency in fasting.

The intellectual-ideological part of the interview is used for identifying the level of religious literacy. It includes questions about belief in the resurrection of the dead, Orthodox concepts of God, Church, sin, and questions on knowledge of Sacraments. The social dimension of religiosity consists of two aspects: the involvement in the parish life, including frequent communication with other church members, and participation in the parish meetings and events. Respondents are also expected to ask the priests for advice with some frequency.

We used cluster analysis to group questionnaires according to involvement in ritual activity, then considered the levels of religious literacy and social activity as additional factors that have an influence on Orthodox believers' attitudes toward non-Orthodox practices. As a result of our data analysis, we divided respondents into four groups: (1) active prac-

---

[23] Glock and Stark 1968.
[24] Chesnokova 2003.
[25] Sinelina 2005: 96–106.
[26] Lebedev and Sukhorukov 2013: 118–126.
[27] Karaseva and Shkurova 2014.

ticing believers (APB group), (2) practicing believers (PB group), (3) seldom practicing believers (SPB group), and (4) formal believers (FB group).

The first group includes respondents who attend services, confess, and receive Communion once a month or more often, who make an effort to read morning and evening prayer every day, to keep all Church fasts, including fasting each Wednesday and Friday. The second group consists of those who attend services once a week and more often, confess and receive Communion several times a year (but not every month) or at least once a year; who do not read morning and evening prayers regularly, and who do not fast all the time. The third group consists of respondents who attend services once or twice a month on average, confess once a year or less often and irregularly receive Communion (once every several years), who rarely read morning and evening prayers and who fast irregularly. The respondents of this fourth group neither confess nor receive Communion; they do not keep fasts and do not read prayers but will attend services from time to time (we refer to this as Orthodoxy as a cultural identity).

The questionnaire group, aimed at studying how non-Orthodox practices spread among Orthodox believers, consists of twelve questions, including six questions regarding magic. We modeled this questionnaire on Beliaev's questionnaire,[28] monitoring the content of bookstores and TV channels (Ren TV, TV3-mystic, etc.). Most questions are single answer (SA) with four possible answers: two answers that do not contradict Orthodox tradition and two answers that define eclectic religiosity. We measure the level of eclectic religiosity according to the number of selected eclectic answers: a zero-level means negative attitudes toward all offered non-Orthodox concepts; a mid-level means positive attitudes toward three of our twelve concepts, on average; and a high level means five non-Orthodox concepts or more.

---

[28] Beliaev 2009: 88–98.

Patterns of religious behavior of Orthodox believers

The Holy Scripture and texts of Sacred Tradition present the Orthodox doctrine that we followed in our analysis. In spite of the strict canonical limitations, the Orthodox tradition is always organized in specific historical and social circumstances. Political, socio-economical, and cultural factors influence religious institutions as well as individual consciousness and behaviors. First of all, there are certain folk beliefs that are transmitted within local religious groups, that is, veneration of new martyrs and non-canonized saints. Second, individual religiosity is always a subjective interpretation of religion with particular intellectual horizons, as well as an extent of practical preparation and integration of Orthodox and non-Orthodox concepts.

Different spiritual and quasi-scientific theories are spread in contemporary Russian society. Orthodox believers form their attitudes based on popular spiritual ideas (such as clairvoyance, extrasensory perception, karma, and reincarnation), and these attitudes are strongly determined by the believer's experiences in life. In some cases, such concepts are consistently incorporated into the believer's worldview. In other cases, they consciously or not create complex, heterogeneous groups of beliefs.

A number of 1,084 respondents took part in our survey; 46% being identified as active practicing believers, 22% practicing believers, 18% seldom practicing believers, and the rest of 14% being formal believers. Out of our total, 37% have zero-level eclectic religiosity, 37% have middle level, and 26% are highly eclectic. The questionnaires split respondents into four groups, depending on correlation between levels of religiousness and eclecticism. We will discuss them in reverse order so as to better formulate our following argument:

1. Respondents who are religiously indifferent (8%): this group is characterized by a low level of religiousness (non-practicing believers) as well as a zero level of eclectic religiosity. These respondents are skeptical about non-Orthodoxy; their answers on questions concerning definitions of God, Church, sin, etc. are closer to the answers of Orthodox believers and are quite different from answers of the two other groups.

The respondents of this group formally identify as believers, considering Orthodoxy a part of their national and cultural identity.

2. Non-Orthodox eclectics (24% of respondents) have a low level of religiousness (seldom practicing believers), and a high or medium level of eclecticism. The respondents of this group keep their confessional identity; some of them are disappointed by institutionalized Orthodoxy and prefer to embark on personal religious journeys, while others have never been involved in church life. As a rule, they know little about Orthodoxy and have a low level of religious literacy, which they tend to compensate for by turning to non-Orthodox practices. This group highly value nondenominational spiritual experiences as the latter offer an opportunity for self-expression, for solving personal problems, etc. At the same time, they see in it a potential to remain free from the "external authority" and strict regulations of Orthodox tradition. The eclectic concepts contradicting orthodox beliefs prevail within this group (e.g. the concept of reincarnation/the Christian idea of soul).

3. Orthodox interpreters (40%) is a group of religiously sensitive respondents with high levels of religiousness (actively practicing and practicing believers) and high or medium level of eclectic religiosity. For these respondents, religious exploration, spiritual experience, and a desire to find their own answers for spiritual questions are significant. This group is characterized, on the one hand, by a high level of religious literacy and, on the other, by acceptance and comprehension of eclectic concepts from an Orthodox point of view. Believers attempt to construct a consistent system of beliefs (e.g. the aura is interpreted as saints' haloes or the Tabor Light, meditation practice—as a prayer, telepathy, and telekinesis—as common properties of saints, etc.

4. Orthodox believers (28% of respondents) are the respondents with the highest level of religiousness (actively practicing believers) and the lowest level of eclectic religiosity. This group has neutral or negative attitudes toward eclectic concepts; their answers fit the Orthodox doctrine the most.

Only the first group is characterized by a lack of significant interest in the supernatural. In contrast, the respondents of three other groups declare high levels of Orthodox and/or non-Orthodox belief. The religiously indifferent type of respondents is least frequent among the Orthodox believers who participated in the survey; the most common type is that of Orthodox interpreters, who combine a high level of religiousness with an increased interest in non-Orthodox practices. J. Sinelina's research has similarly shown that believers with high levels of religiousness most often take into account the various superstitions and signs, compared to people with middle- and low-level groups. From our results, the high level of eclectic religiosity is the third group; they are especially sensitive to the supernatural, which is an essential character of religious believers.

Magic among Orthodox believers in the Middle Ural

It is apparent to us that the attitude toward magic will most depend on the level of religiousness, of religious literacy, and of their involvement in parish life. The results of the research show that believers with a high or middle level of religious literacy are more critical toward magic and express negative evaluations more frequently than those who have a low level of religious literacy. The same tendency can be observed in the fact that believers who are more involved in parish life are more inclined to have a zero level of eclectic religiosity and to be more skeptical about magic than those who are not involved in parish life.

It is a rather surprising that low practicing believers demonstrate the most positive attitude toward magic. They share the idea that water can save positive or negative emotions, believe in auras, horoscopes, talismans, and amulets having tangible results; they leave open the possibility of Spiritism more often than formal believers. In this group, 62% have a low level of religious literacy and 60% are not involved in parish life.

In the area we surveyed, there is a lack of a churched (institutionalized) religious experience, which is compensated by vernacular interpretations. This produces a combination of Orthodox and non-Orthodox beliefs. The answers of the former group of believers are closer to the answers of active practicing believers in terms of their skeptical attitude toward magic. This happens perhaps because of two overlapping reasons: some of the formal believers are not responsive to the supernatural and some are not interested in religion or magic. Second, others who were former active practicing believers with a high religious literacy, have left the Church, but preserved their attitude toward magic. The attitude toward magic in these three Ural cities is slightly different; it does not depend on the level of urbanization, but on local cultural symbols specific to these communities.

Not only do the high level of religious literacy and active involvement in the parish life determine the low level of eclectic religiosity, but the factor of geographical location is also important for people's attitudes toward magic. The percentage of respondents with high and low levels of eclectic religiosity in Nizniy Tagil (350,000 inhabitants) is slightly larger than in Yekaterinburg (1,500,000 inhabitants) and Kirovgrad (22,000 inhabitants). The results of non-Orthodox convictions and practices among Kirovgrad inhabitants are much closer to the results of Yekaterinburg inhabitants. In part, this is connected to the fact that Kirovograd residents often move to Yekaterinburg in search of better job opportunities; further there is often a temporary migration, some of them come back, but adopt megapolis lifestyles. The higher level of eclectic religiosity in Nizniy Tagil is partly connected to the isolated location of the city; people here have fewer opportunities to compare alternative sets of beliefs, which translate into them being more conservative. Mass media is one of the main factors influencing their worldviews; they tend to watch it uncritically and accept messages about supernatural incidents as real and scientifically proven (Table 1).

Table 1: Attitude to non-Orthodox concepts in the Middle Ural

Non-Orthodox convictions	Strongly agree + rather agree (%)		
	Yekaterinburg	Nizniy Tagil	Kirovgrad
1. Aura exists as a special energy in and around the human body	58.4	71.2	59
2. Efficacy of witchcraft and magic	38.5	48.7	47
3. Normal water can save positive or negative emotions	34.9	41	41.9
4. Talismans and amulets have real impact on his/her fortune	23.8	34.2	24.8
5. Contact with ghosts can lead to expected results	20.8	17.4	16.2
6. Belief in horoscopes and astrology	12.6	16.6	7.7
7. Willingness to consult with magic practitioners	5.5	6	7

In Yekaterinburg, Nizniy Tagil, and Kirovgrad, the best known ideas and practices regarding magic are as follows: (1) aura is a special energy within and around human body; (2) witchcraft and magic work; (3) water can save positive or negative emotions; and (4) talismans and amulets have a real impact on his/her fortune. Less popular are opinions that (5) contact with ghosts to gain certain results is possible and (6) people are willing to consult with magicians.

In the perception of most respondents, magic has much in common with science. The popularity of concepts such as aura or special properties of water is mainly determined by their pseudoscientific nature. For example, some respondents interpret aura as a natural biological energy produced by the human body (such as electromagnetic, radio fields, or aural space). Water can save positive or negative emotions through changes in the molecular structure. Some respondents successfully incorporate these concepts into Christian Orthodox discourse. They see the aura as halos and Tabor Light emanating from the saints; they equate energetic-informational properties of water with biblical features of holy water.

Magic became popular in Russia in the 1990s. In the time of the so-called "Religious Renaissance," one could find books on exorcisms and magic rituals on people's bookshelves, while mass media broadcasted numerous advertisements about magic. In all, 38.5% in Yekaterinburg, 47% in Kirovgrad, and 49% of Nizniy Tagil respondents believe that magic is real. The reality of magic is seen as consistent with the Christian worldview, since people know of miracles performed by magicians in the Old and New Testament. For a better understanding of the Orthodox attitude toward magic, it is important to mention that most respondents also identify magic with pagan evil forces. In Yekaterinburg, 92% of respondents consider consulting magicians to be morally unacceptable (91% in Kirovgard and 88% in Nizniy Tagil). In case of emerging problems, 30.2% in Yekaterinburg, 40% in Nizniy Tagil, and 36% in Kirovgrad are willing to see an astrologist, yet in a very difficult situation, most respondents will wait for help from God (88%), priests (66%), or relatives (55%). Only 2% prefer to consult an astrologist in difficult situations. Despite the rather tolerant attitude toward magic practices among Orthodox believers, some respondents have a fairly low degree of confidence in the efficiency of magic. They see it as a kind of fashionable or curious exotic experience, not as a serious and effective help.

The belief in the power of talismans and amulets is another popular non-Orthodox concept: 24% in Yekaterinburg, 25% in Kirovgrad, and 34% respondents in Nizniy Tagil share this idea. Accepting this concept, Orthodox believers have different understandings of the nature of this type of power and will offer Orthodox interpretations. Some respondents assume that only Christian crosses can be considered talismans, or that talismans can influence human acts only with God's permission (positive interpretation), while others underline the negative effects of talismans and amulets because of their pagan origins (negative interpretation). In general, most respondents are rather skeptical about the effectiveness of talismans and amulets; they see them as having a *placebo effect*, based often on autohypnosis.

Less popular concepts among the interviewed populations are Spiritism, horoscopes, and astrology, because of their perceived contradiction with Orthodoxy. The low level of trust in horoscopes and astrology is affected by a ubiquitous use of astrological symbols in public by the everyday broadcasting of horoscope predictions in tabloids, which eventually seems to lead to a loss of interest and a spread of negative or indifferent attitudes toward astrology in general.

Magic is attractive to some respondents because it promises a short, simple way to accomplish clear goals. Its popularity increases during times of social and economic transition. The economic situation in Russia has been unstable since the fall of Eastern regimes, with high levels of social inequality and low levels of social mobility. Many people declare they do not feel able to change, or be in charge of, their lives; they perceive life as determined by external forces, outside their control. Sometimes magic is understood as the only instrument to solve economic problems: different magic rituals, spells, and spiritual workshops aimed to attract wealth are well advertised and quite popular.

Age, gender, and attitudes toward magic

Our analysis shows that there is no statistical correlation between gender and the level of eclectic religiosity. Women were slightly more predominant in the group with zero level of belief (38% and 33%, respectively) than men in groups with medium levels of belief (39% and 36%) and high (27% and 26%) levels. Thus, the correlation between level of eclectic religiosity and gender has qualitative rather than quantitative implications. Men, more often than women, believe that water has special energetic-informational properties and leave open the possibility of contact with ghosts. Women, more often than men, are open to horoscope predictions and consult magicians. At the same time, male respondents are more skeptical of non-Orthodox ideas and practices. The men's interest in magic is different than that of women. They see magic concepts as a way of self-development, and perceive it as part of technological and scientific societal progress. Females: perceive magic as the shortest way to solve their problems, mostly regarding their private lives (Table 2).

Table 2: Distribution of answers according to level of eclectic religiosity and gender

Gender		
	Male (%)	Female (%)
Zero level of eclectic religiosity	33.80	37.60
Medium level of eclectic religiosity	38.90	36.40
High level of eclectic religiosity	27.40	25.90

The level of eclectic religiosity varies by age: in elder age groups, respondents are often skeptical about the non-Orthodox concepts, while younger generations are more open to nontraditional religious concepts (Table 3). Starting from the age group of thirty to thirty-nine years, the percentage of respondents with a high level of eclectic religiosity is lower, while the number of people with zero level is growing and reaches a maximum of 46.8% in the age group of greater than sixty-nine.

An interest in horoscopes, in consulting with magicians, in the concept of energetic-informational features of water is most popular among people aged thirty and younger, and gains less support from respondents aged thirty-five and older. Younger generations seem to be more open to nontraditional concepts, prone to experimenting and innovating; and people generally become more conservative regarding these topics, as they get older (Table 4).

Table 3: Distribution of answers according to level of eclectic religiosity and age

	Age						
	<19 (%)	20–29 (%)	30–39 (%)	40–49 (%)	50–59 (%)	60–69 (%)	>69 (%)
Zero level of eclectic religiosity	34.0	36.3	33.2	30.3	36.0	41.1	46.8
Medium level of eclectic religiosity	23.4	27.5	41.0	43.0	40.2	41.1	38.0
High level of eclectic religiosity	42.6	36.3	25.8	26.8	23.8	17.7	15.2

Table 4: Distribution of answers according to level of eclectic religiosity and education level[29]

	Education level				
	Incomplete secondary education (%)	Secondary education (%)	Special secondary education (%)	High education (%)	Have academic degree (%)
Zero level of eclectic religiosity	50.0	41.2	41.9	32.8	34.6
Medium level of eclectic religiosity	40.6	28.4	39.0	38.0	19.2
High level of eclectic religiosity	9.4	30.4	19.1	29.2	46.2

The level of eclectic religiosity is, based on our research, growing as people obtain higher educational levels: respondents with incomplete secondary, completed secondary, and special secondary education (50%, 41%, and 42%, respectively) express a negative attitude toward non-Orthodox convictions more often than respondents who have a high education or academic degrees (33% and 35%, respectively). Respondents with a higher education will more frequently demonstrate a high level of eclectic religiosity than their less educated peers, but this tendency is not necessarily true when it comes to their attitudes toward magic.

Respondents with a secondary or lower education are more superstitious and less critical of magic than people with higher levels of education; the former more often believe in the power of talismans and amulets, in the energetic-informational properties of water, and are ready to consult magicians. On the other hand, the interest in magical ideas and practices as a component of religious patchwork does not depend on the level of education. For example, people believe in magic forces,

---

[29] The educational system in Russia has five basic levels. The incomplete secondary education is a level of unfinished school education, secondary education—a basic school education that takes ten to eleven years. Students receive special secondary education graduating from technicum (elementary vocational training), or high education graduating from university. The highest level of education is ended with obtaining of academic degree (candidate of science, then doctor of science).

auras, horoscopes, and accept the possibility of Spiritism almost irrespective of their educational level. This shows the universal appeal of old superstitions—but they still have the most influential among lower educated people.

Openness toward certain magic ideas and practices is based on particular interests present in the Russian society today. The concept of energetic-informational properties of water has been intensively discussed on television and online for several years. Many people with high levels of education became more skeptical toward this concept by participating in these debates. The concepts of auras, horoscopes, and the using Spiritism for specific purposes are very appealing, especially to younger generations. Mass media often forms positive opinions toward these concepts through the news, documentaries, films, and cartoons. These concepts also never become a subject of public debates in Russia, so people tend to accept the media portrayals of things like the magic properties of water uncritically.

Conclusion

Magic has historically been an important part of vernacular Orthodoxy; nowadays, it is complemented and supported by pseudoscientific ideas. The eclectic combination of Orthodox and popular non-Orthodox ideas and practices that Orthodox believers maintain is what we call vernacular Orthodoxy. We identified four patterns of Orthodox believers' attitudes toward magic: indifferent attitude in formal believers; conscious or not eclectics, blending Orthodoxy, and magic; interpretations midway between Orthodox and non-Orthodox ideas and practices; and negative attitudes of practicing believers. Belief in the reality of magic does not always coincide with a positive appraisal; magic can be perceived as a convenient, simple way to attain specific goals, as well as a manifestation of demonic forces. Orthodox believers can accept the idea that talismans and amulets are powerful, but can refuse to use them; they may consider magic to be real phenomenon based on past experiences, but refuse to participate in magic rituals.

The attitudes toward magic strongly depend on the respondent's religious behavior. Seldom practicing believers are more interested in magic than active practicing and formal believers: people who seldom practice often combine Orthodox and non-Orthodox ideas and produce vernacular interpretations. Gender, age, and educational levels do not form a strong correlation with one's attitude toward some magic concepts/beliefs. For example, a belief in talismans, amulets, and magic forces depends neither on age nor on gender. This can be explained by acknowledging the lifestyle and personal experience of some respondents, including various events they interpret as encounters with magic, that have a strong influence on the believers' attitude.

One's attitude toward magic strongly correlates with age: respondents younger than thirty years old demonstrate an increased interest in magic. They can accept new knowledge and experience; they more often than older people look at religious tradition as a rigid form without vital content and tend to rebel against it. This study shows older people are more conservative; the positive attitude toward magic decreases as respondents age (to sixty and older). In this age group, the majority of respondents show a zero level of eclectic religiosity.

> This research presents the results of the project "Traditional Religions in Post-Secular Society" funded by the Russian Humanitarian Scientific Foundation (№. 15-13-66601).

Bibliography

Nancy T. Ammerman, "Introduction. Observing Modern Religious Life," in Nancy T. Ammerman (ed.). *Everyday Religion: Observing Modern Religious Lives*, 3–20 (Oxford: Oxford University Press, 2007).

Dem'yan Beliaev, "A Case of Empirical Study of Deterodoxy Religion in Contemporary Russia/Opyt empiricheskogo issledovaniia geterodoksal'noi religioznosti v sovremennoi Rossii," in *Sotsiologicheskie issledovaniia*, vol. 11 (2009), pp. 88–98.

Irena Borowik, "Orthodoxy Confronting the Collapse of Communism in Post-Soviet Countries," in *Social Compass*, vol. 53, no. 2 (2006), pp. 267–278.

Valentina Chesnokova, *Churchiness as a Phenomena and Subject of Study/Votserkovlennost':* fenomen i sposoby ego izucheniia (Moscow: Desiat' let sotsiologicheskikh nabliudenii, 2003).

Karel Dobbelaere, "Towards an Integrated Perspective of the Processes Related to the Descriptive Concept of Secularization," in *Sociology of Religion*, vol. 3 (1999), pp. 229–247.

Emile Durkheim, *The Elementary Forms of Religious Life*. Translated by Karen E. Fields (New York: The Free Press, 1995).

James G. Frazer, *The Golden Bough* (New York: Macmillan, 1950).

Charles Y. Glock and Rodney Stark, *American Piety: The Nature of Religious Commitment* (Berkeley: University of California Press, 1968).

Ekaterina Grishaeva and Anastasia Cherkasova, "Orthodox Christianity and New Age Beliefs Among University Students of Russia: A Case of Post-Communist Mixed Religiosity," in *Religion and Society in Central and Eastern Europe*, vol.1 (2013), pp. 9–20.

Danièle Hervieu-Léger, "In Search of Certainties: The Paradoxes of Religiosity in Societies of High Modernity," in *Gosudarstvo, religiia, tserkov' v Rossii i za rubezhom*, vol.1 (2015), pp. 254–268.

Svetlana Karaseva and Elena Shkurova, "Study of Religion in the Multi-Religious Society: A Case of Belorussia/Izuchenie religioznosti v polikonfessional'noi srede (obosnovanie kontseptsii dlia Belarusi)," in Marinna Shakhnovich (ed.). *Nauka o religii v XXI veke: traditsionnye metody i novye paradigmy. Sbornik statei i dokladov,* 183–201 (Saint Petersburg: Saint Petersburg Philosophical Society, 2014).

Sergey Lebedev and Vladimir Sukhorukov, "Narrow Pass Nowhere/Tesnyi put' ne tuda?," in *Sotsiologicheskie issledovaniia*, vol.1 (2013), pp. 118–126.

Thomas Luckmann, *The Invisible Religion: The Problem of Religion in Modern Society* (New York: Macmillan, 1967).

Roman Lunkin, "The Numbers of the Faith and Values: May 2012. Analytical Review from Research Service 'Sreda'/Cifry o vere i cennostyah: May 2012. Analiticheskiy obzor ot Sluzhby 'Sreda'." *SREDA*. June 5, 2012. Accessed March 15, 2016. http://sreda.org/en/2012/tsifryi-o-vere-i-tsennostyah-may-2012-analiticheskiy-obzor-ot-sluzhbyi-sreda/5293#

Bronislaw Malinowski, *Magic, Science and Religion* (Prospect Heights, IL: Waveland Press, 1992).

John Middleton, *Magic, Witchcraft and Curing* (Austin: University of Texas Press, 1967).

Leonard Norman Primiano, "Vernacular Religion and the Search for Method in Religious Folklife," in *Western Folklore*, vol. 54, no. 1 (1995), pp. 37–56.

Leonard Norman Primiano, "Ratings of Social Institutions." *Russian Public Opinion Research Center.* Accessed March 15, 2016. http://www.wciom.com/index.php?id=123

Jlia Sinelina, "Churchiness and Superstitions in Yaroslavskaya oblast'/Votserkovlennost' i suevernoe povedenie zhitelei Yaroslavskoi oblasti," in *Sotsiologicheskie issledovaniia*, vol. 3 (2005), pp. 96–106.

Rodney Stark, "Reconceptualizing Religion, Magic, and Science," in *Review of Religious Research*, vol. 43, no. 2 (2001), pp. 101–120.

Randall G. Styers, *Making Magic: Religion, Magic, Science in the Modern World* (Oxford: Oxford University Press, 2004).

Larisa Titarenko, "On the Shifting Nature of Religion During the Ongoing Post-Communist Transformation in Russia, Belarus and Ukraine," in *Social Compass*, vol. 2 (2008), pp. 237–254.

Edward Burnett Tylor, *Religion in Primitive Culture* (New York: Harper and Brothers, 1958).

Don Yoder, "Toward a Definition of Folk Religion," in *Western Folklore*, vol. 33, no. 1 (1974), pp. 2–15.

Rosalie Wax and Murray Wax, "The Notion of Magic," in Current Anthropology, vol. 4, no. 5 (1963), pp. 495–518.

How to Become the "Slavic-Aryans": The Founders of the Russian Neo-Paganism and Their Ambitions

Victor Shnirelman

Abstract

The Russian Neo-paganism that emerged in the 1970s and 1980s was a radical ideology, and turned into a mass movement after 1991. In the 1990s, the Russian Neo-pagan communities grew like mushrooms. Who were their founders? What were their basic ideas and goals? How did they arrive at the Neo-paganism? What were their relationships with the Soviet and, later on, Russian states? What was the role of politics, especially nationalism in the emergence and further development of the Russian Neo-paganism? What can one expect from these groups and ideas in the future?

Keywords: Russia, Neo-paganism, nationalism

The Russian Neo-paganism reflects three cultural "positions" which emerged in the last Soviet decades: first, the ethnic Russian nationalism alarmed with what was a "non-Russians' political and economic encroachment" upon what was considered traditional Russian territory; second, an ecological movement concerned with the degradation of the environment; and third, an ethno-cultural movement meant to preserve traditional culture from disappearing in the face of modernization.

The first was the strongest and still affects Russian Neo-pagans, regardless of the diversity of their ideological stances and beliefs. This reflects both Russian and Western intellectual traditions of the xenophobic "Great Aryan Myth," which in the Russian cultural environment has been turned into the "Slavic Aryan Myth." I argue that it was mainly the political dynamics of recent decades that led to the emergence of Russian Neo-paganism, a community concerned more with the destiny of ethnic Russians and their culture than it was with any theological issues. To analyze this trend, I will present intellectual and political biographies of the most influential founders of Russian Neo-paganism, and discuss their successes and failures in contemporary Russia.

The emergence of Russian Neo-paganism was directly connected with the "Russian question," namely a crisis of the Russian ethnic identity that occurred in the late Soviet decades, especially after the collapse of the Soviet Union. As it is well known, ethnic Russians were a dominant majority in both the Russian Empire and the USSR. Further, until very recently they used to associate themselves primarily with the state rather than with any particular ethnicity, and did not separate their history from the history of the state. In addition, the Soviet myth of the time provided ethnic Russians with an "elder brother" status, which focused on them as the civilizers, the bearers of a higher level culture, who generously shared their material and intellectuals resources with all the other ethnic groups, especially the more "backward" ones. This myth was consciously and intensively cultivated by Soviet authorities from the late Stalin times (1940s to early 1950s) on. Further, ethnic Russians were presented by the state as the Messianic people meant to lead humanity toward a new, just civilization.

However, this image has changed in the late Soviet decades, when for various political, social, demographic, and cultural reasons, ethnic Russians began to see themselves as a minority rather than a majority. Ethnic nationalism increased and reflected a particular mythology—essentially a Great Narrative regarding "their" remote ancestors (Shnirelman and Komarova 1997). This is how the Russian Neo-paganism has come into being.

Its ideology emerged and was sharpened in the 1970s when an "anti-Zionist" campaign was launched in the USSR (Laqueur 1993: 107 ff.; Korey 1995). It was at that time that Neo-pagan founders discovered the Nazi racial myth (Agursky 1975). This together with an interest in early philosophical and religious teachings, in particular concerned with Indian ideas and the occult, attracted Russian intellectuals in the 1950s and 1960s (Heller 2012; Menzel 2012) and made up the ideological basis of this pagan movement.

Paganism in the Soviet period helped justify the Communist order, enabled the authorities fight against the universal monotheist religions and supported the idea that treat atheism was a faith (Shneider 1993: 144–148; also see Falikov 1989). This interest in paganism developed side by side with an interest in Russian folklore and tradition. The state propagandists tried to teach the public to perceive pagan beliefs and rituals as a more valuable cultural heritage rather than religion. The Communist Party elite supported this, especially on the eve of the coming Millennium of the Baptism of Rus' (Shnirelman 2015a).

It is in this environment that the chauvinist "Pamiat'" movement was born in Moscow. In 1980–1982, this developed inside the "Society of the Book-Lovers" at the Ministry of Aviation Industry, which then changed its name "Society of the Book-Lovers" to the Patriotic Association of "Pamiat'" in November 1982. Its core was made up of activists from the Moscow branch of the All-Union Society for Security of the Monuments of History and Culture (VOOPIK) and friends of the well-known Soviet artist Ilia Glazunov (Platonov 2012: 160–162). In the early 1980s, many of these people became obsessed with a version of Neo-paganism in which the Russians were believed to be the earliest people on Earth. This was acknowledged by one of the movement's leaders V. Yemelianov who claimed that "Pamiat'," in its founders' view, had to become a pagan anti-Christian organization (Yemelianov 1994). Its leaders were Communist Party members who wished to preserve the integrity of the Soviet Empire. At that time, the movement's links to Russian Orthodoxy and monarchism were of less importance for them (Solovei 1991: 18; Pribylovsky 1992: 165–166; Moroz 1992: 71–72; Verkhovsky and Pribylovsky 1996: 9–10; Mitrokhin 2003: 555–556).

It is in this period that the Russian nationalists discovered "eternal enemies" in the form of the "Zionists" (Jews) and Masons. They were searching tirelessly for the "secret(s)" of these foes that assured their survival, as they were thought to contain some kind of infinite power. To discover this secret they turned to the Aryan myth, which located their own ancestors in the Far North, in the legendary Hyperborea (Shnirelman 2007, 2014, 2015b). They developed the Aryan Myth by including both the occult tradition rooted in the M-m Blavatsky's "Theosophy and the Nazi heritage of occultism and racism." To adapt the myth to the Russian milieu, they slavified it, and the "Aryans" became the "Slavic-Aryan race." In addition, in order to provide the myth with historical authenticity, they used the fake "Book of Vles, that flooded the book market and media during the last quarter of the century (Shnirelman 1998, 2003) which contained numerous versions of the myth. It is noteworthy that the "Book of Vles" was discussed twice as a "mysterious chronicle of the 9th century" at the meetings of the "Pamiat'" in 1983 (Platonov 2012: 165–166). This demonstrated its importance for this new ethnic Russian nationalism.

Who were the promoters of the Aryan/Slavic myth? Valery Yemelianov (1929–1999) was one of the first to promote it. He graduated from the Institute of Eastern Languages at the Moscow State University and then worked for Khrushchev as a referent in the Near Eastern Affairs (Reznik 1996: 61–82). In 1963 he was tried for plagiarism in his PhD thesis, but this did not destroy his career. After Khrushchev had been dismissed him, Yemelianov managed to defend his thesis (again) at the Higher Party School (HPS) in 1967, and went on to teach at the Institute of Foreign Languages and at other higher education schools including HPS. His fluency in Arabic as well as his job helped him establish contacts in Arab countries, including higher-level officials. It is from there that he learned about "Zionism,"[1] and, since then Zionists, became a symbol of absolute evil and a target of uncompromised resistance for him, personally.

As a lecturer of the Moscow branch of the CPSU in the early 1970s, Yemelianov dedicated himself to "unmasking" the "Kike-Masonic plot" which had much in common with the "Protocols of the Elders of Zion" (Nudel'man 1979: 36–37). His lectures on the topic were only cancelled after the American Senator Jacob Javits protested (Vishnevskaia 1988: 85).

This did not stop Yemelianov and he went on to write the book "De-Zionization," first published in Arabic in the Syrian newspaper "Al-Baas" in 1979 by order of the President Hafez Asad. A photocopy of the

---

[1] For the Arabic "anti-Zionism" and popularity of Hitler in the Arabic world, see Lewis 1986: 192–235 and Wistrich 1991: 222–239, 247.

book was allegedly published in Paris by the Palestine Liberation Organization (PLO) and then disseminated in Moscow. The book included reproductions of Konstantin Vasiliev's pictures that represented the struggle of Russian heroes against evil forces. One particular picture there was entitled "Ilia of Murom gains the victory over the Christian plague," and this later became iconic for the Neo-pagans.

The book's narrative was popular among the Russian Neo-pagans as well as other Russian nationalists. According to Yemelianov, the world history was essentially a death struggle of the "Zionists" (Jews) and "Masons" against the rest of humanity led by the "Aryans"—according to a plan devised by King Solomon (Yemelianov 1979: 21). Yemelianov intended to unmask the wicked designs of the "Zionist-Masonic concern," which allegedly planned to build a world state by 2000. In Yemelianov's view, Christianity was Zionism's weapon, created by the Jews to enslave all the other peoples of the world. The author believed Jesus Christ to be simultaneously an "ordinary Jewish racist" and a Mason. He also discovered Prince Vladimir, the Baptist of the Rus', had Jewish blood. He claimed that only the "Aryan world" led by Russia could repel any future "Zionist assault" (Yemelianov 1979: 2, 28).

In 1977–1978, Yemelianov took an active role in the "anti-Zionist club" that had to become the core of the future World anti-Zionist and anti-Masonic Front (VASAMF) "Pamiat'" mass movement. Yet, the project was delayed, and the aforementioned "Society of the Book-Lovers" was established instead.

Obsessed with his "unmasking mission" Yemelianov began to accuse Soviet ruling elites, together with Leonid Brezhnev, of "Zionism." In 1980, he attempted to give copies of his book to members of the Politburo of the CC CPSU and its Secretariat. This was too much for the Soviet authorities—Yemelianov was kicked out of the Party and soon taken to the psychiatric asylum after being accused of murdering his wife (Reznik 1996). Once released in 1986, he initially sided with the Patriotic association of "Pamiat'," headed by Dmitry Vasiliev, and established VASAMF "Pamiat'" in late 1987 (Deich and Zhuravlev 1991: 145–156; Solovei 1991: 28–29; Pribylovsky 1992: 158, 1998a). The Front believed it stood for the "majority of natives of any country" and saw its mission to be a fight against the danger of the "Jewish Nazism (Zionism) rule." Its ambition was to establish an "anti-Zionist, anti-Masonic dictatorship" in every country without endangering the current state order. The Front saw this as a racial struggle, a struggle for democracy that would rescue the world from sufferings already "experienced by the peoples of Russia and Palestine." The Front supported the PLO (Lebedev 1991: 113–126; Solovei 1992: 129), and Yemelianov viewed Islam as a true ally in this struggle (Yemelianov 1979: 34).

Even after the 1989 fall, Yemelianov could not hide his sympathy toward paganism. He helped establish the Moscow Pagan Community and adopted the pagan name of Velemir. In 1992, he proclaimed himself the "Head of the World Russian Government", yet his organization had only several dozen members in the early 1990s. In the late 1990s, Yemelianov argued for the reestablishment of monarchy in Russia and named the retired colonel Eugene Dzhugashvili, Stalin's grandson, as its ruler (Pribylovsky 1998c). In the 1990s, Yemelianov taught in the Academy of Panzer Troops. Even if toward the end of his life, he lost influence as a political figure, his name is still respected by Russian Neo-pagans, who see him as a "founding father."

Alexei Dobrovol'sky (1938–2013) was another important Pagan activist, whose initiation in Neo-paganism occurred in the same Moscow milieu as Yemelianov (Rozhdestvensky 1981–1982: 258; Lugovoi 1996a, 1996b; Verkhovsky, Pribylovsky, and Mikhailovskaia 1998: 24–25; Mitrokhin 2003: 191–198; Shizhensky 2012: 13–42). He was a student of the Moscow Institute of Culture, but never graduated. As an admirer of Stalin, he became involved with various dissident movements from a very early age. In 1956, he made an attempt to organize the "Russian National-Socialist Party" with young workers from Moscow's military plants, in order to "restore the Russian nation." In May 1958, all these activists were arrested, and their leader was given three years in a labor camp. There he met former collaborationists, Nazis, and members of the People's-Labor Union (NTS). Being influenced by them, he was a monarchist for a short time (while in camp, 1958–1961), after which he was a member of an underground political organization (1963–1964). In March 1964, the members of this underground group were arrested, and

Dobrovol'sky, who feigned madness, was committed to a psychiatric asylum for a year. He was released in 1965, and rejoined the NTS in 1966–1967. During this time, he was taken with Nazi ideas, their symbolism, and "Higher Style." His dream was to eliminate all Jews. His new entourage, Nazis and collaborationists, led him to believe that Americans had built gas chambers to accuse Nazis of genocide (Charny 2004: 72–73).

In 1961, Dobrovol'sky was baptized in the Russian Orthodox faith, but his religious devotion did not last long. In the Dubravna labor camp (in Mordvinia), he became acquainted with S. Arseniev-Hoffman, a member of a secret Russian-German society that was established before the Second World War. It is from him that Dobrovol'sky learned about the "ancestors' faith," the "Nordic race" and the swastika. In 1969, he bought rare books, became interested in paganism and the occult, and became an admirer of Blavatsky's teaching. In 1986, he left Moscow for Pushchino and, since then, dedicated himself to folk medicine. In the late 1980s, he enrolled in the Patriotic Association of "Pamiat'," but, after the Russian Orthodoxy took the group over in 1987, he left it for the VASAMF "Pamiat'." In 1989, he helped establish the Moscow pagan community and adopted the pagan name of Dobroslav. During this time, he gave talks and actively participated in the national-patriotic meetings. In 1990, he collaborated with the "Russian Party" of another nationalist pagan Viktor Korchagin.

He later moved to the village of Vasenevo in the Kirov region, where he established his own pagan community around his family. He believed that the Slavic tribe of Viatich populated the area in the pre-Christian era. One of his sons, Alexander, was given the pagan name of Viatich. In 1993–1995, Dobroslav gave "enlightenment talks" in Kirov.

Dobroslav represented the "national-socialist" wing of the Neo-pagans and was highly respected by the nationalists. In 1994, he unsuccessfully attempted to establish a political organization—the Russian National Liberation Movement. On June 22, 1997, he established Veche—the united congress of the pagan communities, and was proclaimed the leader of the Russian Liberation Movement. He later had a fall out with the "Russian Truth" publishers, who had supported him earlier. A culture-historical society called "Yarila's Arrows" was established by Dobroslav's followers. This too disintegrated in the early 2000s because Dobroslav, a loner, was not interested in heading the organization, and there was no other option for a good leader.

In the early 2000s, Dobroslav focused on developing the pagan worldview and visited Moscow several times to give talks. On April 23, 2001, he was accused of stirring up anti-Semitism and religious hatred, and was taken to court. The regional Communist newspaper "Kirov's truth" intervened on his behalf (Putiatin 2001). Nonetheless, in March 2002 Dobroslav was sentenced to two years in prison (Polozov 2002). In March, May, and July 2005, three of Kirov's courts pointed to the extremist nature of several of Dobroslav's books, which led to these books being added to the Federal list of extremist literature in 2007.

The first leader of the Moscow pagan community (established in 1989) was Alexander Belov, whose pagan name was Selidor. Belov. He claimed that his ancestors were Varangians of the early chronicles, and that they originated from the Baltic-Slavic population. Furthermore, he claimed ancestors among the Livonian Order's knights, who took part in the battle of the Chudskoe Lake in 1242, one of the most important battles in Russian history. He argued that he was connected to the Order's knights through a descendant of Polish kings (Belov 2007: 29, 105, 113–114). In the 1970s, he studied martial arts, became a professional athlete, and received his black belt in 1982. Belov graduated from the Library-Bibliographic Faculty of the Moscow State Institute of Culture the same year, and then graduated from the Psychological Faculty of the Moscow State University in 1986. At the turn of the 1980s, he worked in the University of Peoples' Friendship, and later on—in a few Scientific-Technical Information Bureaus. He claimed to have met the famous psychiatrist N. P. Bekhtereva (1924–2008), who taught him nontraditional approaches to human psychology. He also studied magic and came to believe in reincarnation.

During 1989–1990, Belov was a member of the VASAMF "Pamiat'." In 1990, he expelled Yemelianov, Dobrovol'sky, and their followers from his community for political radicalism (Verkhovsky, Papp, and Pribylovsky 1996: 263–264; Pribylovsky 1998b, 1998c). Afterwards, the community changed its name to the Moscow Slavic Pagan Community and made it clear that it had a nonpolitical agenda. The group distanced itself from fascism and claimed that its goal was to restore to the modern era early Slavic spirituality (Belov 1992: 392–393). In addition, Belov wrote stories and novels about remote ancestors, who he identified with the "Slavic-Aryans," and linked them with an unbelievable chronology and advanced cultural advancements.

All these activists were connected to Moscow. Other developments took part in Leningrad (now St. Petersburg), where the movement was started by Viktor Bezverkhy (1930–2000). Bezverkhy graduated from the Mikhail Frunze Advanced Military and Naval High School in 1952. He received his PhD in Marxist-Leninist Philosophy in 1967 from the Leningrad State University, with a dissertation on the Immanuel Kant's anthropological views. He then taught Marxism-Leninism there and at other civil and military colleges. At the same time, he invited his students to informal gatherings in his apartment, where he taught them racist and anti-Semitic concepts arguing that society needed to be delivered from the "defective offspring" that resulted from mixed marriages. These "hybrids" were depicted by Bezverkhy as the "Kikes, Indians or Gypsies, and Mulattos," all of whom allegedly delayed societal development and social justice (Shnirelman 1998). At age fifty-one, he took an oath to "devote all his life to fight against Jews—the mortal enemy of humanity."

Bezverkhy's philosophy of "Vedizm" argued that "in case of a fascist victory, all the peoples will be passed through a sieve to reveal a racial origin: the Aryans will be united, the Asian, African and Indian elements will be put in their place, and the Mulattos will be eliminated as entirely useless" (Solomenko 1993). The "Vedists" believed that "hybrids" enslaved humanity by hiding knowledge and introducing into the world a system of "usurper slavery" based on "Judaism and its daughter branches like Marxism-Leninism, the ecumenical worldview, Krishnaism."

Around 1979, Bezverkhy decided to establish the "Volkhv club," which had to include Nazi-style paramilitary groups. At the same time, he drew on his knowledge about the Gestapo in order to compile files on

Jewish intellectuals in Leningrad (Lisochkin 1988; Solomenko 1993; Verkhovsky, Papp, and Pribylovsky 1996: 242–243). In 1990, his dreams and ideas gained some credibility when the "Union of the Veneds" was established. Simultaneously, he started a small publishing house of "Volkhv" which published Hitler's *Mein Kampf* in 1992. In 1992 and 1995, he was taken to court for stirring ethnic strife, yet managed to escape conviction. Petersburg's artist and publicist Igor Siniavin (1937–2000) is sometimes viewed as one of the founders of Russian Neo-paganism. He graduated from the Military-Topographic School, and later was a student at the Leningrad State University—initially at the Mechanic-Mathematical Faculty, and then—at the Art Department of the Historical Faculty. He began his career in Leningrad as a modernist artist opposing official Soviet art. He later turned to political writing, and became an advocate for Russian Neo-paganism, believing it would be a powerful instrument to mobilize the Russian people. During his lifetime, Siniavin became increasingly radicalized. In the late 1960s, like many other nonconforming artists, he was interested in spiritual traditions, which led him to mystic and occult teachings. He was attracted to the religions of Ancient India and Egypt as well as Christianity, in the spirit of Blavatsky's Theosophy. He was arrested in May 1976, then fled the country, and lived in the United States until 1986.

He found the American lifestyle shocking, and subsequently went through a spiritual crisis, that led him to believe a clash between the West and Russia is imminent. Since then, he portrayed the West as the "historical enemy," incapable of understanding Russia with its Messianic idea, and believed that the West wanted to make Russia a colony or to destroy it entirely. He began to envision a clash between Russia and the West in cultural rather than social-political terms. He came to see Russianness as a cultural, ethnical, and ideological concept rather than one of racial-ethnic dimensions: the Russians were those who wanted to serve Russia (Siniavin 1991: 140–141). Siniavin wanted Russia to be a powerful state, associated democracy with a "Satanic force," demanded that individuality be subordinated to state, while the state had to be ruled by "own, native" authorities. By that time he had drifted away from modernism because of its "anti-national stance" and viewed artistic license as "undermining of any regime" (Siniavin 1991: 147).

Having rejected the United States, Siniavin became a Russian nationalist, whose values were "Homeland, Nation, People" (Siniavin 1991: 149). He associated true Russia with Slavic Rus', and romanticized the early Slavs, arguing that modern Russia should remain loyal to its history. His attitude toward Christianity became ambivalent, as he tried to separate its high moral standards from "fanatic (Jewish) nationalism." His view of Communism was similar: on the one hand, he discovered that it represented the eternal Russian dream of Truth and Freedom; on the other hand, he was embarrassed with its "Zionist stance" (Siniavin 1991: 201–205).

Before his trip to the United States, Siniavin had distanced himself from ethnic-racial issues, but upon his return to Moscow, he attacked Soviet internationalism and believed it led to the "genocide of the Russian people." In his "Soviet period," he began to see remote prehistory in romantic terms ("the more remote, the more light") and was attracted to the early Slavs. By 1990, he rejected Christianity, which emphasized humility. Instead, he demanded an open struggle for "the truth of the Russian Soil." For that, a "genuine early Slavic spirit" had to be restored (Siniavin 1991: 15, 134). He believed that Russian Orthodoxy had lost its ideological power and Christian morals could only be productive in a homogenous state. Siniavin rejected a pluralist and liberal agenda. Instead, he dreamed of a consolidated Russian nation, supported by a powerful state and social unanimity ("the only Truth"). Thus, a new ideology came to life. Siniavin now believed that one had to rely solely on one's own people, the state, and its own geography (Siniavin 1991: 138, 208–214). In the early 1990s, he turned to Russian Neo-paganism and in 1996 published his book "The Way of Truth" (Siniavin 2001).

A journalist, Oleg Gusev, is of equal interest as a case study of how one can come to embrace a right radicalism based on anti-Christianity and paganism. A Khabarovsk native, he graduated from the Khabarovsk Forest Engineering School and had been a correspondence student of the Department of Journalism at the Philological Faculty of the

Far Eastern University since 1969. Simultaneously, he worked as a journalist for a newspaper of the Far Eastern military region. This, plus rumors on the imminent "Chinese threat," especially after the 1969 Soviet-Chinese clashes on the Domansky Island, led him to fear a "world plot" against Russia. Gusev started attending political meetings in the late 1980s in Leningrad. There he met Roman Perin and Eugene Krylov and became part of their small National-Democratic Party. In 1991–1993, he started, together with Perin, a racist and anti-Semitic newspaper called "Russian action." Gusev saw this as a response to "Zionists" who allegedly organized perestroika, and to the democrats who supported them. Before they started the newspaper, Perin and Gusev studied the prerevolutionary Russian anti-Semites and racists as well as their Western counterparts. In this way, they came across the Black Hundred newspaper "Russian action," where they found an attractive agenda and thus gave the same name to their own newspaper (Gusev 2000: 49–50, 96).

The newspaper was banned after the October 1993 putsch. It later appeared under the name "For the Russian action," with the same goal—the "unmasking of the criminal deeds of the world Jewish criminal-political mafia against Russia" (Gusev 2000: 51). Initially the newspaper had close ties with the Bezverkhy's "Union of Veneds," but Gusev had broken ties with the Union for ideological reasons by the mid-1990s. In 1996–1997, both Gusev and Perin tried to establish new political parties but failed.

Gusey's writing career was more successful, and by the late 1990s he was head of the North-Western branch of the All-Slavic Union of Journalists and a professor at the World Slavic Academy. In the early 2000s, Gusev published several "pagan racism" books based on Aryan ideas. This strategy proved to be effective for many like Gusev, and over the last fifteen years many Neo-pagan leaders left the political stage, attempting to make their ideas popular through their books. However, in

2011–2014, Gusev and Perin were taken to court several times for inciting hatred and racial hostility.[2] Recently, Perin acknowledged that their newspaper had lost its large audience.[3]

Several other Russian nationalist leaders, who wanted to shape the "Russian idea," followed the Siniavin's route. Gradually, they rejected their former "Soviet" or "State-Monarchic" illusions and advocated instead a Russian Neo-paganism. They all came to view this as an ideology rather than a religion, and believed this was what the Russian people needed. A poet, Alexei Shiropaev, started his career by advocating for the empire and "Russian Orthodox fascism" (Shiropaev 1995), yet later on, he reinvented himself as a pagan and regionalist. He graduated from the Moscow art school and became a well-known activist of the Neo-Slavophile wing of the Russian nationalist movement in the mid-1980s (Shiropaev 1992). In 1993–1994, he shifted to Nazism and became one of the leaders in the People's-National Party of Alexander Ivanov (Sukharevsky). At that time, he glorified the Russian empire, wrote a manifesto of the "Russian Orthodox Aryanism" (Shiropaev 1994), and evidently wished to become a Russian Gabriele D'Annunzio.[4]

Yet after 2000, he broke away from Russian Orthodoxy and turned to paganism. In 2001, he published "Prison of the People," a book that challenged the beliefs of many of his former associates. He claimed that the main enemy of the Russian nationalists was the "Eurasian Project" of the "Khazars" and "Byzantians," supposedly a political agenda of the Russian Tsars, Red Commissars, and the Russian Orthodox Church for centuries. He himself stood for Russian separatism, not unity, and the existence of separate, racially homogenous Russian states oriented toward Europe. He saw Russianness in racial terms that emphasized the purity of blood, and wanted Europe and Russia to become that "white world" of the SS dreams (Shiropaev 2001).

In January 2007 with Vadim Shtepa, Shiropaev held a meeting of the "national-democrats" in Great Novgorod. They proclaimed themselves "Novgorod Veche" and introduced the Pangolin (Crocodile) as

---

[2] (http://www.zrd.spb.ru/hronika.htm). Accessed on January 3, 2016
[3] (http://spb-politics.livejournal.com/). Accessed on January 3, 2016
[4] For Annunzio's role in Italian Fascism, see Gillette 2002.

their symbol—allegedly because it was a major god of pre-Christian Northern Rus'. Their regionalism has a "white ethno-racial foundation" which unites numerous "Russian nations." Like some other European right radicals, Shiropaev has recently made an attempt to establish contact with Israel to help resist "extremism, religious fanaticism and nationalism."[5] He currently claims that he shifted to liberal nationalism and radically revised his former views (Volchek 2016).

A similar trajectory was taken by another well-known national-democrat, Peter Khomiakov (1950–2014), who initially claimed adherence to Russian Orthodoxy, but turned to paganism for political and ideological reasons. One of the more educated Russian radicals, he graduated from the Geographical and Mechanic-Mathematic Faculty of the Moscow State University, defended a PhD thesis in management and was awarded the title of professor. In post-Soviet Russia, he was affiliated with the Institute of System Analysis.

Khomiakov became a nationalist to protest against Soviet bureaucratic mismanagement (Khomiakov 2006). What started his political struggle was the redirection of the Siberian rivers: he joined the "Pamiat'," but left it after D. Vasiliev became its leader. In February 1992, he sided with the "Russian National Sobor" of General A. Sterligov, yet left it being frustrated with its strong "anti-intellectual tendencies." After that, he joined several small nationalist movements, including national-capitalists grouped around the journal "Golden Lion." In 2002, he was a member of the "Congress of the Russian communities" and was close to its leader Dmitry Rogozin. Later on, he became one of the leaders of the racist "Liberty Party" (Verkhovsky and Kozhevnikova 2009: 231–237).

Being frustrated with Putin, Khomiakov established a network "National Liberation of the Russian People" in the fall of 2006 and soon after became an ideologist for the small radical group the "Northern Brotherhood." Both were pagan organizations and opposed "imperial Russia." They disseminated their views through a website until fall 2009 when the website was closed by the police. In 2008, Khomiakov made contacts

---

[5] Rossiiskie natsional-demokraty nashli ponimanie. v Izraile // Dniester, July 12, 2011. Accessed on January 3, 2016. http://dniester.ru/content/rossiiskie-natsional-demokraty-nashli-ponimanie-v-izraile.

with Ukrainian radical nationalists and together they started the "Confederation of equal and free East Slavic territories" with a headquarters in Kiev. In October 2008, he was elected the president of "Russians for the Ukrainian Guerilla Army." The Russian Federal Security Service (FSB) tracked his activities and Khomiakov was arrested and tried in March 2009, but soon released. To escape prosecution, he left for Ukraine (Sergeev and Trifonov 2009). Then he moved to Georgia, but returned to Russia in 2011 and was immediately arrested. In October 2012, he was imprisoned to four years for financial fraud and the establishment of extremist organization[6] and died incarcerated.

An original version of Neo-paganism emerged in Omsk led by Father Alexander (A. Yu. Khinevich), who graduated from the Omsk Polytechnic Institute. In time, he became more attracted to psychology than technology, became an actor and focused on hypnosis and parapsychology. He became well known in the late 1980s occult wave when he gave lectures in esotericism and became interested in folk medicine and UFOs.

In 1990, he established a Center for the study of paranormal phenomena "Jiva-Astra" where the members performed exorcisms and practiced folk medicine. This center became the Neo-pagan Church "Jiva Temple of Inglia" and was promoted the World Truth, a religion allegedly brought from the Cosmos by "white people—the Aryans." The Church, which borrowed the term "Inglings" from Scandinavian folklore, has no branches outside Russia and was registered in Omsk in October 1992 (Yashin 1994, 1997, 2001; Tkach 1998).

Khinevich then opened there an "early Russian temple" as a "Temple of Perun's Wisdom" (Khinevich 1999: 152; Vladimirov 1994). Its interior decorations showed a scene of syncretic nature of the "Slavic-Aryan myth." A sign above the entrance reproduced paleography from the "Book of Vles," and Russian icons were placed side by side with Konstantin Vasiliev's pictures[7] and swastikas inside. The church exhibits

---

[6] Lider "Severnogo bratstva" poluchil chetyre goda kolonii // Lenta.ru, October 15, 2012. Accessed on January 3, 2016. http://lenta.ru/news/2012/10/15/homyakov/
[7] Konstantin Vasiliev's pictures dwelt on the Nazi artistic style are highly appreciated by both Neo-pagans and right radicals in Russia.

other religious symbols, such as statues of Perun, Krishna, and the Yin-Yang. The temple sponsored two (male and female) seminaries and a Sunday school, which focused on the Occult (Chanysheva 1999). By 1999, about 3,000 students graduated from Khinevich's school and his community had some 500 permanent members (Yashin 2001). By 2009, the community had grown to 600 people. Its members were shocked by the Soviet Union's dissolution, but were also attracted to Khinevich's teachings, that linked them to the "Great Race," and a glorious "Aryan" past. Sometimes the school children in town would visit the Temple, and some became infatuated with Ingliism (Chanysheva 1999).

Following Blavatsky, Khinevich believed that Earth's different races originated from the aliens from different planets, and these mixed marriages caused spiritual and intellectual decline. He also claimed that "Russian Slavs" had secret Vedic knowledge, argued that Christianity was a "Kike-Masonic plot," which aimed at Slavic degeneration. Therefore, he sees swastikas as "signs of defense of the Native land and Holy Faith" (Khinevich 1998). Khinevich shared his ideas in a book entitled "Ingliism. Short course" in 1992 and then in a series of books under the "Slavic-Aryan Vedas" published later. In 1992, Khinevich visited the United States and claimed he established branches of his Church there. Being an admirer of A. Asov, the major advocate of the "Book of Vles" Khinevich attempted to get in contact with Neo-pagans in Moscow and elsewhere, but without much success. However, back in St. Petersburg he was named a "honorary Vened."

Initially Khinevich's movement had a political dimension that focused on the Russian nation, paganism as a national ideal and was an infatuated with Aryanism. Khinevich expressed sympathy for the chauvinist "Russian National Unity" of Alexander Barkashov, which kept guard at the mass actions of Inglings. In general he was politically active in 1990–1993. Since then, he found a loyal audience and became more careful—he shared his ideas now only with trusted people, and his "holy books" opened only for the initiated. From time to time, he arranged mass pagan festivals and rituals (Khinevich 1999: 216–235), where people started bonfires shaped as swastikas.

Khinevich's Church's hierarchy was led by "Pater Dii" (Khinevich). In an attempt to make his teachings attractive, and to keep the community intact and homogenous, he claimed that the church was for "white people." He introduced a rule stating that if Inglings withdrew, it would not only consider an act of betrayal but a renunciation of their Clan, parents, and ancestors. According to Khinevich, this would lead to the death of everyone in the Clan (Khinevich 2000: 124).

Khinevich was charged with racism and anti-Semitism because of his teachings. As a consequence, tensions developed between Khinevich and municipal authorities in the early 2000s. This first occurred in 1997 when the authorities accused Inglings of displaying swastikas and extreme nationalism (Yashin 2001). After a court verdict of May 5, 2004, the Khinevich's Church and two other pagan bodies (Slavic community of Asgard and Slavic community of the Temple of Perun's Wisdom) were closed."[8] By June, Khinevich had reopened his community and website. In late 2006, he republished the book "Slavic-Aryan Vedas," which a court found to be extremist (Lidera 2008). In June 2009, he was sentenced to one and a half years in prison, but continued his religious activity. In November 2015, the court labeled "Slavic-Aryan Vedas" an extremist organization once again.[9]

Discussion

Many founders of the contemporary Russian Neo-pagans opposed the Soviet regime, and a search for new models of political and social organization led them to paganism. They were initially inspired by Russian nationalism, at least more than by any spiritual concerns. Some of them were attracted to folk medicine, magic, and parapsychology and tried to develop their own esoteric traditions. It was these figures who became

---

[8] Sudebnoe reshenie o likvidatsii pravoradikal'nykh organizatsiii v Omske // Tsentr "Sova," April 30, 2004 (http://www.sova-center.ru/racism-xenophobia/docs/2004/04/d8899/). Accessed on January 3, 2016. Also see Verkhovsky and Kozhevnikova 2005: 113.

[9] Voitovich V. Omsky sud priznal "Slaviano-Ariiskie Vedy" extremistskim materialom // superomsk, November 6, 2015. Accessed on January 3, 2016. http://super-omsk.ru/news/24018

founders of the first pagan communities, such as Belov, Bezverkhy, Dobroslav, and Khinevich. Others emphasized the political dimensions of Russian (re)nationalization Ie (Yemelianov, Siniavin, Shiropaev, Khomiakov, and Gusev). All of them were urban intellectuals and most well educated. Still they held on to the imaginary image of the "enemy," and all of them were enthusiastic about the remote Slavic past that they learned about—more from myth and folklore than scholarly knowledge. They attributed unbelievable depth to this past and located in it the roots of Russia's present dilemmas.

They saw themselves as marginal on the Soviet political stage and were often persecuted by the police. Their activities became much more of a success after the dissolution of the USSR, when state security became more lax and the Communist ideology was discredited. Once Soviet atheism was weakened, its place was taken by mass enthusiasm about various religious teachings. This occurred against a background of a deep political, social, and economic crisis, including wide-scale threats to the Soviet system of values. A growth of ethnic tension led to the ethnic wars along Russia's borders and a sense that ethnic Russians themselves were becoming victims. This made people frustrated with the Soviet internationalism. Such an environment led to a renewed interest in Russian (Slavic) values and this in turn gave rise to Neo-pagan communities.

These Russian (Slavic) values had been controlled and defined by the Russian Orthodox Church in the past, which allowed it to dominate Russia for centuries. In response, the Russian Neo-pagans depicted the Middle Ages as a period when the genuine pre-Christian culture fell victim to a barbaric pogrom, people lost their freedom and found themselves oppressed by the Church and state. This narrative extended the Golden Slavic Age in pre-Christian eras, which, based on esoteric accounts, was represented by 2,000 years of the terrible era of Kali-Yuga. They accused Christians and Jews of brutality and viewed them as unwelcomed guests who arrived in Rus' to enslave and eliminate the Slavs. This narrative had parallels links to the Aryan Myth, which glorified the Aryans, the supposed ancestors or close relatives of the Slavs, and stigmatized the Jews. Christianity was associated with the Jews, while the "Slavic-

Aryans" were depicted as the bearers of pre-Christian wisdom and some of the earliest religious traditions, ones thought to be the basis for all other religions of the world. Neo-pagans wished to restore this original faith and knowledge to Russia and bring harmony to the world by establishing a new Golden Age. Yet, while celebrating the democratic values of their remote ancestors, these Neo-pagan leaders wanted to impose upon Russia their own fascist dictatorship. Their ideology was often xenophobic and racist. Their discourse, especially their overt anti-Christianity, led Neo-pagans to oppose (and be opposed by) many in contemporary Russia, and to be, as in the Soviet period, persecuted.

At the same time, not all Neo-pagan communities, which have emerged in the last twenty years, follow the agenda set down by the Neo-pagan founder-fathers discussed here. Nonetheless, all of them occupy marginal niches in the Russian Orthodox environment and are often attacked by the Church and state.

Acknowledgments

The chapter is a result of the project "The problems of interethnic contacts and interactions in the texts of both oral and written culture: the Slavs and the Jews" (the Russian Scientific Foundation grant no. 15-18-00143).

Bibliography

Mikhail Samuilovich Agursky, "Neonatsistskaia opasnost' v Sovetskom Soiuze," *Novyi Zhurnal* (New York, 1975) 118: 205-218

Alexandr K. Belov, "Poklonenie Perunu," in *Nauka i religia*, vol. 11 (1992), pp. 16–17.

Alexandr K. Belov, *Udar iz niotkuda azbuka boevoi magii* (Moscow: Russkaia panorama, 2007).

N. O. Chanysheva, "Russkoe neoyazychestvo (na primere drevnerusskoi pravoslavnoi ingliisticheskoi tserkvi i dvizheniia 'Troianova tropa' v g. Omske)." 1999. Accessed January 29, 2010. http://www.ic.omskreg.ru/religion/kult/neoyaz/trop_main.htm

S. Charny, "Natsistskie gruppy v SSSR v 1950–1980-ye gody," in *Neprikosnovennyi zapas*, vol. 5, no. 37 (2004), pp. 71–78.

Mark Deich and Leonid Zhuravlev, *Pamiat' kak ona est* (Moscow: Tsunami, 1991).

Boris Zinoviyevich Falikov, "Neomistitsizm v SSSR," in Dimitri Efimovich Furman and Mark Smirnovk (eds.). *Na puti k svobode sovesti*. T.1, pp. 478–492 (Moscow: Nauka, 1989).

Aaron Gillette, *Racial Theories in Fascist Italy* (London: Routledge, 2002).

Oleg Gusev, *Belyi kon' Apokalipsisa* (St. Petersburg: LIO Redaktor, 2000).

Leonid Heller, "Away from the Globe. Occultism, Esotericism and Literature in Russia During the 1960s–1980s," in Birgit Menzel, Michael Hagemeister, and Bernice Glatzer Rosenthal (eds.). *The New Age of Russia. Occult and Esoteric Dimensions*, pp. 186–210 (Berlin: Otto Sagner, 2012).

Alexander Khinevich, "Svastika. Istoricheskie korni," in *Rodnye Prostory*, vol. 1, no. 36 (1998), p. 7.

Alexander Khinevich, *Slaviano-Ariiskie Vedy. Kniga vtoraia. Kniga Sveta. Kharatii Sveta: Kharatii 1–4* (Omsk: Izdanie Drevnerusskoi Ingliisticheskoi Tserkvi Pravoslavnykh Staroverov-Inglingov, 1999).

Alexander Khinevich, *Slaviano-Ariiskie Vedy. Kniga tretia. Ingliizm. Slovo mudrosti volkhva Velimudra. Chast' 2* (Omsk: Izdanie Drevnerusskoi Ingliisticheskoi Tserkvi Pravoslavnykh Staroverov-Inglingov; Arkor, 2000).

Petr Khomiakov, *Otchet Russkim bogam veterana Russkogo dvizheniia* (Moscow: Belye Al'vy. 2006).

William Korey, *Russian Antisemitism, Pamyat, and the Demonology of Zionism* (Chur: Harwood Academic Publishers, 1995).

Walter Laqueur, *Black Hundred. The Rise of the Extreme Right in Russia* (New York: Harper Collins, 1993).

Alexander V. Lebedev, ed., *Ruskoe delo segodnia. Kniga 1 'Pamiat'*, pp. 12–95 (Moscow: TsIMO IEA RAN, 1991).

Bernard Lewis, *Semites and Anti-Semites. An Inquiry Into Conflict and Prejudice* (New York: W. W. Norton & Company, 1986).

"Lidera zapreshchennoi obshchiny staroverov-inglingov privlekaiut k otvetstvennosti za popytku narushit' zapret"//News.ru, November 11. Accessed January 7, 2016. http://www.newsru.com/religy/11nov2008/zapret.html

Igor Lisochkin, "Neispovedimy puti "vedizma," in *Leningradskaia pravda*, December 22 (1988), p. 3.

E. Lugovoi, Ogneved: "Slava Yarile!," in *Sovety Baby Yagi*, vol. 2, no. 6 (1996a), p. 4.

E. Lugovoi "Pis'ma redaktoru," in *Sovety Baby Yagi*, vol. 1, no. 5 (1996b), p. 4.

Birgit Menzel, "Occult and Esoteric Movements in Russia from the 1960s to the 1980s," in Birgit Menzel, Michael Hagemeister, and Bernice Glatzer Rosenthal (eds.). *The New Age of Russia. Occult and Esoteric Dimensions*, 151–185 (Berlin: Otto Sagner, 2012).

Nikolai Mitrokhin, *Russkaia partiia. Dvizhenie russkikh natsionalistov v SSSR, 1953–1985 gody* (Moscow: Novoe literaturnoe obozrenie, 2003).

V. L. Moroz, "Bortsy za 'Sviatuiu Rus'" i zashchitniki 'Sovietskoi Rodiny'," in Rafail Sh. Ganelin (ed.). *Natsional'naia pravaia prezhde i teper'*. Chast' 2, vyp.1 (1992), pp. 68–96.

Rafail Nudel'man, "Sovremennyi sovietsky antisemitizm. Formy i soderzhanie," in *Antisemitizm v Sovietskom Soiuze. Ego korni i posledstviia* (1979), pp. 24–52. (Moscow: Publisher, Biblioteka Allia, 1979)

Oleg Platonov, "Voina s vnutrennim vragom" (Moscow: Algoritm, 2012).

A. Polozov, "Yazychnika iz Shabalinskikh lesov osudili na dva goda," in *Viatsky krai*, March 8, 2002.

Vladimir Pribylovski, "Pamiat'," in Rafail Sh. Ganelin (ed.). *Natsional'naia pravaia prezhde i teper'*. Chast' 2, vyp.2 (1992), pp. 151–170.

Vladimir Pribylovski, "Russkie yazychniki," in *Ekspress-khronika*, February 21, 1998a.

Vladimir Pribylovski, "Russkie yazychniki," in *Ekspress-khronika*, March 7, 1998b.

Vladimir Pribylovski, "Novye yazychniki—liudi i gruppy," in *Russkaia mysl'*, April 30–May 6, 4220 (1998c), p. 21.

A. Putiatin, "Borets s khristianstvom opravdan," in *Viatsky nabliudatel'*, May 18, 2001.

Semen Reznik, *The Nazification of Russia: Anti-Semitism in the Post-Soviet Era* (Washington, DC: Challenge Publications, 1996).

S. D. Rozhdestvensky, "Materialy k istorii samodeiatel'nykh politicheskikh ob'edinenii v SSSR posle 1945 goda," in *Pamiat', Moscow-Paris*, vyp. 5 (1981–1982), pp. 226–283.

Nikolay Sergeev and Vladislav Trifonov, "'Severnyi brat' Khomiakov bezhal v Kiev," in *Kommersant*, August 14, 2009.

Roman Shizhensky, *Filosofiia dobroi sily: zhizn' i tvorchestvo Dobroslava, A. A. Dobrovol'skogo* (Penza: Sotsiosfera, 2012).

Aleksei Shiropaev, "Revoliutsiia prodolzhaetsia...," in *Russkii vestnik*, vol. 24 (1992), p. 11.

Aleksei Shiropaev, "Plot' i krov'," in *Zemshchina*, vol. 99–100 (1994), p. 15.

Aleksei Shiropaev, "Sverkh-natsional'nyi sotsializm," in *Nasledie predkov*, vol. 1 (1995), pp. 27–33.

Aleksei Shiropaev, *Tiur'ma naroda: russkii vzgliad na Rossiiu* (Moscow: FERI-V, 2001).

G. Shneider, "Ot ateizma k iazychestvu," in Mikhail Naumovich Epstein (ed.). *Novoe sektantstvo: tipy religiozno-filosofskikh umonastroenii v Rossii* (70–80-ye gg. XX v.), pp.144–148 (Holyoke: New England Publishing Co, 1993).

Victor A. Shnirelman, *Russian Neo-Pagan Myths and Antisemitism* (Jerusalem: The Hebrew University, 1998).

Victor A. Shnirelman, "Aryanism, Neo-Paganism, and the Jews in Post-Soviet Russia," in *Jews in Russia and Eastern Europe*, vol. 2, no. 51 (2003), pp. 69–102.

Victor A. Shnirelman, "Russian Response: Archaeology, Russian Nationalism and Arctic Homeland," in Kohl Ph. L., Kozelsky M., and Ben-Yehuda N. (eds.). *Selective Remembrance: Archaeology in the Construction, Commemoration, and Consecration of National Pasts*, pp. 31–70 (Chicago: Chicago University Press, 2007).

Victor A. Shnirelman, "Hyperborea: Arctic Myth of the Contemporary Russian Radical Nationalists," in *Journal of Ethnology and Folkloristics*, vol. 8, no. 2 (2014), pp. 121–138.

Victor A. Shnirelman, "Perun vs Jesus Christ: Communism and Emergence of Neo-Paganism in the USSR," in Ngo, T. and J. Quijada (eds.). *Atheist Secularism and Its Discontents. A Comparative Study of Religion and Communism in Eurasia*, pp. 173–189 (Basingstoke: Palgrave Macmillan, 2015a).

Victor A. Shnirelman, *Ariisky mif v sovremennom mire*. In 2 vols (Moscow: NLO, 2015b).

Victor Shnirelman and Galina Komarova, "Majority as a Minority: The Russian Ethno-Nationalism and Its Ideology in the 1970s—1990s," in Hans-Rudolf Wicker (ed.). *Rethinking Nationalism and Ethnicity: The Struggle for Meaning and Order in Europe*, pp. 211–224 (Oxford: Berg Publishers, 1997).

Igor Siniavin, *Glas* (LIO "Redaktor": Leningrad, 1991).

Igor Siniavin, *Stezia pravdy*, Second edition (Moscow: Russkaia Pravda, 2001).

Valerii Solovei, "Pamiat'": istoriia, ideologiia, politicheskaia praktika," in Alexander V Lebedev (ed.). *Ruskoe delo segodnia. Kniga 1 "Pamiat"*, pp. 12–95 (Moscow: TsIMO IEA RAN, 1991).

Valerii Solovei, "Sovremennyi russkii natsionalism: ideino-politicheskaia klassifikatsiia," in *Obshchestvennye nauki i sovremennost'*, vol. 2 (1992), pp. 119–129.

Ye Solomenko, "Adolf Hitler v Sankt-Peterburge," in *Izvestiia*, June 10 (1993), p. 5.

V. A Tkach, "Orden-missiia 'Jiva-Khram Inglii'," in N. A. Trofimchuk (ed.). *Gosudarstvo, religiia, tserkov' v Rossii i za rubezhom*, vol. 5 (1998), pp. 39–44.

Alexander Verkhovsky and Galina Kozhevnikova, "Tri goda protivodeistviia in Alexander Verkhovsky (ed.). *Tsena nenavisti. Natsionalizm v Rossii i protivodeistvie rasistskim prestupleniiam*, pp. 111–129 (Moscow: Tsentr "Sova.", 2005).

Alexander Verkhovsky and Galina Kozhevnikova, eds., *Radikal'nyi russkii natsionalizm: struktura, idei, litsa* (Moscow: Tsentr "Sova.", 2009).

Alexander Verkhovsky, Anatoly Papp, and Vladimir Pribylovsky, *Politicheskii extremizm v Rossii* (Moscow: Institut experimentalnoi sotsiologii, 1996).

Alexander Verkhovsky and Vladimir Pribylovsky, *Natsional-patrioticheskie organizatsii v Rossii* (Moscow: Institut experimental'noi sotsiologii, 1996).

Alexander Verkhovsky, Vladimir Pribylovsky, and Ekaterina Mikhailovskaia, *Natsionalism i ksenofobia v rossiiskom obshchestve* (Moscow: Panorama, 1998).

Yu Vishnevskaia, "Pravoslavnye, gevalt!," in *Sintaksis*, vol. 21 (1988), pp. 82–101.

V. Vladimirov, "Sooruzhaetsia khram," in *Omskii vestnik*, July 5.(1994), p. 1.

"Preobrazhenie natsionalista", *Radio Svoboda*, January 16, 2016. Accessed January 16, 2016. http://www.svoboda.org/content/article/27489657.html

Robert S. Wistrich, *Antisemitism. The Longest Hatred* (London: Themes Methuen, 1991).

V. B. Yashin, "Predstavleniia o severe Omskoi oblasti v sovremennykh netraditsionnykh religioznykh ucheniiakh," in A. A. Kozhukhar', B. A. Konikov (eds.). *Tare—400 let. Problemy sotsial'no-ekonomicheskogo osvoeniiia Sibiri*. Chast' 2, 88–93 (Omsk: Administratsiia Omskoi oblasti, 1994).

V. B. Yashin, "Ario-sibirskie kontakty v drevnosti i sovremennye marginal'nye dukhovnye ucheniia," in *Rossiia i Vostok: filologiia i filosofiia. Materialy IV mezhdunarodnoi nauchnoi konferentsii "Rossiia i Vostok: problem vzaimodeistviiia*," 243–246 (Omsk: Omskii gosudarstvennyi universitet, 1997).

V. B. Yashin, "Tserkov' pravoslavnykh staroverov-inglingov kak primer neoyazycheskogo kul'ta." in Victor Shnirelman (ed.). *Neoyazychestvo na prostorakh Yevrazii*, 56–67 (Moscow: Bibliesko-Bogoslovsky Institut, 2001).

V. Yemelianov, *Desionizatsiia* (Parizh.1979).

V. Yemelianov, "Nastoiashchaia 'Pamiat' zhiva," in *Russkaia Pravda*, vol. 3 (1994), p. 3.

The Curse Prayers of Saint Vasile or How to "Declare War to the Devil"

Alexandra Coțofană

Abstract

This chapter sets out to explain the use of curse prayers against the Devil and other cultural manifestations of evil in Christian Orthodox faith in Romania. The chapter represents an anthropological analysis of various linguistic elements of the *molifte*, or curse prayers. The chapter will start with a discussion of the text of the curse prayers, moving on to poetics and finally, to a short discussion about how the use of voice is important in this ritual. While the chapter encourages further research for comparative data from neighboring Orthodox countries and diaspora on the use of curse prayers, it does present the extensive research done on the use of witchcraft as a tool against evil and of "special prayers" used to rid laity of the effects of witchcraft[1] along the Ukrainian-Romania border. Furthermore, Kivelson and Shaheen discuss the use of prayers by witches in Muscovite magic.[2]

Keywords: Romania, witchcraft, priest, exorcism, Christian Orthodoxy

The lay name of the curse prayers used in the Romanian Orthodox Church is *molifte*, a Slavic word. The official purpose of these prayers is to be read out loud as a curse cast on the Devil, his work, and all his minions. There are three such prayers in current use within the Romanian Orthodox Church: the molifte of Saint Vasile, the molifte of Saint Ciprian, and the molifte of Saint John Golden Mouth. This chapter will focus of the molifte of Saint Vasile, because they are considered to be the most powerful and effective tool against evil. While in most instances, evil means any influence that demonic powers are understood to have over a person or a household, the molifte of Saint Vasile are most often

---

[1] Worobec 1995: 179.
[2] Kivelson and Shaheen 2011: 25.

used in exorcisms. Exorcising a person with the help of molifte is often referred to as an *unbinding ritual.*

Reading the molifte is usually done by an Orthodox priest on January 1, when Orthodox Christians celebrate Saint Vasile. The mass and the reading of the molifte are understood to be a ritual cleansing ritual for the entire community. A tiny, pocket prayer book called the *Moliftelnic* contains all three prayers. The priest does the reading in the church, after the mass. All the parishioners must be on their knees and touch the priest's clothing during the uttering of the prayers. Those who cannot touch the priest directly need to touch someone who touches the priest, in a gesture of cleansing contagion. Everyone in the church must be "connected" this way before the reading starts. It is common for a priest to be called in for spiritual emergencies that disturb the general flow of life and read the molifte in someone's house and at another times than the January 1. However, it is the church reading of the molifte will concern this chapter.

Text

The complete text of the molifte of Saint Vasile is comprised of three parts: (1) a summoning of God, (2) curses addressed to the Devil, and (3) a prayer to God. In this chapter, I will discuss the second part of the text, which is comprised of all the curses aimed at the Devil.

I have done a preliminary translation of the text (Table 1) and a semiotic partition that I will try to explain. Translating texts, especially ritual texts, such as the molifte, can often be difficult, as text can lose its meaning when changing languages. Anthropologists and linguists present similar cases across cultures—Anthony Webster analyzes an instance, when a Navajo poem no longer makes sense, once translated into English.[3] Some repetition, assonance, and phonetic representations can be literally lost in translation. For the molifte, I have tried to mirror the original, unaltered text in the translation as much as possible, keeping in mind that a text must make sense within the context of a certain culture. More attention will be given to the structure and meaning of the text, as

---

[3] Webster 2006: 39.

deeper linguistic matters would be better addressed in another longer piece.

A comprehensive definition of text is given by William Hanks who states that texts are any configurations of signs that are coherently interpretable by some community of users.[4] Hanks also discusses the importance of textuality as a concept related to text. Textuality is the connection between the forms of signs that comprise a text and a broader context that establishes its coherence. This could mean that some texts are only coherent and have meaning in particular contexts, which applies to religious texts, as they are linked to the personal beliefs of a certain individual or group and serve their purpose there, lacking much if any universality. Religious text often uses regional or archaic texts, together with unusual syntax in a way that enforces the idea that priests are bestowed knowledge beyond the understanding of the congregation. This helps enforce their authority in a parish, where they set the rules on the language and communication.

Dell Hymes notes the importance of what people choose to do with their language and that the role of the sociolinguist is to describe the linguistic societies in their own terms and according to their rules of communication.[5] People often interpret their own languages emotionally, among other ways, which is an important part of the way culture is represented and experienced. Turino similarly discusses the interpretation of sign effects in Pierce and defines the emotional interpreting as an unreflected effect upon feeling. Together with the energetic interpreting and the sign interpreting, such emotional interpreting helps explain the dichotomy between mind and body.[6]

Reading the molifte is an important religious ritual for Romanian Christian Orthodox congregations and is used as a solution to the various sociocultural divergences that people experience in their everyday life. Whether it comes in the form of bad luck, illness, or a third-person breaking up a family, many people will describe the cause of their misfortune to be the Devil, who often works through human agents and magic.

---

[4] Hanks 1989: 95.
[5] Johnstone and Marcellino 2009: 3.
[6] Turino 1989: 226.

The reason why I chose to focus mainly on the second part of the molifte is because in interviews with Romanian Christian Orthodox people who have attended the reading of the molifte, many claim that this is the part when they start feeling different in the reading of the entire prayer. I have asked DN, aged twenty-nine, a Romanian Orthodox Theology graduate about the molifte. She has participated in many masses, some of which were done specifically for the molifte reading. When asked about the most powerful parts in the molifte, she answered:

> You can answer this question yourself when you read the molifte ... because I am certain that they will impress you as much as they impress me. Sometimes, when the priest would scream, "I curse you," the people (n.a. present in the church) would start to scream as well. They are fearful, run, leave. ... This is what I remember everyone said.

This second part of the Saint Vasile molifte is divided into three parts that I separated based on their structure and message. This second part is entirely devoted to cursing and challenging the Devil, or to declare war on the Devil, in the words of a few exorcist priests I interviewed. It is the most powerful prayer, in the words of my respondents, and thus the focus of my analysis. Its first subsection is made up of four sentences, following the same structure.

Table 1: Curse prayers: Section one

Te blestem pe tine, inceputorul rautatilor si al hulei, capetenia impotrivirii si urzitorul vicleniei.	I curse you, starter of malice and blasphemy, chief of opposition and author of ruse.
Te blestem pe tine, cel aruncat din lumina cea de sus si surpat pentru mandrie in intunericul adancului.	I curse you, the one thrown from the higher light and collapsed in the deep darkness for the sake of pride.
Te blestem pe tine si pe toata puterea cea cazuta ce a urmat vointa ta.	I curse you and all the fallen power that followed your will.
Te blestem pe tine, duh necurat, cu Dumnezeu Savaot si cu toata oastea ingerilor lui Dumnezeu, Adonai, Eloi, Dumnezeul cel atotputernic; iesi si te departeaza de la robul lui Dumnezeu.	I curse you, unclean spirit, to God Almighty and all the army of angels of God, Adonai, Eloi, God Almighty; get out and distance yourself from this servant of God.

As discussed previously, some of the words in the molifte are not in current use in Romanian, but can often be found in religious texts. They are uttered by a single speaker, the priest, to whom the audience may answer at times, in short phrases meant to enforce the message, as noted in DN's interview except.

The next subsection of the curse prayer in Table 2 is formed of five sentences that start with "I curse you with God/with He who ..." speaking once again directly to the Devil. In sentences two and three of this section, Jesus and the Holy Ghost are also invoked in the curse and in fighting the Devil. This is extremely important as it offers cultural insight—as Webb Keane states, very often, into cultural representations of objects and beings appear in texts.[7]

Table 2: Curse prayers: Section two

Te blestem pe tine cu Dumnezeu, Care prin cuvant toate le-a zidit si cu Domnul nostru Iisus Hristos, Fiul Lui cel Unul-Nascut, Care, mai inainte de veci, in chip de negrait si fara patima, S-a nascut dintr-insul; cu Cel ce a facut faptura vazuta si nevazuta si a zidit pe om dupa chipul Sau si, mai inainte, prin legea firii l-a invatat acestea si cu priveghere ingereasca l-a pazit; cu Cel ce a inecat pacatul cu apa de sus si a desfacut adancurile de sub cer si a pierdut pe uriasii cei necucernici si turnul faradelegilor l-a sfaramat si pamantul Sodomei si al Gomorei cu foc si cu pucioasa l-a ars si spre marturie fumega fum nestins; cu Cel ce marea cu oastea cea impotrivitoare lui Dumnezeu, tabara paganatatii, sub valuri de veci a inecat-o.	I curse you with God, who through the use of the word built everything and with our Lord Jesus Christ, the only begotten Son, that, before the ages, in unspeakable guise and without passion, was born from himself; with He who made the visible and invisible creatures and built man in His image and, earlier, through the law of nature taught him these things and protected him with the aid of angels, with the One who drowned sin in waters from above and opened the depths beneath the sky and lost the un-devout giants and crushed the tower of all injustice and the land of Sodom and Gomorrah with Fire and brimstone and burned to witness smoking smoke un-extinguished; with Him that the sea with the army that opposes God, the heathen camp under the waves forever drowned her.
Te blestem cu Cel care, la plinirea vremii, din Fecioara in chip de negrait S-a intrupat si pecetile	I curse you with the One who, at the coming of time, from the Virgin, in His unspeakable way was embodied

---

[7] Keane 1985: 101.

curatiei intregi le-a pazit; Care a binevoit sa spele prin botez intinaciunea noastra cea veche, cu care noi prin neascultare ne spurcasem.	and guarded the seals of all purity; Who deigned to wash through baptism Our ancient impurity, which defiles us through our disobedience.
Te blestem pe tine cu Cel ce S-a botezat in Iordan si ne-a dat noua in apa, prin har, chipul nestricaciunii; de Care ingerii si toate puterile ceresti s-au mirat, vazand pe Dumnezeu cel intrupat smerindu-Se, cand Tatal cel fara de inceput a descoperit nasterea cea fara de inceput a Fiului si cand pogorarea Sfantului Duh a marturisit unimea Treimii.	I curse you with the One who was baptized in the river Jordan and gave us in water, by grace, the image of incorruption, he who all the angels and heavenly powers were in awe of, seeing God Incarnated and humble, when the Father without beginning found the Son's birth without beginning, and when the coming of the Holy spirit confessed the Union of the Pentecost Trinity.
Te blestem pe tine cu Cel ce a certat vantul si a linistit viforul marii; Care a izgonit cetele diavolilor; Cel ce prin taina a dat vedere ochilor lipsiti de lumina ai celui orb din nastere si a innoit zidirea cea veche a neamului nostru si celor muti le-a dat grai; Cel ce a curatit ranile leprosilor si pe morti din groapa i-a inviat; Cel ce pana la ingropare cu oamenii a vorbit si iadul prin inviere l-a pradat si toata omenirea a intocmit-o sa nu mai fie cucerita de moarte. Te blestem pe tine cu Dumnezeu atottiitorul, Care a insufletit pe oameni si cu grai de Dumnezeu insuflat dimpreuna cu Apostolii a lucrat si toata lumea a umplut-o de dreapta credinta.	I curse you with Him who scolded the wind and calmed the sea whirlwind; Who drove the minion divisions away; He who gave light to the eyes of the man born blind and renewed the old building of our nation and gave voice to the dumb, He who cleaned the wounds of the lepers and raised the dead from the pit, who until burial spoke to the people and diminished hell by resurrection and to all mankind that he created so that it would not be conquered by death. I curse you with God Almighty, He who animated the people and with the speech blown by God inspired the Apostles who worked together and everyone filled it with righteous faith.

The difference in how subsections one and two are formulated, and in how the beings there are represented, is obvious. The reader (priest) uses the beings mentioned in subsection two to enforce the curse started in subsection one. The priest acknowledges having little power alone, so he summons higher powers, of positive cultural representation, in order to fight off evil.

The third subsection addresses the Devil directly and consists of three sentences of similar structures that begin with "Fear," used as a single, second-person imperative verb. The first sentence describes all the many shapes the Devil can take and all the ways in which it can reach a person. The second sentence is a threat of what would happen if the Devil chooses to return and repossess someone. The third sentence tells the Devil where to go once it leaves the body of the victim of possession (Table 3).

Table 3: Curse prayers: Section three

Teme-te, fugi, pleaca, departeaza-te, diavole necurate si spurcate, cel de sub pamant, din adanc, inselatorule, cel fara de chip, cel vazut pentru nerusinare, nevazut pentru fatarie, oriunde esti sau unde mergi, de esti insusi Beelzebul, sau de te arati ca cel ce scutura, ca sarpele, sau ca fiara, sau ca aburul, sau ca fumul, ori ca barbat, ori ca femeie, ori ca jiganie, ori ca pasare, sau vorbitor noaptea, sau surd, sau mut, sau care infricosezi cu navalirea, sau sfasii, sau uneltesti rele, in somn greu, sau in boala, sau in neputinta, sau pornesti spre ras, sau aduci lacrimi de dezmierdari; ori esti desfranat, ori rau mirositor, ori poftitor, ori facator de desfatare, ori fermecator, ori indemnator spre dragoste necurata, ori ghicitor in stele, ori sezi in casa, ori esti fara de rusine, ori iubitor de vrajba, ori fara astampar; sau te schimbi cu luna, sau te intorci dupa un oarecare timp, sau vii dimineata, sau la amiaza, sau la miezul noptii, sau in orice vreme, sau la revarsatul zorilor, sau din intamplare te-ai intalnit, sau de cineva esti trimis, sau ai navalit fara de veste; sau esti din mare, sau din rau, sau din pamant, sau din fantana, sau din daramaturi, sau din groapa; sau din balta, sau din trestie, sau din noroaie, sau de pe uscat, sau din necuratie; sau din lunca, sau din padure, sau din copaci, sau din pasare, sau din tunet, sau	Fear, run, leave, stay away, unclean and defiled devil, from the underground, from the depths, deceiver, you without a face, you known for shamelessness, unseen for calving, wherever you are or where you go, for you are Beelzebub himself, or if you show yourself like the flick, the serpent, or beast, or steam, or like smoke, or as a man or as a woman or as a prodigy, or the bird, or speaker night, or deaf, or dumb, or frightening others with invasion, or tearing, or conspired bad deeds, in deep sleep or disease, or helplessness, or start to laugh, or bring tears of caress, or are adulterous, or bad smelling, or lustful, or maker of delight, or charming, or a lure to impure love or fortune-teller, or sit in the house, or you are without shame, or hatred lover or restless, or you change with the month, or you come back after some time, or come in the morning, or in the afternoon, or at midnight, or at any time or at dawn, or randomly you met, or someone sent you, or you invaded without warning, or you're from the sea, or river, or earth, or fountain, or debris, or pit, or the pool, or cane or mud, or on land or impurity, or of meadow, or the forest or the trees, or birds, or thunder, or the cover of the bath, or from bathing water, or from the idols' grave or from where we may know, or from where we may not know, known or unknown, or from some unsuspected

din coperamantul baii, sau din scaldatoare de ape, sau din mormant idolesc; sau de unde stim, sau de unde nu stim, cunoscut ori necunoscut, sau din vreun loc nebanuit, pieri si te departeaza, rusineaza-te de chipul cel zidit si infrumusetat de mana lui Dumnezeu.	place, perish and go away, be shameful at the face that God built and decorated.
Teme-te de asemanarea lui Dumnezeu celui intrupat si sa nu te ascunzi in robul lui Dumnezeu (N), ca toiag de fier si cuptor de foc si iadul si scrasnirea dintilor te asteapta, ca rasplatire pentru neascultare.	Fear the likeness of God incarnate and don't hide in God's servant (N) as an iron rod and a fire oven and hell and gnashing of teeth await for you, as a reward for disobedience.
Teme-te, taci, fugi, sa nu te intorci, nici sa te ascunzi cu vreo alta viclenie de duhuri necurate, ci du-te in pamant fara de apa, pustiu, nelucrat, unde om nu locuieste, ci este cercetat numai de Dumnezeu, Cel ce leaga pe toti care vatama si uneltesc aupra chipului Sau; Cel ce in lanturi te-a aruncat in aflatorul tuturor rautatilor. Ca mare este frica de Dumnezeu si mare este slava Tatalui si a Fiului si a Sfantului Duh, acum si pururea si in vecii vecilor. Amin.	Fear, shut up, run, do not come back or you hide with any other wickedness of evil spirits, but go into the earth without water, into wilderness and uncultivated soil, where man does not live, but is only known God, He who ties all those who plan to harm His image, He who threw you in chains in He who knows of all evils. How great the fear of the Lord and great is the glory of the Father and the Son and the Holy Spirit, now and ever and unto ages of ages. Amen.

Repetitions of specific signs and words are common in ritual texts and, as Webb Keane suggests, they can offer clues as to who is meant to read the texts.[8] In the case presented by Keane, the living would send a message to the dead through a ritual speaker. In this case, the message of the living must reach spirits and tell them that their possession is abusive. The ritual speaker remains a strong element in reading the text.

Poetics

Performance in the linguistic act is a very important element of the poetics of a text, as noted by Bauman and Briggs. They join McDowell in

---

[8] Idem, 103.

THE CURSE PRAYERS OF SAINT VASILE 107

analyzing how the formalization of the ritual act diminishes its accessibility to other performers and to the audience.[9] However, in the case of reading the molifte, this formalization is necessary because it helps, the reader however powerful/religious he might be, to withstand any consequences that come with what SC, aged thirty, another Theology graduate believes is a very strong prayer:

> Think of it as a way of declaring war on the Devil.

He further goes to say:

> Each priest who reads the Holy Molifte has been bestowed a gift from God. You cannot start doing this work (n.a. reading molifte) just like that. You have to prepare yourself for it. You have to go through constant praying and fasting for at least three days, eat no food, only drink water. You have to cleanse your body and your soul and have to go through all the requirements that are asked from a priest, including doing good deeds. Also, a layperson cannot come to an unbinding unprepared. They too have to fast and to have a pure body, which means not having laid with someone else ahead of the mass. If these conditions are met, then the mass will help all the people present, not only the possessed people. For those who come unprepared, the mass can cause harm, even destroy them. There are cases of priests who tried reading the molifte and quit, because it made them sick.

Voicing

Voices are another tool used in the molifte ritual and are meant to carry the text or inform reactions to it. Webb Keane discusses the dialoguing voices and their importance in the ritual act.[10] The priest must read with intonation, both to prove his strength that can overcome evil and to give hope to the lay people. Jane Hill notes how the voices we choose to use in a certain context can help get our message across, when discussing the case of a peasant, the last speaker of Mexicana language interviewed in the area where Hill did research. Don Gabriel, the peasant, used personal meanings and voices to tell the story of how his son was

---

[9] Bauman and Briggs 1990: 63.
[10] Keane 1999: 272.

murdered.[11] Similarly, Tanya Luhrmann (2014) has found that the (nonhuman) voices people hear (and we can say, by extension, reproduce), are shaped by their culture.[12]

When reading the molifte, the priest dialogues with the Devil through the text of the curse prayer. He also dialogues with the crowd, in different ways. The crowd will respond to his reading by saying "Amen" throughout the entire prayer and will repeat the priest's words when he starts the actual curse in order to help secure his position in the war he is declaring on the Devil. Even though the mass may be intended for particular victims of possession, there will be frequent cases of a small number of people taking part in the mass as audience members, who discover they too are possessed. When the curse prayer starts, they start behaving outside of the norm, their bodies twist, and they voice nonhuman actors. Some will swiftly exit the church screaming, others will start cursing at the priest and the church, as an institution. At this point, the priest must be strong and start a dialogue with the Devil that the new victims unknowingly host. Impromptu exorcisms thus happen during the masse, revealing the power of ritual dialogue.

The voices of the newly discovered possessed parishioners change during the reading. They can use their human voice, to complain about how the Devil inside torments them and the next second shift to a very different voice, their demon voice, to swear and claim their power over the human body they now inhabit. Referring again to Keane's work, it often happens that in religious rituals the speaker may not always control their voice. At the same time, they can avoid claiming responsibility of the voices they use.[13] When the ritual ends, (if) the demonized person is freed, the victory is attributed to the priest, with the help of the entire congregation, thus entrusting these exorcisms with social value.

---

[11] Hill 1995: 109.
[12] Luhrmann et al. 2014.
[13] Keane 1999: 273.

How uttering the curse and being a priest drive demons away. Speech acts and professional vision in Christian Orthodox exorcisms

In a therapeutic community of demonized people set up in Northern Romania by a priest, the molifte are used weekly in an exorcism ritual. Again, this ritual consists of a priest reading to a group of people from a small prayer book, called moliftelnic. These prayers have some (symbolic) resemblance to the Pseudepigrapha and the New Testament Apocrypha in the Western Christian traditions. In Romania, the molifte are used in adult exorcisms or at baptisms, to banish demons from a child's body. What exorcisms mean in Romanian belief and practice is not necessarily congruent with either Western Christian ideas or mass media portrayals like that in Roman Polanski's 1969 horror film Rosemary's Baby.

The molifte will normally only be uttered in the church once a year, on January 1, when Saint Vasile is celebrated, only by priests who have a particular God-given gift. They are thought of (and think of themselves as) strong enough and sufficiently spiritually cleansed to successfully perform the ritual. However, if the parishioners request additional masses, they can be done at different times in the year—my data shows no consensus in the priests' opinions on whether these extra readings should be allowed or not. The event analyzed further is an exorcism performed in July 2014, in a small church in Romania. The church and housing around it are owned by Father H, a priest who created a community of possessed parishioners who live there for an indeterminate period of time.

Father H (now eighty-four years) used to preach in a village, in Northern Romania. In recent years, he has devoted most of his time to performing exorcisms, instead of the regular Christian Orthodox masses. He left the village church in the care of his son, also a priest. Father H built another church and a small living complex outside the village, which can host and feed around twenty people.

The fences around the private property are very high and new comers can only go in with special permission from one of the monks working there, in case a prior meeting with the priest has not been set.

Most of the possessed people in the community are permanent residents, since their spirit possessions are culturally treated as a chronic illness. Epileptics also live here. (The culturally perceived chronicity of demon possession deserves more exploration from medical anthropologists.) Father H claims that once a witch sends a demon to torment a person, the demon will not rest until the job is done and even if they are chased out through exorcism, the witch who sent the demons will not take them back, so they must return to the victim over and over again until they fulfill their assignment. Although gendered roles of the devils have not been discussed in depth during the interviews, Father H referred to all the demons with masculine pronouns.

Father H, like other priests I have talked to, acknowledges that not a lot of priests choose to dedicate their life to performing exorcisms, as it is a path filled with danger. He says he often does not sleep because the Devil comes to visit at night and as they quarrel; sometimes, the Devil will pull the blanket from his bed, out of spite. At night, he lights candles and sings religious songs in order to drive the Devil away. Priests who start a war with Satan, cursing him with the molifte, make it unsafe for their families. He states that the only reason why his family is still alive is because he always lived far away from them. When asked if he needs to protect himself during masses, he claims the demons only have one human target, the victim they initially possess. If, after an exorcism, they are chased out, they will go back home to the witch who summoned them—because "we all go back home."

Roman Jakobson's principles (1960) are useful to analyze the speech event represented by an exorcism. Jakobson states that language must be investigated in all variety of its functions. The structure of the language and its functions can be represented through the following design:

```
                    CONTEXT
ADDRESSER           MESSAGE            ADDRESSEE
                    CONTACT
                    CODE
```

The addresser sends a message to the addressee. In order to get across, the message requires a context, understandable to the addressee, one that is either verbal or able to be verbalized. A code must be used, one that is common to both addresser and addressee, that helps encode and decode the message. Finally, a successful speech act needs a contact, a physical channel, and a psychological connection between the addresser and the addressee, which allows the two each other.

In the exorcisms performed by Father H, the addressee and the addresser are constantly changing, and the same voice can shift between the two roles in a very short time. The context has to be a church mass attended by parishioners, who trust in the priest's power and his knowledge of liturgical procedures. The church also forms a sort of trap for the demon(s). Being in "God's home" can weaken the demon and a successful exorcism can be performed with more ease.

The fact that all the voices involved speak the same language helps communicate the speech act. While the priest reads the molifte, each of the other voices involved reacts according to their status and given social role(s). The demon voice will express distress but will verbalize the fact that the ritual is not strong enough to stop them, while the human voice will use interjections and words to express pain. Furthermore, Jakobson notes, each of these factors determines a different function in language—but they do not have to be present in the same speech act.

The referential function identified by Jakobson focuses on the context. In this case, the church represents the physical context, as exorcisms rarely happen elsewhere. They also must have an audience, as the priest needs support during the ritual, and to summons God's help. The parishioners support the priest, by adding "Amen" at the end of his every sentence and crossing themselves at certain points in the service.

The emotive function focuses on the addresser, and is an expression of what the speaker's attitude is toward what they are saying. This layer of language is present in the demon's voice and their use of interjections, which are bound to express emotion. Although they sound like interjections to the listeners, their intended purpose is different—they are imperative statements or demands. For example, when the priest takes on the role of speaker, the emotive layer is not as clear—in part due to the fact that he is reading his utterances from a book and is following a set of formalized, institutionalized procedures. However, when he is no longer the addresser, the two voices understood to be inside of the possessed parishioners (their human voice and their demon voice) start to talk to each other, mostly in interjections. Here we have the addressee and the addresser in the same (physical) body, yet claiming different identities. The human voice will ask the demon:

> Iesi! Iesi afara! Iesi ca nu mai pot! Iesi sa nu te mai vad, iesi!
> (Translation: Get out! Get out! Get out! I cannot bare it anymore! Get out, I no longer want to see you, get out!).

Although the voice is very deep and raspy, it is the voice that the human in the body claims, and that is culturally understood as sounding different than their talking voice because of all the pain they are experiencing at the time of the exorcism. Consequently, the embodied voice of the demon can be pitchy and feminine and voices most of the interjections. According the Roman Jakobson's six functions of language, the two speakers can be identified by the utterances involved in the speaking acts of exorcisms.

The pitch of possessed people's demon voices expresses their feelings, anger, or pain and is a marker of the emotive function. As Jakobson notes, the emotive function is aimed at the addresser, while being a direct expression of the addressee's feelings. This is achieved with the help of interjections, of elongating vowels in words, and through body language—specific gestures and facial expressions that stress and express the specific feeling of the addressee.

The second function that can be noticed during an exorcism is the conative function, expressed through the demands that the addressee (here represented by the possessed and the demons they voice, each taking turns) makes to the addresser—the priest. Although the statements they make are directed at the priest, they are messages about the self, in reaction to the messages they receive. In this case, it is the cursing done through the molifte that makes both the possessed and the demons uncomfortable. The message of the possessed is direct; they state exactly how the uttering of the molifte makes them feel. The demons, on the other hand, use an implicit form of speech, acting aggressive and irritated, but asking the same thing, that the ritual stops.

As the exorcism continues, the priest's voice becomes firmer and stronger when reading the text of the prayer, making the demon voices utter their interjections louder and louder, until finally they soft en again. During some exorcisms, the crowd hears the Devil voicing sentences addressed to the priest. The Devil voice often says:

> Gata! Gata! Gata! Gata! Ehe, gura bai!
> (Translation: Stop it! Stop it! Stop it! Stop it! Hehe, shut up, you!).

Several people can be exorcised at the same time. The mass will last for as long as the priest can keep his strength up or until the demons give up. There are three identifiable moments in the exorcism, in terms of addressees and addressers changing roles. They will fluctuate in intensity and order, but are repeated over and over, until the ritual is over:

Addresser	Addressee	What is being communicated
Human voice	Demon	The human voice asks the demon to leave and no longer torment her.
Demon voice	Priest	The demon voice asks the priest to stop the ritual or mocks him/the institution he represents.
Priest voice	Demon	The priest curses the demon and by doing so, forces him to come out.

Absences in the ritual are represented by the fact that the demon never replies to the human voice when being asked to leave, nor does the priest reply to the demon or the possessed human's voice, but instead, carries on with the ritual.

The conative function focuses on the addressee, often directly and imperatively vocative and imperative. The human voice expresses fatigue, pain, and need for liberation, while the demon voice uses the invocative and imperative to express both concern and impudence. The priest voice is always to be confident and firm.

The phatic function in the speech act refers to the contact, and may be expressed through a deep exchange of ritualized formulas. The channels of contact may be face-to-face, on stage/to audience, or indirect (writing to or telephoning the addressee). The exorcism ritual mainly involves the face-to-face channel for the three main voices involved, but the ritual also needs an audience, that is present there and sees the whole act progress. Phatic communication is present, some of the sounds made by the people possessed are to show that the human is tired, that the demon not impressed or, on the contrary, that the demon is concerned on the defensive. At the same time, the speakers talking to the priest, namely the demons and the humans, will use changes in tone, pitch, and talk to show when the speaker himself or herself has changed.

In terms of bodily roles within the ritual, the possessed and the priest are using their bodies to communicate their messages to each other. At the same time, because the demons do not have their own physical bodies, they use the possessed bodies to mediate their communication. In doing so, they violate the possessed humans' authority over their bodies, as they are not welcome or accepted to take over. The raspy vocal quality helps let everyone know that it is the demon speaking and not the humans, meaning that the vocal qualities also serve a phatic function.

The metalingual function focuses on the code used—meaning the addressee or addresser need to check if they are using the same code, by asking each other direct or rhetoric questions. As part of the ritual, the priest will use metalinguistic verbs, i.e., "curse", "exit", "fear", "keep away") several times in the ritual. The text has several parts, each with their own function. The metalinguistic verbs are used throughout, and are repeated so as to enhance their power. The priest's tone changes when these verbs are used—he highlights them by using a stronger tone of voice.

Charles Goodwin analyzes three practices that every professional must learn, as part of their trade. Coding, or transforming observations into objects of knowledge will mean, in our case, the way that priests interpret the manifestations of the people who are thought to be possessed. The famous Romanian 2005 case of the Tanacu Orthodox monastery, where a young nun died during an exorcism[14], shows that too much coding can lead to unwelcome situations and unpredicted outcomes. However, all the people who attend the mass where the molifte prayers are read, go there knowing that when the reading begins, they themselves could start uttering words and sentences that would normally not make sense to them, in a different voice, twitching, or any other bodily manifestation that can tell the priest they are possessed. The coding scheme that the priest uses means that there are two categories of people in the church: those possessed, who need his help, and the others.. The cognitive and social world of the priest, like that of any other professional, is limited to the parameters of the system they work in, as Goodwin goes to argue.

A second linguistic practice used by professionals is that of highlighting, which means that the professional (here a priest) will emphasize specific phenomena within a larger perceptual field which makes the relevant events stand out. When some features are hard to distinguish, the professional will try to point out what they believe is relevant and persuade the audience that these have been identified. Examples of highlighting are the moments when Father H raises his voice while reading the molifte and expects the demons to react accordingly. When the demon voices respond in a raised tone, he considers it as a sign of confrontation and lifts two wooden crosses above his head, continuing to curse the Devil. Every time he draws shapes in the air with the crosses, his voice becomes more authoritarian. He repeats it until the demon voices become softer, and proceeds then to read in a softer voice. At random intervals, he raises his voice and the two crosses again, waiting for a reaction from the demon voices. Whenever he does this, he stresses on words like "diavol," meaning "devil/demon," which is when he expects the demon voices to scream in response.

---

[14] http://www.cbsnews.com/news/nun-dies-after-convent-exorcism/ accessed February 12th, 2017

The third practice is what Goodwin calls *material representations* and defines as activities like making transcripts, tables, articles, databases, graphics, giving lectures, etc. which taken altogether, helps constitute the collective knowledge base of a profession. Goodwin argues that most researchers will focus too much on the writing of words, sentences, and written language and too little on graphic representations. The place where the exorcism is held is filled with expressive material representations: the religious paintings on the church walls, the crosses that Father H holds over the possessed bodies and ultimately, the holy book that he is reading. In terms of professional tools, the only one that is used solely for the exorcisms and is recognized as such is the small book containing the molifte. All other objects serve often-different roles in exorcisms than the ones they are usually assigned.

Crucial to the whole ritual is the presence of the audience, who knows when and how to react. An outsider would have trouble understanding when crossing yourself is appropriate, or when "Amen" should be said. These are all acquired linguistic practices that assume a person has have attended such a ritual before, e.g., an experienced parishioner and so learn appropriate behavior. The audience is external to the professional vision, but not completely. They must have the same cultural background to be able to understand what the procedures are. The fact that everyone attending the ritual must also be "strong enough" has been mentioned in several interviews. So what does this mean to an outsider? How do you prepare for something that is coded in a few words that may mean almost anything? A well-trained, cooperative audience seems to be part of whether the ritual will be a success or not. Could we then talk about professional vision among parishioners?

They, the audience, are expected to have read the material representation of the text or at least be familiar with it; they are also expected to understand the larger context of Orthodoxy, together with how to act appropriately during such a ceremony. This does not solely mean to know when they are expected to be quiet but also when they are expected to be vocal. They must also be familiar with at least part of the priest's technical language.

The technical language of an Orthodox priest is mostly comprised of archaic words, that are no longer is use today. Maurice Halbwachs (1980) discusses how Christianity's religious memories and the type of life they propose are from what social life is like today. The religious memory does not acquire new information, nor does the information migrate from within other religious groups. The use of archaic words in an exorcism stresses the fight between good and evil and the fact that this fight started very early in history (perhaps invoking Biblical and early Christian exorcism chronicity?). If starting war with the Devil with these words was powerful then, there is no reason to believe that these "weapons" would no longer be effective today.

The priests must learn the correct language for fighting the Devil and for identifying spirit possession. How do they acquire this competence, if most priests seem to avoid this practice for the safety of their families? Priests are initiated in performing the exorcisms in much the same way that witches are initiated in binding and conjuring evil. The young priests need to be around older priests "who have the gift" and observe the procedures repeatedly, until they learn how to perform them. But how do they know that they are "strong" enough to spend a lifetime helping the chronically possessed? Father H recalls when he recited the Third Gospel to a woman possessed by a demon. He recalls being so overwhelmed by God's power entering his body that he started crying—"priests are charged like batteries," he says. They need good energy to be charged again, and are exhausted when they have to fight evil and negative energy.

> *I would like to thank Jim Nyce and Jessica Pollock for being companions in discovering those who benefit from and those who are plagued by witchcraft.*

Bibliography

Richard Bauman and Charles Briggs, "Poetics and Performance as Critical Perspectives on Language and Social Life," in *Annual Review of Anthropology*, vol. 19 (1990), pp. 59–88.

Charles Goodwin, "Professional Vision," in *American Anthropologist*, vol. 96, no. 3 (1994), pp. 606–633.

Maurice Halbwachs, *The Collective Memory* (New York: Harper & Row Colophon Books, 1980).

William Hanks, "Text & Textuality," in *Annual Review of Anthropology*, vol. 18 (1989), pp. 95–127.

Jane H. Hill, "The Voices of Don Gabriel: Responsibility and Self in a Modern Mexicano Narrative," in Dennis Tedlock and Bruce Mannheim (eds.). *The Dialogic Emergence of Culture*, 97–147 (Urbana: University of Illinois Press, 1995).

Roman Jakobson, "Concluding Statement: Linguistics and Poetics," in Thomas Sebeok (ed.). *Style in Language*, 350–377 (Cambridge, MA: MIT Press, 1960).

Barbara Johnstone and William M. Marcellino, "Dell Hymes and the Ethnography of Communication," in Ruth Wodak, Barbara Johnstone and Paul Kerswill (eds.). *The Sage Handbook of Sociolinguistics*, 57–67 (London: Sage, 2010).

Webb Keane, "The Spoken House: Text, Act, and Object in Eastern Indonesia," in *American Ethnologist*, vol. 22, no. 1 (February 1995), pp. 102–124.

Webb Keane, "Voice," in *Journal of Linguistic*, vol. 9, no. 1–2 (1999), pp. 271–273.

Valerie Kivelson and Jonathan Shaheen, "Prosaic Witchcraft and Semiotic Totalitarianism: Muscovite Magic Reconsidered," in *Slavic Review*, vol. 70, no.1 (2011), pp: 23–44.

Anthony Webster, "The Mouse That Sucked: On 'translating' a Navajo poem," in *Studies in American Indian Literature* ser. 2, vol. 18, no. 1 (2006), pp. 37–49.

Christine D. Worobec, "Witchcraft Beliefs and Practices in Prerevolutionary Russian and Ukrainian Villages," in *Russian Review*, vol. 54, no. 2 (April 1995), pp. 165–187.

Thomas Turino, "Signs of Imagination, Identity, and Experience: A Peircian Semiotic Theory for Music," in *Ethnomusicology*, vol. 43, no. 2 (1999), pp. 221–255. 24.

Maternity Rituals in the Soviet Western Ukrainian Borderland

Dzvenyslava Hanus

Abstract

The formation of the Western Ukrainian borderland emerged from some was significant territorial disputes, which led to lengthy negotiations and the signing of several agreements between the USSR and Poland (1944–1947, 1951). The border between Ukraine and Poland was set at the Curzon Line with some minor deviations of several kilometers in favor of Poland, that is, it was a political decision based on the earlier Entente border of December 8, 1919 (Kulchytskyi 2004: 507). Neglecting ethnic, historical, and other aspects in establishing the border resulted in mass deportations of Ukrainians and Poles during the "Vistula" operation in 1947 and in the exchange of national territories between the USSR and Poland in 1951. This border, in other words, results from a series of political compromises: "The tragedy of the two nations consisted in the fact that having suffered the greatest human and material losses during the Second World War, they found themselves hostages of the geopolitical confrontation between the Soviet Union and Western powers" (Kalakura 2007: 323).

Keywords: maternity rituals, borderlands, Ukraine, Christian Orthodoxy, magic

For the Ukrainian and Polish population the postwar era was a hard time, one filled with uncertainty and little hope for the future. The population shifts were associated with fears of violence, injustice, individual and group tragedies, tortures inflicted on innocent people, loss of family and property, forced deportations from their native land, few opportunities to hold church services, to pray, to take care of their churches or the graves of their ancestors (Chmelyk 2011: 949). All this comes up in the interviews conducted with many respondents:

> I lived in the Krakiw region, abroad. We were all loaded on a train and taken away. It was already after the war, after (19) 45 when we were taken to Kharkiv. We spent a year there and then my mother and I moved here. There, in Kharkiv, there were few people and we were brought there to increase the population. Some people were even given apartments and some were lodged in the houses of the people living alone. We lived with two old people. And then we went to Drohobych district, while everybody fled. We came in (19)47 and stayed there till (19)58. After that, our apartment was taken away and we moved on. When the Poles moved out, they left the house and we moved in that house.

The last territorial and border changes were made in 1951. They were based on the exchange principle "kilometer for kilometer," resulting in the (Ukrainian) Drohobych region going to Poland in exchange for part of the (Polish) Liublin province (the modern Sokal district of Lviv region of Ukraine including Chervonohrad, Belz, and Uhniv). The agreement concerned not only a transfer of land but also the mutual displacement of the population. This is said about the deportation:

> In 1952 we were resettled. Poles were given land there, and it was necessary to resettle people here and to take from there. So some people were resettled to Donetsk, others to Kherson and we were resettled here. At first we did not believe that we would be resettled, and then they began, everybody was taken out.

The memories of Western Ukrainian citizens living along the borderland about the past recount the destruction of traditional ways of life and being forced to start life all over again.

Redrawing the Ukrainian-Polish border led to the disappearance of a number of settlements. The population was resettled to the south and east of Ukraine, yet people did not give up hope that they could return to their homes. Still, the Ukrainian culture of the migrants who came back from the south or east of Ukraine was enriched with traditions from other regions. The resettled population had to adapt to new climates and methods of farming. People with different historical experiences and mentalities surrounded them. As a result of the new borders, the traditional life, material, and spiritual values, as well as other cultural features were in part displaced or destroyed in the Ukrainian-Polish territories.

The policy of the Soviet government along the Western Ukrainian borderland attempted to destroy the traditional Ukrainian rites and traditions and replace them with "Soviet" ones, to create the Soviet man imbued with the communist ideology. They created a common festive and ritual culture for all Soviet people, meant to replace local traditions and erase cultural differences. It was proclaimed "the Soviet rites are the heritage, the general moral value of the entire family of Soviet peoples. Every nation enriches the new ritual and contributes its best elements to it, everything that promotes a sense of socialist brotherhood" (Orlyk 1983: 11).

The establishment of the Soviet rites in the territory of UkrSSR occurred in several stages (Kurochkin 1988: 208–212). The first one lasted from 1917 until the mid-1930s. This was the period of intense state activity against church holidays and religion. In place of the traditional religious rites, new Soviet ceremonies were instituted: "red wedding," "red christening" (*oktiabryny, zirkovyny*), and "red funeral." The second stage was from mid-1930s to 1950s. At this time, the so-called professional holidays (Teacher's Day and Miner's Day) were introduced. The third stage was 1950–1980s. At this time, academic researchers created community rituals, described the methodological basis of each rite, published study guides, and formed special commissions to introduce and control these ceremonies and rituals.

The introduction of Soviet holidays and ceremonies in the territory of Western Ukraine occurred in two stages. In the first stage (1939 to late 1950s), national holidays and community rituals were established, and during the second one (from the early 1960s to until the end of 1980s), they were integrated into the daily life of the population (Mykhalchuk 2008: 97).

The formation of these new rites happened in two ways. They were observed intentionally so that they organically supplemented each other; the first set of rites merged traditional rituals with Soviet meaning ("red christening" and "red wedding"), and the second set of rites altered the content and form of traditional ritual, removed "unnecessary archaic" elements from them and introduced "necessary" Soviet elements. This so-called transformation of rites meant that there was no need for "religious, old, conservative rituals that neither by their content nor form, nor symbolic, philosophical, and ideological basis meet the socialist reality" (Kelembetova 1984: 188).

The destruction of the traditional culture was closely connected to the anti-religious campaigns. Given the large extent of popular support for the Greek Catholic Church, the struggle in Western Ukraine was different from other parts of the UkrSSR. First, the government disestablished the Greek Catholic Church, a decision made by the councils in Lviv (1946) and Uzhgorod (1949). Then there was the elimination of the Orthodox Church, which was seen as the ideological enemy of the state, since an important social marker of the communist society was its secularity. Churches were closed for a variety of official reasons—the need to build new rows of shopping stalls on the site of the church, the need for a village club or a cinema, and the "threatening proximity" of churches to schools (Shlikhta 2000).

Despite this massive rejection of institutionalized religion, the heritage of churches continued but church rituals were now interpreted in a different way, according to the new Soviet ideology; a ceremonial meeting replaced liturgy, revolutionary songs replaced acathisti and religious songs; galleries of portraits of party leaders, not saints, now embellished the meeting halls on holidays, while the columns of demonstrations and parades turned into "red iconostasis" (Riznyk and Hrytsenko 1998).

A command planning principle introduced the new rites. The holiday culture was controlled by the regulations of Politburo. Conferences were held on Soviet festive rites and a Special Committee on Soviet traditions, festivals, and rituals was set up in 1964 by the Presidium of the Verkhovna Rada of the UkrSSR, and continued from 1978 on by the Council of Ministers of the UkrSSR (Hromova 2010: 134). Special ritual commissions were also established by other state organizations, buildings were erected especially to perform these new rites.

Whether people accepted the new rites varied according to the type of settlement they lived in; the rural population would more often keep the older religious traditions, while the urban population adapted to new conditions sooner, as the Ukrainian traditions came under attack the most in urban centers. A special commission was composed from village deputies and activists (farmers, farm workers, and the rural professionals) for the introduction of new rituals, and given the task of organizing holidays. The commission members were to develop a detailed plan for all ritual events and to appoint people responsible for carrying out individual sections of the plan (Kuveniova 1957: 107).

The main innovations in Soviet holidays were; secularism (a rejection of the traditional religious holidays); mass character (almost all the holidays were "national"); the cult of work (a new attitude toward work as a holiday); state status (the holidays became an expression of the state ideology); a compulsory character (attendance at demonstrations and holidays was mandatory); and new regulations (special committees developed regulations for celebrating holidays) (Haievska 2012: 168).

Over time, the rituals became more ideological and internationalized. This is most clearly seen in the rites depicting life cycles. Weddings were held without a church ceremony and marriages were performed under the "symbols of communism." Instead of baptizing a child in the church, a family would now have to take part in civil ceremonies where a birth certificate would be issued.

Traditional Ukrainian folk ritual is based on an amalgamation of Christian and pagan components. This complex cosmology was formed because after the adoption of Christianity, the church ideology spread only among small groups and only fragments of the religious discourse reached the local people. The population uses a mix of worship objects, ancient gods with Christian saints (Bulashev 1992: 41). In the first steps of Christianization, people started practicing Christian rites by adapting them to the local, pagan rites, as Christianity "did not entirely meet the local ideology and its values, people viewed the new religion through their own lens, which is why they were making significant adjustments in Christian realities" (Hrymych 2000: 36). This fusion of pagan magic and Christian rites can be observed in examples of traditional maternity rites, which underwent further changes as a result of the Soviet policy.

This chapter is written based on ethnographic interviews recorded by the author based on fieldwork done in the villages of the Western Ukrainian/Polish borderland. Significant attention was paid to the respondents' age. Older generation memories (eighty–ninety-five years old) were valuable in understanding magical beliefs that existed in the early 20th century, in contrast to a younger generation (sixty–seventy-five years old), whose stories relate more to changes in community rites due to the Soviet regime.

In Ukrainian maternity rites, there are generally three main ritual stages; (1) rituals related to pregnancy and childbirth; (2) (the ritual) acceptance of a newborn to the family; and (3) ritual purification of the mother and the baba-povytukha (midwife) (Zelenin 1991: 319).

Prenatal rituals

Prenatal customs and rituals blend both rational knowledge and magical practices. These are performed during the wedding in order to ensure a boy is born. There are also traditional ways that help predict pregnancy and the gender of the baby, as well various restrictions to protect the health of the mother and child (Hvozdevych 1998: 278).

The population of the Western Ukrainian borderland performed a wide range of rituals to influence the gender of the baby. It is worth noting here that the birth of a boy was always seen as more desirable than the birth of a girl, as boys carry on the family name.

Concern for the gender of the child was already shown in wedding rituals, allowed before the Soviet period. For example, to help ensure a male child, the bride had to sit on a belt before going to the church for the wedding; a young boy was seated on the bride's lap during the celebration; the bride's father would put a hat on her head; the bride had to sit on a pair of man's pants at the table during the wedding reception; and many other similar symbolic rites were practiced. After the introduction of the new "Soviet" marriage ceremony, these rituals gradually disappeared from the marriage ceremony.

Rituals were also carried out before conceiving the child. They involved laying various objects on the bed. Man's clothes and tools were traditionally used to help guarantee the birth of a baby boy. There were two ways of using male clothes: the first involved a sheepskin coat, pants, a hat, a belt laid on the bed, while a second narrative suggests a woman had to put on a belt and pants before intercourse. A hammer or an ax would often be placed under the bed, both symbols of masculinity. If the woman wanted to have a girl, she would insert a needle in a pillow or would put a kerchief or an apron on before intercourse. These symbolic actions, given their mysticism, did not change over time. However, a gradual understanding that they did not always work led to people abandoning them.

Ritual prohibitions were very important among the prenatal traditions. These were based in a belief that there is a putative relationship between the behavior of the pregnant woman and the unborn child. A violation of these prohibitions could have dire consequences for both the mother and the child. The expectant mother tried to protect herself and her baby from danger by respecting ritual constraints; these continue to be practiced today.

One of the primary ritual requirements for a pregnant woman was not to get angry or to quarrel. The woman was not even supposed to be present during quarrels or fights as this could lead to the child being born a bully. Thus to insure correct behavior for the baby, the mother was not to quarrel, not to get angry, she also had to be tidy and honest because doing otherwise predestined the newborn child to act out.

The pregnant woman was not to look at ugly, sick, or disabled people, as their physical traits might be passed on to the child. The expectant mother was also warned against begging and borrowing. To do so could affect the child's future: they could in the future become a beggar or acquire large debts. If the pregnant woman stole anything, her child was predestined to become a thief, or, according to another tradition, a stolen thing could affect (deform) the body, particularly the baby's hands.

Another group of beliefs, still held to the present, are associated with a pregnant woman being frightened. The generally accepted consequence of fright was that moles would appear on the child's body. A spot could occur on the child's body when a pregnant woman got scared of fire and then touched her body. There was a similar, widespread belief that a fear of mice and reptiles (lizards, snakes, etc.) could mark an unborn child. A fear of mice, for example, would lead to the child being born with a mark, a mole covered in hair.

A pregnant woman was also not to work on holidays, including Sundays. In particular, she was not to sew on holidays or work in the vegetable garden. Depending on the holiday, there could be various consequences for the child: when working during an important holiday such as Christmas, Easter, or Trinity, the child could be born without hands, in case of a minor holiday, the child could be born with defects corresponding to the work being done. In the Soviet times however, these kinds of prohibitions broke down completely.

Such holidays (feasts and Sunday) were considered unacceptable in the new socialist society, since they were based in religion. For example, a pregnant woman on a collective farm had to work (almost) all the time, which often led her to violate traditional prohibitions against her will:

> A holiday has come, I know that today is a holiday, I am not supposed to work as it does harm to the child, but I have to go to the collective farm and I had to work.

The prohibitions not to gather and cultivate cucumbers, beans, and pumpkins were also violated on collective farms. The pregnant woman was traditionally forbidden to walk and climb under a wire or fence, to hang clothes out to dry, or to step over a horse harness. These acts, it was believed, would cause the umbilical cord to wrap around the baby, causing his/her asphyxiation at birth. The work conditions often led to these prohibitions being completely neglected:

> I worked on the collective farm and stepped over wires, ropes. I had to do it; nobody paid attention to it anymore.

The public life of a pregnant woman was limited by ritual prohibitions regarding the most important stages of a family's life cycle: baptism, weddings, and funeral rituals. Until recently, the borderland population considered it dangerous to ask a pregnant woman to be a godmother. To do so could result in death of either a born or unborn child, or the child being sentenced to a hard life. A pregnant woman was forbidden to attend weddings. If she did, the newlyweds would have a hard life and her child would not follow in their footsteps. Nor could a pregnant woman attend funerals. If she did, a child might die, could become pale, and could have cold hands and feet. These prohibitions disappeared along with the religious rites associated with baptism and weddings.

Maternity rituals

In the mid-20th century, maternity rituals changed, because of the gradual loss of the baba-povytukha as an assistant in childbirth. First, the authorities allowed women to choose if they wanted to give birth with a baba-povytukha or a midwife. In this case, the people of the Western Ukrainian borderland preferred a baba-povytukha, due to long-term local traditions. The Soviet authorities were not pleased and the role of the baba-povytukhas in childbirth began to be monitored and banned by the authorities. If found assisting in childbirth, a baba-povytukha could be arrested. Also, giving birth to a baby at home with the help of the baba-povytukha caused considerable difficulties when it came to getting a birth certificate. State policies opened more hospitals, which also played a role in the loss of childbirth rituals. The location of a settlement, its distance from the city, road conditions, the availability of medical personnel played a very important role in where new hospitals were located (Boriak 2009: 91).

The rituals that the baba-povytukha performed to help a woman deliver a baby disappeared when the baba-povytukha could no longer practice. Prior to this, they would, for instance, break an egg at childbirth or pour some water through the woman's marriage ring three times. "If the egg easily broke, this was a sign that the woman would go through labor easily," "if water poured easily through her ring, she would go through labor easily." A few traditional birth rituals are however still practiced today. Some such practices, meant to aid in childbirth, involve the woman unbraiding her hair, undoing knots and buttons on clothes, taking off rings, earrings.

The tradition to preserve the umbilical cord continues even if the child is born in a hospital. The mother has to keep it for seven years and then give it to the child, to ensure that the child is clever. The disappearance of many other maternity rites can be explained because it is not possible to perform them in the hospital. Often, for example instead of burying the placenta under the threshold of the house or stables, it was disposed of by hospital staff.

Postpartum rituals

There are a number of rituals associated with a child's first bath, swaddling, and baptism. These all are intended to give the child health, beauty, good character, happiness, and prosperity. There are a number of amulets a child also has to wear to be protected from danger (the evil eye or death).

The first bath rituals remained unchanged during the Soviet period as they could be performed in private by family members, mostly by the child's mother and grandmother. During the first bath, both parents would place various items in the bathwater to ensure the child's good looks. They believed that the qualities of the items they chose would be passed on to the baby. When bathing a boy, oak leaves were placed in the water, symbolizing strength; peas were meant to give the baby boy curly hair. When a girl was bathed, berries of viburnum were placed in the water to ensure her beauty; birch leaves were to make certain that she will be slender; marigolds that she will have dark eyebrows; a mirror that she will dress well.

The first bath was a moment when the family would show much care for the child's future. Typically, coins were added into the water "for the child to be rich"; sometimes they were placed under the tub. Wheat grains were thrown into the water "for the child to always have bread."

In order to help decide the future talents of a child, the parents would place various objects in the water. Given the economic and business conditions in the 19th and early 20th centuries, parents placed different male and female tools into the water or under the tub depending on the gender of the child. When a boy was bathed, an ax, a hammer, or a nail was added in the bathwater, for the boy "to know how to work," "to grow as a craftsman." When a girl was bathed, a needle, scissors, and thread were placed there, to ensure she will be good at sewing, a rolling pin and an apron for her to know how to cook, "to be a hazdynia (a good wife)."

Once the Soviets took over, these items changed and the focus shifted more toward the child's intellectual abilities: a pen or a pencil was meant to help the child write and study well, as well as paper, a copybook, or a book if they wished the child to be a teacher, a pointer, or a syringe if they wanted the child to be a doctor. During the Soviet period, the gender roles and expectations were no longer the same, thus neither were the objects used in the bathwater rituals. The ritual items (and dreams) for the children changed to fit the ideal Soviet man and woman.

After bathing the baby, the water used to be poured under a fertile tree for the child "to grow well and quickly." The tree under which the water was poured was chosen based on the gender of the child: if it was a boy, the water was poured under an oak or nut tree, and if the child was a girl under the apple or cherry tree.

Since the mid-20th century and the new Soviet routines being put in place, the rituals associated with the first baby swaddling disappeared, in particular, swaddling the baby on the sheepskin coat. On main reason for the disappearance of the ritual was its symbol—the sheepskin coat was a symbol of wealth: the child was placed on the sheepskin coat and swaddled for him or her to have much money slowly became discredited. This practice however disappeared faster in some borderland villages largely because of its social stigma: "some people have the sheepskin and do it, but I did not have it and did not do it." In the new Soviet reality, this ritual was less performed because more and more children were born in hospitals.

The tradition of visiting a recently confined mother and her baby was another maternity ritual that the Soviet administration changed in the Western Ukrainian borderland. A new ritual appeared, which consisted of only the immediate family being allowed to visit the recently confined woman and child in the hospital. Prior to this, anyone in the village could visit a recently confined woman at home after she returned from the hospital. The ritual elements of this visit included presents given to the baby, as it was considered that visiting the baby with "empty" hands meant that the child would have "hungry and poor life." Traditional gifts consisted of money, sweets or bread. The guests would put them under the baby's head in the cradle and wished him/her "to have money," "to have a sweet (good) life," and "to [always] have something to eat." The gifts too, changed during the new Soviet rule, as the traditional ones were seen as not ideologically correct.

While the tradition of visiting a child has persisted, this is not the case with baptizing a child. For the Soviet regime, it was particularly important to suppress this ritual because of the regime's opposition to organized religion. Furthermore, baptism was believed to give the church monopoly on the child's conscience and thus strengthen the religious influence on the young (Kelembetova 1974: 127). Not surprisingly then, rituals associated with baptism—in particular, the choice of the child's name and godparents, the celebration in honor of the newborn, were also reduced in significance or prohibited altogether.

The new Soviet ritual that replaced the church baptism was a piece of theater scripted by the state. This was as follows:

> The child was not baptized in church. It was performed in the village club, giving the child's birth certificate. The child was given a personal soviet star, the name of the child was written there. It was so nice; the girls were dressed in the embroidered Ukrainian dresses and were holding rushnyks. The mother with her child would walk to the stage under rushnyks, and the girls kept rushnyks over her head. There was a presenter. She solemnly presented the mother with the child's birth certificate. A pram was given from the collective farm. But it was that way [for] only three years, and then everything stopped.

These state rituals failed however to completely displace church baptisms because its secular character made it too similar to the workers' rallies, with their report-lectures and greetings (Darmanskyi 1975: 57). As well, the population continued to exhibit a high degree of religiosity and ritual practice. Church baptisms became a secret practice dependent on finding a priest willing to perform the service:

> It was forbidden to baptize children. It was done secretly for nobody to know. We looked for a priest, brought him home and he baptized children. I worked as a teacher and did not baptize my children for a long time, because I was afraid of losing my job. When my boys were already two, my husband found the priest and we went to his home with the children, and he baptized them.

The reluctance to keep a child unbaptized for a long time led to home baptisms being done by family members, in particular, "praying" and "baptizing with water." Here the mother or father would say a prayer over the newborn baby, sprinkle them with holy water, and give them a name.

However, this ritual did not replace the church rite, which was still done whenever it was possible.

Some changes happened in the ritual of choosing a name for the baby, which was intended to bring good luck and happiness to the new family member. Traditionally, in choosing a child's name people were mostly guided by two rules: (1) the child was to be named after the ancestors (grandparents) who had had good fortune and (2) the child was given the name of the birthdate saint, who would become his/her protector. The Soviet authorities tried to dictate that the names of Soviet heroes be used by parents instead.

The ritual of choosing godparents for the child also was significantly changed in the Soviet era. This ancient rite has been traced by some authors to the transition from matriarchy to patriarchy, so when the father could not perform his parental role properly, this meant that the mother's blood brother had to take responsibility for bringing up his sister's child (Kosvin 1963: 104). By the middle of the 20th century under Soviet rule, the choice of godparents who held the baby in their arms during the church baptism mainly reflected the parents' desires, meaning they could be relatives, neighbors, or friends. When the church baptism was prohibited, relatives became godparents more often, as relatives were more trusted than anyone else in the community:

> Once it was quite different. Relatives were not allowed to be godparents. Neighbors, bridesmen were chosen as godparents for the family to form a network of support. But during the Soviet regime, you would only choose family members, as you were afraid to be reported to the authorities. Such practices were punished, jobs could be lost.

From the second half of the 20th century onward, "honorable fathers and mothers" were also chosen for the state registrar to witness the church rite, in addition to the godparents of the child, which minimized the role of the latter. Close friends or colleagues were chosen as godparents for the state registration. Accordingly, the child had two pairs of godparents: the first one for the baptism and the second for the state registration.

The tradition of swaddling the child in kryzhmo (a piece of white cloth used for holding a baby during baptizing) was also no longer carried out. In the past the kryzhmo was always a piece of white cloth, but the color of the cloth for the state registration did not matter much. Now both white cloth, the traditional meaning of which became completely lost, and cloth of other colors, such as, of course, red, could be used: "The child was carried to the village club and wrapped in the red envelope."

The rituals that were performed before and after a church baptism also slowly lost their relevance and changed over the years. They began for example to be performed on the day when the woman and child came back home from a maternity ward.

By the middle of the 20th century, there was a popular rite of placing objects on the floor to increase the professional status and intellectual abilities of the child. When leaving the house and/or after returning from church, certain objects, which reflected mental abilities (such as a copybook, a pen, or book) and professional status were placed at the threshold to the house at the godmother's feet:

> When I came back from the hospital, my mother put different items on the floor, and I entered the house with the child and stepped on them for the child to be able to do everything.

Other birth rites changed too. For example, traditionally there was the ritual of placing the child on the table after returning from the church and reciting a prayer for the child to have good health: "for the baby to be healthy/strong as a table." In the new Soviet version, this ritual was performed after returning from the hospital and the child would be placed on the table leaning their head against bread so they would "always have bread." This table should not be very "clear, with crumbs of bread" spread everywhere. Sometimes sugar was scattered in the table as well.

Before the Soviet period, the baba-povytukha, and later the godmother, would bring the child from church, and place them on the broom near the stove to ensure a healthy sleep for the baby. In some borderland villages, the broom was put under the house's threshold when the child was carried to church and taken out upon the family's return. The broom was used to help "the child be quiet as a broom in the corner." Later, in the Soviet era, this ritual was performed when the woman returned from the maternity hospital: the broom was then put at the threshold and taken away after bringing the child into the house.

The secret baptism of the child in the Soviet era also led to the rituals performed during the baptism meal—originally intended to ensure wealth for the child—to be simplified. Money and bread were considered the main attributes of wealth and so there were rites of presenting the child with money and giving guests bread. In the Soviet period, members of the community more frequently just gave gifts to the child. When coming in the house, guests put money near the child or "congratulated" the mother giving her the money and offering clothes as well as a gift. These changes were in part due to difficult economic situation of the times and fewer numbers of guests (often only the parents and godparents were present) at the christening. According to one respondent, "when two people came to the christening, there was nobody to collect money from, so they just placed gifts near the child."

By the mid-20th century, depending on local traditions, these rituals continued at the christening; collecting money on a plate, giving porridge to guests, selling "flowers," and sharing bread among guests. The main performer was the baba-povytukha, also an important actor at the childbirth. At the end of the celebration, she came up to each guest with the plate in her hands and asked money "for shoes" for herself. Then she divided the collected money into two parts. She took the smaller part and gave the larger to the child. When the baba-povytukha lost her role in childbearing (in the middle of the 20th century), the godparents, the child's grandmother, and in some villages the woman who cooked for the christening, or even the mother collected the money for the child. The main christening ritual was now their walking among the guests with an empty plate to collect money. Sometimes various other things could be put on the plate; embroidered cloth or a piece of bread. The guests gave money to help the family purchase things for the baby. Some borderland villages even simplified this ritual too; the godfather or a guest would put a plate on the table and ask guests to give money for the child. After this, the collected money was wrapped in a handkerchief and put into the cradle near the child "for him or her to be rich."

Before the Soviet epoch, there was a local rite of cooking millet porridge for the christening. This was later given to guests; an exchange "porridge → money." The person who generally cooked porridge and treated guests to it at the christening was the baba-povytukha. She personally gave guests porridge or put it on the table for each guest to take and gave money in return. Today, remnants of this ritual have survived: the child's grandmother (a guest) walks among the guests holding the plate and asks guests to give "money for the child for porridge." The porridge itself is absent, because baba-povytukha who prepared this dish often is no longer part of the christening rituals.

Another local variant associated with christening is selling "flowers" a bouquet actually. This ritual consisted of selling to guests a specially made bouquet; there was an exchange here: "flowers → money." The "flower" was a symbol of health, happiness, prosperity, luck, beauty, and fertility (Boriak 2009: 195). A baba-povytukha (till the mid-20th century) performed this rite. In the summer she would make the bouquets from fresh flowers, viburnum, and periwinkle, in the winter she would use dry flowers and periwinkle. When the role of the baba-povytukha decreased during the childbirth, this ritual changed in two ways. First, the role of the baba-povytukha was assumed by the child's grandmother or an old woman at the christening. Second, the ritual with flowers has almost entirely been replaced by the ceremony of the godparents collecting money.

The desire to insure the child's future welfare is clearly expressed in the baptism and christening rites associated with bread. These rites have two components: bringing bread to church with the child and its sharing among the guests at the christening. This was to guarantee that the child would have always have bread in the future because of the guests' having bread at the christening. If the rituals associated with baptism continued in the Soviet era, this ritual did too. If not, the bread ritual could be performed after the mother and child's return from the maternity ward, then the baby's grandmother came out of their home to meet them with bread which was later divided among all the people present.

Even when the baptism ritual was prohibited, other ways to protect a child including both traditional and Christian aspects continued to be practiced. The most common were the use of amulets such as water blessed at Epiphany, flowers consecrated at Trinity, and willow branches blessed on Palm Sunday. They were put in the baby's cradle, added in the bathwater. The state's religious prohibitions made it gradually impossible to use these amulets, as their contents had to be blessed in a church. The traditional amulets were a cross or an icon placed in the child's cradle.

Given the magic protective properties of iron, the parents would often place a knife, scissors, or an ax in or under the cradle. A safety pin could be fastened or a needle inserted into the baby's pillow. If a child had to be left unattended or was taken out of the cradle, these items were put in the cradle "not to be empty"; during the child's first bath they were often put under the tub.

The color red has long had magic properties. A traditional practice in the borderlands was to tie a red thread around the child's hand or to tie a red ribbon on the cradle.

In the Western Ukrainian borderlands, there were other rituals to protect the baby and to prevent their early death. The parents would try to deceive death by ritually denying the birth of the baby and by performing others rituals than the traditional ones. Many of these rituals in the Soviet period lost their meaning as people began to see rational reasons behind a child's death. Also these rituals disappeared because they were so closely connected to baptism, which the state discouraged as well.

Godparents could protect the child from death. Choosing "counter" godparents was traditional in the Western Ukrainian borderlands. This ritual was performed a few days before the child's baptizing or on christening day before going to church. In this ritual, the child's father would go out of the house in the morning and invite the first person they met to be part of "the real" couple of godparents. When baptizing children become prohibited, this ritual was carried out circumspectly because the parents were afraid the authorities could punish them. Also, a brother or a sister could be named godparents, that is, "godparents from one house." This was often a safer option as these godparents came from the family and their godparents' role was easier to conceal from the state authorities.

Also, to deceive death, the child was given away through an open window at his/her parent's house. This was performed before or after the baptism of the child. Traditionally, this ritual was performed by the mother, who would give the baby to the person who carried the child to church (the godmother or father). After returning from church, the godmother/father would again pass the child to the mother through the window. This was seen as a new birth of the child because the window ritually became a border between the two worlds: the previous world, where there was death, and the new one, without it. When the baptism rituals become prohibited, this ritual was performed after the mother and child returned from the maternity ward. The intent here is to conceal the fact of childbirth.

The rite of the child being passed through the window after returning from church often included the custom of "buying-selling" the baby. The parents simulated selling the baby to the godfather or a relative, or a man from another village. Paying money to the child's parents, they took the child in their arms and said that now it was their child. The mother in turn gave this money to the church "to God." This selling of the child and parents' formal rejection of him/her was carried out to deceive death, which after the ritual believed the child belonged to the other parents. In the Soviet times, this ritual was performed very rarely. If performed at all, it was done only when baptizing the child.

Changes also occurred in the ritual linked to the child's first haircut. Traditionally, the godfather of the child cut his/her hair for the first time. In their absence, the father cut the child's hair first. On the borderland, this haircut was done either when the child was one-year-old or after the child began to speak. The cut hair was then most often burned. Some traces of ritual initiation can be seen here: "we could confidently call it this ritual symbolizing the child's transition into a more mature age" (Niderle 1956: 184); one that marked a child's transition from his/her mother's care to the father's. In the Soviet times these rituals lost their importance and, no ritual meaning was linked to a child's first haircut.

The purification rituals associated with a woman's childbirth also disappeared. In the past, "a woman came to church where the priest was reading a prayer over her." This prayer ritual was performed forty days after childbirth. Given the state's prohibition of religion, this ritual too lost its relevance: "when I gave birth to the first child, there was still a priest in the village, he brought me in church. But when I delivered the second baby, there was no priest and it was not allowed, so there was not this ritual."

Because of the Soviet authorities, many of the traditional maternity rites were lost. The prenatal rituals underwent minor changes, in particular, the taboo prohibitions imposed on the pregnant woman. Major changes occurred in maternity and postpartum rituals however, because of the gradual disappearance of the baba-povytukha and the prohibition of church baptism. Most ritual actions carried out during the childbirth as well as the ritual purification of the mother disappeared. The rituals performed before and after the child's baptism were simplified like the choice of the child's name and of godparents, celebrating after the baptism of the child, and ritual ways of protecting children from the death. Magical actions intended to influence the child's future, particularly his/her professional and mental abilities continued began to be performed after the mother's returning from the maternity ward. The practices of the first bath remained unchanged. New state rites appeared in accord with Soviet ideology, including the ritual of "red christening."

Western Ukrainian borderland communities now perform many of these rituals again. However, they lost much of their magical and traditional meaning and today have more value as entertainment and performative events.

Bibliography

Olena Boriak, *Baba-povytukha v kulturno-istorychnii tradytsii ukraintsiv: mizh profannym i sakralnym* (Kiev: n.p., 2009).

G.O. Bulashev, *Ukrainskyi narod u svoikh legendakh, relihiinykh pohliadakh ta viruvanniakh. Kosmohonichni ukrainski narodni pogliady ta viruvannia* (Kiev: Dovira, 1992).

R. Chmelyk, "Vidobrazhennia v pamiati mistsevoho naselennia protsesu tvorennia radiansko-polskoho kordonu v Ukraini (1939–1951rr.)" in *Narodoznavchi zoshyty*.vol. 6, no.(102 (2011), pp: 947–952.

Pavl Darmanskyi, *Obriad u zhytti liudyny* (Kiev: n.p., 1975).

Tetiana Illivna Haievska, "Do pytannia stanovlennia radianskoi sviatkovoi kultury," in Tetiana Illivna Haievska (ed.). *Visnyk Derzhavnoi akademii kerivnykh kadriv kultury i mystetstv: nauk. zhurnal*, 194–198 (Kiev.: Milenium, 2012).

N. Hromova, "Radianska istoriohrafiia kalendarnoi obriadovosti ukraintsiv," in *Etnichna istoriia narodiv Yevropy*, vol. 32 (2010), pp: 133–141.

Maryna Hrymych, *Tradytsiinyi svitohliad ta etnopsykholohichni konstanty ukraintsiv* (Kiev: n.p., 2000).

Sergey Hvozdevych, "Deiaki aspekty dopolohovykh zvychaiv ta obriadiv ukraintsiv Karpat" in *Narodoznavchi zoshyty*, vol. 3 (1998), pp: 278–280.

Oleh Kalakura, *Poliaky v etnopolitychnykh protsesakh na zemliakh Ukrainy u XX stolitti* (Kyiv: Znannia Ukrainy, 2007).

Valentina Kelembetova, *Pobut i relihiini perezhytky* (Kiev: n.p., 1974).

Valentina Kelembetova, *Suspilno-pobutovi funktsii radianskoi obriadovosti* (Kiev: n.p., 1984).

M. Kosvin, "Kto takoj krestnyj otec," in *Sovetskaya jetnografiya*, vol. 3 (1963), pp: 95–107.

S. Kulchytskyi, "Ukrainsko-polskyi kordon: trydtsiat rokiv protystoiannia," in Viiny i Myr, Abo *"Ukraintsi—poliaky: braty/vorohy, susidy"*, 502–511 (Kiev: n.p., 2004).

Alex V. Kurochkin, "Jetapy formirovaniya sovetskoj obryadnosti," in Avt. V. Alekseev; Hudozh.-oform. I. Shatalova; Red, ed. *Sovetskie tradicii, prazdniki i obryady* (Kiev: n.p., 1988).

O. Kuveniova, "Novi sviata kolhospnoho sela," in Natsional'na Akademiia Nauk Ukraïny. Instytut Mystetstvoznavstva, Fol'klorystyky ta Etnolohiï im. M. T. Ryl's'koho: 51–68 *Narodna tvorchist ta etnohrafiia* (Kiev: Naukova dumka, 1957).

O. Mykhalchuk, "'Nova obriadovist' na Volyni v 1960–80-kh rokakh," in *Etnichna istoriia narodiv Yevropy*, vol. 26 (2008), pp: 97–102.

Lubor Niderle, *Slavyanskie drevnosti* (Moskva: n.p., 1956).

Oleksandr Riznyk and Oleksandr Hrytsenko, "Obriady i sviata," in *Narysy ukrainskoi populiarnoi kultury/za red. O. Hrytsenka.* (Kyiv, 1998). http://culturalstudies.in.ua/knigi_11_23.php

Rozvyvaty novi radianski obriady, Interviu z zastupnykom Holovy rady ministriv URSR, holovoiu Komisii po radianskykh tradytsiiakh, sviatakh ta obriadakh pry Radi Ministriv URSR M. A. Orlyk // Liudyna i svit.vol. 7 (1983), p: 11.

Natalia Shlikhta, "Tserkva za umov Khrushchovskoi antyrelihiinoi kampanii: sytuatsiia v Ukraini ta ii polska paralel," in *Ukraina moderna*, vol. 4, no. 5 (2000).

Dmitry Konstantinovich Zelenin, *Vostochnoslavyanskaya jetnografiya* (Moskva: n.p., 1991).

"Media Witches" in the 21st-Century Russia

Tatiana Khoruzhenko

Abstract

The 2000s in Russia were characterized by an increased interest in the "supernatural" and all its manifestations. Current polls show that Russian people still believe in magicians and witches. Nowadays, more than 55% of respondents state that warlocks are a modern reality. The number of people who believe in the supernatural has been constantly growing over the last twenty-five years. In 1990, only 43% of Russian citizens were interested in magic. Numerous types of witches and wizards have active roles in Russian mass media today. Furthermore, their names can be found not only in entertainment media but also in the official press releases.

Keywords: Russia, supernatural, magic, New Age magic, media, tabloids, witches

Police reports present witches as quacks, but even in bureaucratic documents, the folkloric elements regarding the supernatural are evident. Police reports present the witch as always harming a person, taking away their money and/or health. Second, the witch's side of the story is never presented, since the case is based on the confession of the victim.

Russian tabloid press presents practitioners of magic as opposed to official state discourses. In advertising their trade, "Media Witches" tell viewers and readers that they use dark magic. Given all this, it is necessary to point out that traditionally, witches, magicians, and their activities are hidden from the public eye, often occur off stage and the manner in which today's magical figures present themselves breaks any number of traditional taboos related to magic.

Today, these magic figures are often ooze sex appeal and often are actors or models, showing that the interest in the "supernatural" is constantly expanding in media outlets. The influence that this phenomenon has on modern Russian society is a question opened here and inviting future investigation.

The interest in the "supernatural" and all its manifestations has rapidly grown in the first decades of the 21st century in Russia. The belief in sorcery and witchcraft is widespread in post-Soviet Russia, in both urban and rural settlements, according to Russian folklorist S. Adonieva. She points out that belief in witchcraft coincides with a new wave of interest in the occult in general. "In the post-Soviet period, many people rejected Soviet values and sought new sources of morality and spirituality, which led to the flourishing of a number of religious sects and lifestyle orientations, as well as the resurgence and public acceptance of faith healers" (Olson and Adonieva 2013: 223). A growing belief in sorcery and magic began in the 1990s and seems to have achieved its peak in 2015.

The latest opinion polls (VTsIOM 2015) show that Russian people maintain strong beliefs in the power of magicians and witches. Today's media interest in the supernatural has helped legitimatize this interest in magic and witchcraft. Following Todd Gitlin's theory, this shows that news frames simplify, prioritize, and structure the narrative flow of events. "Media frames are persistent patterns of cognition, interpretation, and presentation, of selection, emphasis, and exclusion, by which symbol handlers routinely organize discourse, whether verbal or visual" (Gitlin 1980: 7). Thus, it comes as no surprise that media narratives concerning magic and witches will use motifs found in folklore. On the one hand, the media tries to reject that witchcraft and magic exist; on the other hand, numerous TV shows have increased Russians' appetite for stories concerning the supernatural.

Mass media often portrays the witch in two ways. Police reports and news articles present witches as quacks. Tabloids, on the other hand, present witches as authentic keepers of knowledge. Yet folkloric concepts can be found in both these portrayals.

In the police reports, these folklore elements are evident in the way the background story unfolds: first the witch harms a person, taking away their money and/or health; second, the report never presents the side of the accused, only that of the victim. Similarly, folklore narratives about witches are based on the victim's account. A victim usually recounts his or her misfortune and explains it to be the result of someone's "supernatural" interference. To go on, folk tales present a witch's ability to both harm and cure people, for example cursing with and removing porcha (evil eye).

Curing women from porcha is the most common story in police reports. As an example, I will cite here headlines from several news articles informed by police reports: a resident of Tatarstan cured porcha for 420,000 rubles (December 1, 2015), In Stavropol, fraudsters cured porcha with money and gold (November 30, 2015); a sixteen-year-old girl from Volgograd gave the "healer" a half thousand rubles for the removal of porcha (November 26, 2015). As we can see, news about witches and porcha are common across Russia.

However, tabloids present witches presented very differently than the skepticism of news accounts based on police reports. Women tabloids often hire witches to predict the future of Russian pop stars. Witches' extrasensorial powers are used by tabloids to inform female audiences of the pregnancies and love affairs of celebrities. Interestingly enough, witches always use prosaic, not "magical" terms to inform the readers of their latest findings. As an example, we quote here a witch's advice to a popular Russian singer, who is going to have her third child in April. The fortune-teller Natalia Efimova is sure that

> the singer and her husband are going to be wonderful parents, but they should not forget that the child is another soul, given to us for a while. Excessive guardianship can only hurt children. To make pregnancy uneventful Jasmine needs to adjust the timetable for their travel and surround herself with people who sincerely hope for both mother and infant's health and happiness, [she adds] no harm will come to her from wearing an amulet [to protect her] from the envious and detractors (Jasmine 2015).

In tabloids, unlike newspaper accounts from police reports, readers are acquainted to the "voice" of the witch. Russian people's curiosity about the supernatural is partially satisfied through numerous TV shows, where viewers can become familiar with diverse practices. Magicians and witchcrafts not only present their abilities on public television, they also make claims about the authenticity of their powers in interviews. The TV show "The Battle of Extrasensory(ies)" represents an important outlet for post-Soviet Russian Media Witches. The show is inspired by the British TV series "Britain's Psychic Challenge" and is extremely popular in Russia. The fall of 2015 welcomed the sixteenth season of the show into Russian homes. Russian sorcerers and diverse magical figures from the former USSR appear on the show, boosting the success of the TV series and thus reflecting the widespread interest of Russians in the occult.

Anthropologist Galina Lindquist claims that "while the occult, by definition, is a hidden knowledge, urban magic in big cities is a conspicuously public phenomenon. As such, it is often created by the media and upheld by the market as a thriving field of service and commodity exchange" (Lindquist 2006: 23). She also notes "the contradiction between the occult character of magical knowledge and its spread and visibility as a social and economic field in post-perestroika urban Russia" (idem). It is necessary to point out once more that, traditionally, witches and magicians rarely advertise their powers publicly, and that their ways are generally hidden from mainstream society. The way these figures are presented by Russia's media industry today breaks these taboos. In her analysis of the market for the folk helpers in Russia, Lindquist notes, "the ideas on which magic rests are made public through media channels become the new infrastructures of business and marketing" (Lindquist 2006: 24).

The public knowledge of Media Witches today is unique—not only do they use television shows and tabloids to advertise their powers; they also construct their magical biography and identity publicly. It is not surprising then that most of these magical figures are young and good looking, ooze sex appeal and are, more often than not, actors or models.

In my analysis of their interviews from the popular TV show "The Battle of Extrasensory(ies)", I found that their stories are often quite similar, offering the possibility to construct a biographical plot and narrative around which the modern witch fashions her identity.

Miraculous birth

In almost all the interviews that I have analyzed, witches recount the strange circumstances of their birth. Usually they are brought into this world as sick babies, so they live "marked" by the threat of death throughout their lives.

Julia Vang[1] recounts:

> My mother knew immediately that I am an unusual child, even when she was first pregnant. The story of her pregnancy and my birth is mysterious. Secondly, her pregnancy lasted eleven months. And thirdly, I had to die three times before I was born. My mother had an accident, then during her pregnancy, she underwent surgery for appendix removal, after which, a doctor tried to kill me while she was in labor. My mother tried to find out what the reason was [for his actions], but this man had mysteriously disappeared from the hospital (Zubkova 2014).

Natalia Vorotnikova[2] suffered two clinical deaths. These deaths are proof of her unusual talent:

> My first clinical death, according to the doctors, happened during my birth: a fourth degree asphyxia occurred, as the umbilical cord was wrapped around my neck three times. This is a fairly rare event. But, apparently, it was my destiny to stay alive ... when I was only two weeks old; I choked with the mother's milk because of an obstruction in my throat and pharynx (Vorotnikova 2011)

If the birth of future witches occurs without trouble, then their stories describe major injuries suffered during childhood. These physical traumas are, much like the miraculous birth, meant to be a sign of their magical abilities. Merilin Kerro[3] was struck by lightning at age six. Elena

---

[1] Julia Vang (thirty-four years old) is a Latvian model, actress, and the winner of the fifteenth season of "The Battle of Extrasensory(ies)." She personifies herself as a spirit of Chaos.
[2] Natalia Vorotnikova (thirty-nine years old) is folk-healer and fortune-teller, the winner of the first season of "The Battle of Extrasensory(ies)."
[3] Merilin Kerro (twenty-seven years old) is an Estonian witch and model, practices Voodoo magic. She took part in fourteenth and sixteenth seasons of "The Battle of Extrasensory(ies)," but never won.

Yasevich[4] was accidentally burnt with boiling water at age ten, and subsequently was in a coma for two months. Zulia Radjabova[5] began to lose her sight at age ten. She believes that she inherited the gift of healing from her ancestors, as well as a protection from becoming fully blind.

For the Media Witches, their magic abilities usually emerge after clinical death or a traumatic event, so these trials function much like a (traditional) witch's initiation. After death, they are believed to be reborn. As such, clinical death and injury is a crucial point in the discourse of every Media Witch.

Family gift

> [In] Russian folk belief, the means of acquiring occult knowledge for a sorcerer happened by way of inheritance or a pact with the devil and occasionally was acquired unwittingly or unwillingly (Wigzell 2009: 72).

Despite Wigzell's claim, most Media Witches believe they gain magical knowledge through inheritance from an elderly relative, mainly from grandmothers. Even here, the discourse is led by folklore concepts: women inherit magical powers from their female relatives, usually their mother or grandmother (Tolstoi 1999: 297). Witches tend to show signs of their magical powers early in life. As a child, Merilin Kerro could see the souls of the dead. This Estonian witch got her gift and first lessons of witchcraft from her aunt, who was also a witch:

> As a child, I used to play with my sister in an abandoned house. I once saw a woman and realized in horror that nobody else could see her except for me. It was very scary. As it turned out later, it was the spirit of a woman who died exactly in that house (Kerro 2014a).

Elena Yasevich got her abilities from her great-grandmother, who also taught her various rituals. In her practice, Elena uses candles made according to her great-grandmother's recipe. Natalia Vorotnikova and Zulia

---

[4] Elena Yasevich (thirty-seven years old) is a witch, fortune-teller, folk-healer, and the winner of the twelfth season of "The Battle of Extrasensory(ies)." She uses the magic of fire.
[5] Zulia Radjabova is "The best fortune-teller of Russia" and "The best folk-healer of Russia," the winner of the second season of "The Battle of Extrasensory(ies)."

Radjabova both claim that the gift of fortune telling was passed down in their families. Natalia's mother and brother could predict the future, while all of Zulia's ancestors and relatives were healers.

Natalia Banteeva[6] similarly inherited her magical powers from her grandmother. She realized she is a witch when she was four and a half years old.

> It was in the village, I went to a wake with my grandmother. While there, I went to her and said, "I do not like this man who is looking at me."—"Where is this man? No one is there!"—my grandmother said. "But how can it be? He is standing in the corner, so gray." Grandma immediately understood everything, because she, too, had psychic abilities. All she said was: "Well, everything has started." Years later, she gave me all her gift (Banteeva 2010).

Inheriting the gift caused conflict between Natalia and her mother. As a result, during adulthood, Natalia broke all ties with her mother. Natalia's history is not typical for a Media Witch biography. While at first the families are scared by their daughter's gift, they eventually learn to accept her, but try to hide her supernatural powers from others.

For example, Julia Vang recounts:

> My mother treated me with love and understanding of what I am. I was a strange and unusual child, compared to others. For example, I talked to animals. Yet she did not constrain my development, and was happy when I learned how to read at the age of two and a half (Vang 2014).

The most interesting part of the witches' interviews in the TV show is when they talk about how they understand magic and their role in the society. Mainly, they see themselves as helpers. The most socially oriented are those who identify as folk healers and bioenergists. Lindquist argues that by advertising their abilities, witches "try to create for themselves an acceptable social identity and a worthy place in the moral domain. The strategies of legitimation that are used to these ends are in-

---

[6] Natalia Banteeva (forty-one years old) is a witch, fortune-teller, and the winner of the ninth season of "The Battle of Extrasensory(ies)." Now she works as a producer of her own magic center "Banteeva Group." She is also attempting to establish her own Coven.

dispensable for practitioners' self-construction as attractive and desirable, as charismatic individuals, which, ... is the main precondition of the effectiveness of their healing" (Lindquist 2006: 24).

To help validate the authenticity of their supernatural powers, witches can affiliate themselves with central religious figures. For example, Julia Vang insists that her spirit is the same as Jesus or Buddha:

> The god Radomir, who is called Christ, Buddha or Mohammed is the same entity as me, they were all sent here to bring the light of love from supreme chaos (Vang 2015).

Elena Yasevich calls herself a dark witch. She insists that she received her powers from the World of Death and argues that the energy harnessed by the dead can be used for good:

> In fact it is all the stereotypes and ignorance. What is darkness? It is, in fact, the world of the dead. So someone who receives power from the Dark is someone who draws strength from the dead, and then manages it. Darkness is not bad. It does not mean that, if met, the Dark bestows you with thousands of curses at once. The power of the dead can be used for good. You need to always remember the law of the boomerang: Everything you do, will come back (Yasevich 2012).

Zulia Radjabova says that she is not an ordinary witch, but exists on a much higher plane than other witches. On her website she claims that she is not a magician, nor extrasensorial, but an Initiate, of which there are only seven in the world. As seen so far, the ways in which the Media Witches describe themselves can vary, often greatly, from one witch to another.

While folk healers or fortune-tellers prefer to open their own centers, where they cure people and make predictions, and even tour the country to give master-classes, Media Witches often refuse to help people—Julia Wang says that divination bores her. Merrikin Kerro helps people, but claims that after she helps, people's pets may die.

> Of course, I know that you can change something in the life of another person, for example, help someone avoid death, but then you leave a karmic debt. This means that your interference might affect someone else. If you save people from death by use of black magic, you must have something to give in return, to prevent this karmic debt. I always tell people who are asking for help about it. And if they are willing

to give something, I tell them what and how to proceed ... I always warn them that their pets can die. I had three cases of pets dying (Kerro 2014b).

In their interviews, none of the witches define magic, but instead describe which supernatural power(s) guarantee good results. Most Media Witches attempt to use dark magic to help people; they claim to receive it from the primordial chaos or from the world of dead. Very few claim they are helped by angels in their work. Angels and prayers appear only in the interviews of folk healers who use conventional religious paraphernalia in their rituals, such as the rosary.

Tursunoy Zakirova,[7] is an ethnic Tajik, whose helping angels speak to her in a foreign language:

> The Guardian Angels that I see speak to me only in Uzbek. ... It's hard to explain, but they are dressed in white and pink Turkmen robes. I see them when I pray or just close my eyes and silently ask that they come and talk to me. They appear as both men and women and are so beautiful. God, the Lord Allah helps me. God is one, but there are a lot of angels. I have particular guardian angels who constantly come to me—a woman and a man. Even in my dreams I see them, they tell me what will happen the next day (Kuprina 2008).

Zulia Radjabova says:

> Nobody can harm me; I have a powerful defense—my angels (Radjabova 2015).

In her work, she uses Orthodox idioms and religious materials; her website shows her standing in front of the icons.

> I see my mission as helping people. God has given me skills, and I have to use them—this is my destiny. Learn to forgive. Help each other. Everything should be done through love and faith. And do not be afraid—the Bible says: "The one who fears is not perfect in love" (Radjabova 2015).

All witches, regardless of how they described themselves, have tools that they use in their magical rituals. Voodoo witch Merrikin Kerro and folk healer Tursunoy Zakirova both use knifes in their rituals. Kerro uses a

---

[7] Tursunoy Zakirova is a Tajik folk-healer, fortune-teller, and the winner of the season of "The Battle of Extrasensory(ies)."

knife and animal parts to make sacrifices for the spirits, while Zakirova says that a vision of a knife came to her while praying.

Tursunoy's gift was bestowed after the death of her mother. She had a vision while praying of a rosary with 121 beads. She went and ordered one identical to the one in her vision. Tursunoy uses the rosary in prayer to obtain more information. She always carries a rosary and a knife that came to her in prayer and a vision. This knife she found quite by accident after her mother's death" (Zakirova 2008).

Almost all the witches interviewed claim that every person has supernatural powers that they can develop, mostly by reading esoteric literature and staying positive. Elena Yasevich says:

> Magic is an illusion, a temporary "backup" or light illuminating the way. If you really want to change something in your life, you need to develop yourself with the help of spiritual practices, routine, and a positive emotional state (Safronov 2013).

Tursunoy Zakirova has similar beliefs:

> When a person does bad things, or thinks about Evil, when they carry envy, their aura becomes spoiled. In general, you always have to have good thoughts and give thanks to God, by saying, "Thank God!" (Kuprina 2008).

Some witches see themselves as moral leaders and spiritual teachers called on to bring about the evolution of the world, or at least of Russia (Lindquist 2006: 44). Given this, it is interesting to explore the activity of several witches in Natalia Banteeva's so-called "Banteeva Group," who have their own website and claim they create "new magic." Their website encourages those who desire to be successful to join them—"Our new magic is for those who are willing to own the world" (Banteeva Group 2015). This new magic is rooted in numerous traditional magical practices:

> After examining a series of magical systems, including tarot, runes, Cabala, Shamanism, and Wicca, and guided by the scientific development of quantum physics and genetic research, we embark upon a quest for new magic. New magic is a symbiosis of traditional techniques, and provides much material for individual research and improvisation. Using new magic, you'll be able to build your personal magic symbols like Papus or Crowley, create your own language and philosophy

as Castaneda and Gurdjieff, invent your own methods and tools to gain business capital, like Pavel Durov and Robert Kiyosaki (Banteeva Group 2015).

The Banteeva Group invites those visiting their website to attend their school of magic, to learn how to make personal horoscopes, to work with one's aura, and to make online taro predictions. The representatives of the Banteeva Group are certain that

> the witch is an archetype, a woman endowed with special knowledge. In some way, this is another aspect of femininity, which has long been repressed by society, so we are absolutely convinced that the time has come to reverse the situation. Through creating the "COVEN" project, we look for modern "reincarnations" of witches in Russia. We wish to show how multilayered the spiritual life of our society can be. We are able to use this knowledge in modern society (Banteeva 2015a).

All witches involved in the Coven project insist they help people, but admit that before joining Coven they practiced dark magic. According to group leader Natalia Banteeva's autobiography, she too used to practice dark magic, mainly love spells and porcha to make a living. Eventually she came to terms with the fact that her use of black magic was harmful, and went to a monastery to cleanse her spirit, after which she started to work with white magic. Nowadays, Banteeva and her Coven group tour the country to offer consultations and master classes.

> When you read my biography, it immediately becomes clear that I once worked with black magic. But life has taught me the right use of this gift, and gave me an opportunity to confirm that black magic should not be used... because it is very dangerous for both the sorcerer and clients. That is why I stopped doing dark wizardry, and I'm diligently trying to convince anyone who comes to me with such requests to stop as well. Currently, I only work with white magic, so I organized my own sessions in which everyone can gain positive energy that can resolve all problems and hardship of one's life (Banteeva 2015b).

All witches described here, except Merrilin Kerro and Tatiana Larina, became famous after being part of "The Battle of Extrasensory(ies)" TV show. Following their media success, they became active on social media. They use Instagram, Facebook, Vkontakte, etc. to post pictures from their everyday life, to promote themselves, and to advertise their services.

Some of them started working in magic schools or centers, while others became healers for the Russian government. Zulia Radjabova claims that she works for the Kremlin, while Natalia Banteeva says she has refused to work for politicians. In Zulia Radjabova's words:

> I will not name them [clients from the Kremlin]. All I can say is that despite the fact that high-ranking politicians have the best hospitals and doctors at their disposal, they often turn to practitioners of non-traditional medicine (Kuzina 2007).

Natalia Banteeva goes on to suggest that

> any political problem in Russia [can be magically hidden]. Magicians raise strong energy walls between clients and their surroundings. It is done not just by sorcerers, wizards and soothsayers but also by famous magicians. Almost all of them do government work. This is not a hunch, it's a fact. You saw such people in the "Battle of Extrasensorial," for example, Zulia Radjabova. She received an invitation. I, too, was invited to various places. But I refused every offer. Why would I accept them? (Livsi 2010).

Other witches, for example, Tursunoy Zakirova, work with the police to help solve crimes. She claims to only assist the police in emergency cases and in the investigations dealing with murders and the disappearance of people.

As shown, the phenomenon of witchcraft is gaining momentum in modern Russian media. In this chapter, I have analyzed some of the practices of women who use magic and have been part of a witchcraft-themed TV show. It is worth mentioning that males and females, however, discursively create different magic personas. Men tend to present themselves mainly as esoterics, and gain supernatural knowledge through studying written works. They practice spiritual techniques to obtain supernatural experiences. In their biographies, they often praise a certain Master, yet never name him. Their discourses of the (magical) self are constructed quite differently than those of the females witches presented here, which could be a topic for another study.

This chapter has focused on female discourses of the self in practicing magic, with case studies of witches made famous by TV shows and who are active on social media. The study cases presented here show that modern witchcraft operates differently than traditional magic. In the past, for example, magical figures did their magic in secret and never revealed, except to their apprentices, their knowledge, and the source(s) of their abilities.

Nowadays, some magical figures in Russia prefer to demonstrate their powers publicly by taking part in reality shows and by discussing their history with the supernatural through diverse media outlets. The occult tendencies in contemporary Russia reflect aspects of both the global and local societal crises, with people outsourcing their spiritual growth to others to manage.

The interest toward the occult, which has experienced constant growth in post-Soviet society, illustrates the depth of the spiritual crisis of Russians. Russians, it seems, will turn to numerous glamorized ideologies, individuals and faiths in their search for inner peace.

Bibliography

The Official Website of Natalia Banteeva's Producing Center. Banteeva Group 2015. Banteeva Group. Accessed December 10, 2015. http://banteeva.ru/

Natalia Banteeva, "Banteeva: Making Arrangements with Diavol Is Dangerous". *Express-gazeta*, June 8, 2010. Accessed December 10, 2015. http://www.eg.ru/daily/cadr/19799/

Natalia Banteeva, "Witchcraft Exists in Different Cultures". VKontakte, November 22, 2015a. https://vk.com/wall72155373?offset=40&own=1&w=wall72155537 3_21357

Natalia Banteeva, The Official Website of Natalia Banteeva 2015b. Accessed December 10, 2015. http://banteeva-natalya.ru/#_teststudio

Todd Gitlin, *The Whole World is Watching: Mass Media in the Making & Unmaking of the New Left* (Berkeley: University of California Press, 1980).

Jasmine, "Jasmine Told About Her Pregnancy for the First Time". *7 Days*, November 18, 2015. Accessed December 13, 2015. http://7days.ru/lifestyle/family/zhasmin-vpervye-rasskazala-o-svoey-beremennosti.htm#ixzz3tGXauMwP

Merilin Kerro, "Merilin Kerro: Interview After 'Bitvy extrasensov'". Krasaru.ru, January 28, 2014a. Accessed December 10, 2015. http://krasaru.ru/gadanie/1224-merilin-kerro-intervyu-posle-bitvy-ekstrasensov.html

Merilin Kerro, "'The Star o Bitvy extrasensov' Merilin Kerro: One Should Pay a Sacrifice for Using the Dark Magic". *Sobesednik.Ru*, January 31, 2014b. Accessed December 11, 2015. http://sobesednik.ru/incident/20140131-zvezda-bitvy-ekstrasensov-14-merilin-kerro-za-chernuyu-magiyu-cheloveku-prikhodits

Julia Kuprina, "Extrasens Tursunoy Zakirova: Sobchak Will Get Married If She Changes Her Character". *Komsomol'skaya Pravda*, May 29, 2008. Accessed December 10, 2015. http://www.msk.kp.ru/daily/24106/331847/

Svetlana Kuzina, "New Russian Vanga Cures People From the Kremlin". *Komsomol'skaya Pravda*, July 17, 2007. Accessed December 10, 2015. http://www.kp.ru/daily/23935/70170/

Galina Lindquist, *Conjuring Hope: Magic and Healing in Contemporary Russia* (New York; Oxford: Berghahn Books, 2006).

Elena Livsi, "Extrasens Natalia Banteeva: The Most Powerful Maguses Work for the Government". *Komsomol'skaya Pravda*, September 20, 2010. Accessed December 10, 2015. http://www.spb.kp.ru/daily/24560.5/734751/

Laura Olson, and Svetlana Adonieva, *The Worlds of Russian Village Women: Tradition, Transgression, Compromise* (Madison, WI: University of Wisconsin Press, 2013).

Official Website of Zulia Radjabova. Accessed December 10, 2015. http://zuliy aradjabova.ru/

Sergey Safronov, "Elena Yasevich: I Prefer to Live for Good". *Tele.ru*, September 23, 2013. Accessed December 10, 2015. http://www.tele.ru/liniya-sudby/elen a-yasevich-vybirayu-zhit-po-dobru/

Nikolai Tolstoi, ed., *Толстой, Н. И., ред. Славянские древности. Этнолингвистический словарь в пяти томах* [Slavic Antiquities. An Ethnolinguistic Dictionary in Five Volumes]. Т. 1 (Moscow: Mezhdunarodnye Otnosheniia, 1999).

Julia Vang, "Mother Was Glad That I Was Different Compared to Others". *VokrugTV*, October 17, 2014. Accessed December 10, 2015. http://www.vokr ug.tv/article/show/Ekstrasens_Dzhuliya_Vang_Mama_rada_tomu_chto_ya_ ne_takaya_kak_vse_45123/

Julia Vang, "Vang: Priests Will Burn Me Gladly". *Sobaka*, February 9, 2015. Accessed December 10, 2015. http://www.sobaka.ru/fashion/heroes/32987

Interview of Natalia Vorotnikova to "MK v Tule". *Bitva extrasensov*, May 5, 2011. Accessed December 10, 2015. http://www.bitva-extrasensov.su/10-putin-snova-stanet-prezidentomintervyu-mk-v-tule.html

VTsIOM, Press release no. 2964 issued October 30, 2015 by Vserossiiskii tsentr izucheniia obshchestvennogo mneniia". Accessed November 30. http://wciom.ru/index.php?id=236&uid=115446

Faith Wigzell, "Traditional Magic or European Occultism? Commercial Fortune-Telling and Magic in Post-Soviet Russia and Their Relationship to Russian Tradition," in *Folklorica, Journal of the Slavic, East European and Eurasian Folkore Association*, vol. 14 (2009), pp: 57–90.

Elena Yasevich, "Elena Yasevich: Magic Means Everything in My Life". *MediaZavod*, April 5, 2012. Accessed December 10, 2015. http://mediazavod.ru/articles/daily/drugie-rubriki/tendentsii/116212/

Tursunoy Zakirova, "Bitva Extrasensov", February 28, 2008. Accessed December 10, 2015. http://www.bitva-extrasensov.ru/57/

Tursunoy Zakirova, "Tursunoy Zakiriva: I Helped to Find the Murderer". *Asia-Plus*, May 16, 2011. Accessed December 10, 2015. http://news.tj/ru/newspaper/interview/tursunoi-zokirova-da-ya-pomogla-naiti-ubiitsu

Julia Zubkova, "Julia Vang: I've Died Many Times in My Life". *StarHit*, December 1, 2014. Accessed December 10, 2015. http://www.starhit.ru/interview/djuliya-vang-v-etoy-jizni-ya-umirala-mnogo-raz-113701/

(Un)orthodox Practice: Magic and Retraditionalization in Post-Socialist Serbia

Sarah Rafailjovic

Abstract

This chapter investigates the popularization of traditional healing practices and urban sorcery in post-socialist Serbia.[1] Owing to frequent economic crises, traditional ethno-medical treatment has become increasingly popular after the breakup of Yugoslavia and the Civil Wars of the 1990s and has now become part of medical pluralism in the Balkans. New forms of magic have evolved in urban areas, joining the already traditional forms of rural sorcery. Unlike many Neo-pagan practitioners of Western esotericism, who often claim to revitalize an ancient belief system suppressed by the Inquisition during the Middle Ages, popular healers in Southeastern Europe primarily legitimize urban magic by situating its roots in ethno-medicine and rural sorcery. Additionally, religion often increases the legitimacy that urban magic has in society. The existence of institutionalized belief, traditional sorcery, and alternative religious movements are complementary features in the context of contemporary Southeast Europe. Syncretism is deeply rooted in the culture of the region, as the Ottoman rule stopped the influence that the Inquisition could have had on the region. This chapter focuses on the dynamics of the pluralistic belief system in contemporary Serbia and questions' assumptions about rural and urban magic in the region.

Keywords: post-socialism, Southeaster Europe, ethno-medicine, traditional sorcery, popular magic, syncretism

---

[1] The article is based on of my doctoral thesis.

Strolling through urban Belgrade, with its mix of historical facades and imposing socialist buildings, one might find it strange to ask a *baba*[2] for help. The many bookshops in the city center sell books entitled "Vlach magic" or "love spells," yet sorcery and magic seem to fail to fit into this asphalt gray modernity. The multitude of graffiti walls, restaurants, and chic fashion boutiques make one forget about the possibility of urban magic. Admittedly, there is nothing magical about the recent socioeconomic situation. The collective feeling of resignation makes hope for socioeconomic advancement seems like nothing more than an illusion. Nevertheless, people still wear bracelets to protect them against the evil eye. When asked, they claim that a bracelet is nothing more than a holiday souvenir from Sarajevo or Istanbul. Yet one question has to be asked: Why do people still believe in magic, even after all the years of communist atheistic education?

In January 2003, an article in the *Glas javnosti* magazine claimed that old women from rural Eastern Serbia could "remove black magic on demand."[3] At the same time, Serbia has experienced a revitalization of institutional belief, with virtually every car displaying a massive rosary and an Orthodox cross, meant to protect the vehicle and its owners.

The social symbiosis of Serbian magic, Christian Orthodoxy, and modern medicine is due to many factors. Syncretic elements of everyday belief together with economic aspects have played a decisive role in the continuity of these practices through different political regimes. This is an equally important phenomenon in other post-socialist countries, coinciding with the shift from communism to capitalism.[4]

In the Western Balkans, the growing influence of institutional religion after the fall of communism and the popularity of sorcery remains

---

[2] *Baba* literally means grandmother as those who practice traditional sorcery are older women beyond their childbearing age. It is a quite common term and, compared to many other social forms of address, free of negative connotations. When speaking of traditional women healers, I will therefore use this term
[3] Divac 2003: 111–112. My translation.
[4] Cf. Radić and Vukomanović 2014: 191.

closely linked to issues of identity and ethnicity. Within this specific context, the use of magical practices seems to allow for the restoration of social order, which seems for the most lost.[5]

> One of the motifs of turning to one's roots is the return of the traditional ways of healing. [...] In this way, charms, which were recorded by a local ethnologist in the 1950s as being a disappearing phenomenon, are flourishing once again, in a somewhat altered way.[6]

However, such accounts represent more a popularization of traditional healing methods than actual revitalizations. Although ethno-medical practices were prohibited under the communist regime, they were still practiced in secret.[7] This claim is supported by the rich ethnographic data gathered during the socialist period, as well as by the fact that consulting a traditional women healer was generally preferred to seeing a doctor.[8] Ethno-medical practices[9] are deeply influenced by the region's specific sociocultural context. During the 19th century, allopathic medicine was solely available in the country's urban centers, while rural areas only later received allopathic practitioners.[10] Furthermore, the Inquisition never reached this region of the Western Balkans, as it was under Ottoman rule for centuries. Even if Serbian women in the 18th and 19th centuries were sometimes accused of witchcraft and punished by village councils, such accusations remained rare and cannot be compared to the witch hunts that took place in early modern (Western) Europe.[11] As a result, many of those suspected of using malevolent sorcery were allowed to continue their life as village healers after publicly confessing their deeds.[12]

---

[5] Cf. Radulović 2009: 238–239.
[6] Vivod 2009: 244.
[7] Cf. Kerewsky-Halpern 1985: 319.
[8] Cf. Kerewsky-Halpern 1987: 319.
[9] The term "ethno-medicine" means traditional healing methods. Ethno-medical practices are often passed on orally and combine different ritual elements. Among them, for example, are the use of special herbs, charms, prayers, and drums.
[10] Cf. Schubert 1987: 220. For instance, the first medical faculty in Belgrade was established in the 1920s.
[11] Cf. Radulović 2008: 285.
[12] Ibid., 289–290.

Serbia and other Southeast European countries that experienced Ottoman occupation have not carried in their culture the Western dogmatic and pejorative meanings attached to magic. Magic was not equated with heresy, but instead was considered an ambiguous force, which could both harm and benefit individuals. The local pagan traditions slowly merged with Christian Orthodoxy, meaning that people would often consult a conjuror, that is, *baba* for medical treatment.[13] This syncretism still plays a central role in Southeast Europe's everyday life. Magical thought and Christian Orthodox faith did not develop as contradictory systems of belief. This was particularly evident in rural areas, where priests actively participated in the social life of their communities.[14] However, based on official policy set by the Orthodox Church, *vračanje* (witchcraft, sorcery) is classified as superstition. Even so, individual attitudes about witchcraft tend to vary today, often influenced by the popularity of the occult in the entertainment industry.

Medical pluralism and the emergence of the occult market

> [...] for some things, what do doctors know? Injections, injections—nothing else! For some things, *treba da se baje* (you have to cure with charms).[15]

Broadcasting formats focused on witchcraft and divination have gained growing popularity since the 1990s. Magic is discussed as possible, even real, by the urban and the educated, who were brought up according to the atheistic ideology of communism, or the younger generation, raised after the fall of Yugoslavia. Although this may not be in line with a Western, modern and enlightened understanding of the world, it is in part a reaction to the broader sociopolitical context.[16] In short, magical practices are often sought when a social system seems out of balance and sickness can no longer be understood or healed by regular social means.[17]

---

[13] Cf. Radulović 2009: 125.
[14] Cf. Bandić 1997: 58–59.
[15] Kerewsky-Halpern and Foley 1978: 905.
[16] Cf. Radulovic 2008: 293.
[17] Cf. Lindquist 2006: 2.

With living conditions drastically deteriorating after the Civil Wars of the 1990s, Serbia experienced a temporary shortage of resources, which resulted in among other things witchcraft businesses booming, especially in urban areas.[18] The quality of services in the public healthcare system declined, particularly in large cities, which forces many to seek alternative ways of healing. The instable sociopolitical context led to a rapid loss of social values as well as certain institutions, positions, or activities losing their legitmatizing social capital.[19]

Various social titles no longer held the same social status, the legal system was collapsing and people were paid infrequently for their work.[20] This process is often referred to as "decivilization" or simply as "destroyed society," in the sense that people's lives become defined by a "culture of survival" (kultura preživljavanja).[21] As a result, in many areas of former Yugoslavia, the population was temporarily dependent on their families, not money or barter.

In recent years, the economic situation in the Western Balkans has been slowly improving. Still, because of the weak labor market, debts are rarely fully repaid, but settled instead through exchanging goods and services.[22] The healthcare system is more often than not corrupt, meaning that people with lower incomes have to wait long periods of time to be cared for or may never be able to afford adequate healthcare.

When I was living in Belgrade, there was an old woman in my neighborhood whose husband used to work as a musician in the kafanas (restaurants) downtown. A few years ago, both fell chronically ill, but could not afford appropriate healthcare and drugs. The woman told me that she could not even afford a visit to the doctor's office when she broke her leg. This is no isolated case, but part of today's post-socialist reality. On top of the economic reasons, people mistrust public or state institutions, which can result in them seeking the services of witches. What

---

[18] Cf. Papić 1999: 164. For more on the spread of alternative religious movements in Serbia during the 1990s, see Radulović 2007: 261–262.
[19] Cf. Bolčić 1994: 142.
[20] Ibid., 142–143.
[21] Ibid., 144.
[22] Cf. Jasarević 2012: 935.

Larisa Jasarević describes for the current situation in multiethnic Bosnia applies to the entire region:

> Amidst the diversity of the biomedical and magic markets circulate stories of professional malpractice and medical scams, exuberant costs, frightening health stories, flawed technologies, and forged, black market professional degrees.[23]

In competing with the public health system, women healers must remain "affordable," if they want to financially survive in their village or community.[24] Their services provide an alternative to often lengthy and expensive medical treatments. At the same time, the post-socialist-free media has favored the growth of the occult market by offering new advertising platforms.[25] Many of those practicing magic during the communist era secretly, now offer their services openly.[26] Appearing in the media is an important aspect of their work as well as a way to reach more potential clients.[27]

The treatment of physical diseases has traditionally played an important role for state institutions, but recently witches have expanded their work to cure people suffering from mental disorders, traumas or to help with issues in their private life. The work of clairvoyants even offers searches for missing persons or victims of the Civil War.[28] Conditions that have been historically diagnosed by traditional women healers as malicious supernatural attacks are defined today by using psychological terms that relate to the unconscious or the psyche.[29]

Many across the Western Balkans share the feeling of experiencing one's own life in terms of "survival".[30] Misfortune and illness are defined as results of a difficult life, uncertainty, and instability that have cast their dark shadows on people's privacy and autonomy. Previous studies

---

[23] Ibid., 927.
[24] Cf. Eikemeier 2000: 247.
[25] Cf. Lindquist 2006: 35.
[26] Ibid., 37.
[27] Ibid., 23.
[28] Cf. Radulović 2007: 79.
[29] Cf. Jovanović 2000: 23.
[30] Cf. Jasarević 2012: 924.

show people's difficult living conditions and subsequent excessive worrying as the key reasons for why they use the services of sorcerers.[31] But the clients of a *baba* are also the people who see themselves as victims of witchcraft or malicious curses.[32]

Similarly, the *strava* therapy that women healers use in Bosnia is thought to eliminate deep-seated fears,[33] while, "in global clinical practice, *strava* symptoms would be related to psychological, affective, or nervous disorders under the general rubrics of anxiety and depression."[34] In Serbia, the same magical method is known as *salivanje strave* (melting the fear away), because the term *strava* generally means "a terror, a fear, a spell, or evil eye."[35] Since these conditions are believed to result from acts of malevolent sorcery, the conventional treatment prescribed by psychiatrists is sometimes perceived to be less effective than methods using magic.[36]

It is often believed that allopathic medication only treats the symptoms of a disease, whereas sorcery always considers the life and thought patterns of the patient and thus cures their social suffering.[37] As such, it is not surprising that while sorcery is often referred to as disappearing knowledge, urban and rural healers prefer it.[38] But what exactly are the differences between rural and urban practitioners?

Popular magic: Just a "reference to the roots"[39]?

An old proverb says you can tie an ox by his horns and people by their tongue. From this it follows that the *basma* (power to charm) can only be

---

[31] Ibid., 922. Based on Tone Bringa's research on the Bosnian *strava* therapy.
[32] Cf. Vivod 2009: 239.
[33] Cf. Jasarević 2012: 925.
[34] Ibid., 925.
[35] Vivod 2009: 238.
[36] Cf. Jasarević 2012: 925 and 929. According to Jasarević, *strava* mainly treats ailments caused by sorcery on behalf of others, by someone's evil eye or by ill-wishing, generating from people's jealousy and envy
[37] Ibid., 925.
[38] Cf. Jasarević 2012: 926.
[39] Lindquist 2006: 39.

passed on orally and down the matrilineal lineage. Usually, women inherit their powers from their mother or a granddaughter learns from a grandmother.[40] If there are no direct female descendants, a mother-in-law may also teach her daughter-in-law charms.[41] This does not mean that other family members do not know these charms, since the rituals will frequently be performed in their presence.[42] The end of a woman's childbearing years usually marks her ritual purity and the time when she can start using charms.[43] Power comes with age—only older women are called *baba*, indicating not only their ritual power but also their family and social status.[44]

According to Jelena Čvorović, magic remains as individual as its texts and charms, because it is handed down "from knee to knee" over generations.[45] Yet there is another reason for magic being passed on. "It is believed that a woman who has performed magic should bequeath her knowledge in order to die easier."[46] The expectation of a painful death for practicing witches reflects the Church's position, which condemns sorcery as a morally reprehensible act.[47] In order to avoid a painful death and find peace of mind, a dying *baba* has to distance herself from her past practices.[48] Furthermore, sorcery and ethno-medicine are known as *ženska posla* (female tasks) and therefore receive negative connotations in public, more patriarchal domains.[49] This association is often reinforced by the belief that strange things can take place during magic sessions.[50]

According to local belief, illness can be caused by the harmful influence of mythical beings that possess ambivalent moral features, and therefore can both harm and help people.[51] However, since the majority

---

[40] Cf. Kerewsky-Halpern and Foley 1978: 906.
[41] Cf. Radenković 1996: 16–17.
[42] Cf. Kerewsky-Halpern and Foley 1978: 917.
[43] Cf. Radenković 1996: 16.
[44] Cf. Kerewsky-Halpern 1987: 320.
[45] Cf. Čvorović 2006: 186.
[46] Radenković 1996: 18. My translation.
[47] Ibid., 18.
[48] Ibid., 18.
[49] Cf. Radulović 2009: 238–239.
[50] Ibid., 238–239.
[51] Cf. Bandić 1997: 382.

of mythological figures are feminine by nature, a *baba*'s activities follow one simple axiom: "Female demons are fought by female healers."[52] While cures meant to fight such demons can be made using various ingredients, the cause of an ailment can only be detected through divination. If the victim experiences physical symptoms, the affected body region is treated with herbal medicine, after an appropriate *basma* is uttered.[53] Charms can help fight physical disease, but there are also rituals against anxiety or the evil eye, because—as they say—every illness has its *basma*.[54] Yet these rituals do not remain unchanged. As a result of urbanization and due to post-socialist social change, especially the growth in influence of the institutionalized religions, the shape of traditional medicine has changed.[55]

Yugoslav communism attempted to suppress any form of religious belief, which in part resulted in Neo-pagan movements forming relatively late in Southeast Europe, compared to Western urban areas, where they had spread in the early 1970s.[56] In the beginning of the 20th century, occult philosophies permeated intellectual circles in the Balkans, and found a space for dissemination in a number of publications.[57] However, this was not a case of the "re-enchantment of the world," as it happened in other parts of Central Europe, but rather of an adoption of Western spiritualism.[58]

The biggest difference between rural and urban magic can be found by comparing the ritual behavior and the characteristics of practitioners. For instance, in rural magic, the practitioners are often pre-menopausal middle-aged women who have acquired their knowledge autodidactically.[59] As the movement emerges in urban areas, prior education

---

[52] Kreuter 2007: 235.
[53] Cf. Kulišić et al. 1998: 25–27.
[54] Ibid., 25–27.
[55] Cf. Jasarević 2012: 928.
[56] Cf. Truzzi 1972: 16–17.
[57] Cf. Radulović 2007: 63. Publications about spiritualist themes often appeared around the turn of the century and in some cases even up to the 1930s in magazines with titles like *Novo sunce* (The new sun), *Život* (Life), and *Dva Sveta* (Two Worlds). There was also Branislav Petronijević's 1918 published edition *Spiritizam* (spiritism).
[58] Ibid., 63–64.
[59] Ibid., 72.

and social independence play a significant role in the lives of these modern sorcerers.[60] The matrilineal heritage of charms is not a mandatory requirement, yet with a few exceptions, traditional magic still remains the domain of older women, with only a small number of men found among the practitioners of popular magic.

A practitioner of urban or popular sorcery as Maria Vivod calls it, can be a person of any age, sex, or religious orientation, who is most likely self-taught and has been initiated.[61] In urban settings, calling a witch *baba* may seem off the mark, since magic is no longer the exclusive domain of older women. This change raises a series of analytical questions, as the practitioners of modern, urban magic correspond to neither the classical image of the *baba*, nor can they be categorized according to the criteria of Western Neo-paganism. Modern sorcerers create their practice based on individual preferences, adapt new methods, or simply reinterpret traditional techniques. As such, they reach heterogeneity in their activities in an entirely different way than traditional women healers, whose knowledge and charms differ from each other only due to variations in inheritance and initiation.

For the majority of modern sorcerers, their work allows them economic security.[62] One may be tempted to categorize them as Western Neo-pagans, practicing esotericism or part of New Age movements. Yet their philosophy is different from that of Neo-pagans, who celebrate the "revival" of pagan faiths in Wicca covens or as individuals. Urban popular Serbian magic is not a legitimated as a return to an old magic cosmology, interrupted by the Inquisition, but the exact opposite. The narrative of modern, urban sorcerers begins where their parents or grandparents still live—in the countryside.[63] So popular magic is in fact a reinterpreted form of traditional practices and techniques, to which elements of alternative

---

[60] Ibid., 180.
[61] Cf. Vivod 2009: 239–240. Vivod uses the term "popular healer" for neo-pagan practitioners in order to distinguish them from traditional conjurors.
[62] Cf. Radulović 2007: 72–73. Radulović has interviewed several women healers aged from thirty to fifty-five years during her fieldwork, who admitted to economically benefit from their work.
[63] Cf. Lindquist 2006: 29.

religious belief or Western esotericism are added.[64] The reference to the rural origins of their abilities and their magic is of central importance for the authenticity of urban, popular sorcerers, as it increases not only their credibility but also provides their clients with guarantees of their magic's efficacy and legitimacy.

In Russia, for example, modern healers will claim legitimacy by referring to the rural roots of their magic, which the *magi* will skillfully use.[65] They draw their magical knowledge from old and new books on Russian folklore, scientific publications, or spiritualist literature.[66] Modern Russian women healers often choose the self-designation of *babka* or *babushka*—the term means grandmother and sorceress at the same time.[67]

> Modern urban *babki* can present themselves as wise old women with a veneer of village homeliness and a simple and familial charm. [...] But they can also be elegant and successful young women. [...] Taking the name of *babka,* the modern practitioners position themselves both on the market and in the moral domain, subscribing to a certain strategy of legitimating.[68]

Analogous to the term *babka*, men often label themselves as folk healers, generating their own identification to rural magic.[69] In this context, the use of the term *narod* (the people) gets mystified, as it suggests the existence of a collective, indigenous wisdom, of which only a magician can make use.[70] Thus the term emphasizes the ethnic character of religious belief and simulates authenticity. The Orthodox Church also frequently uses it, because it symbolizes an ethnic community different than the concepts of civil society or bourgeoisie.[71] In Serbian academia, this nationalist connotation of the term *narod* leads to new categories in 1990s social anthropology, such as *narodna religija* (folk religion) and

---

[64] Cf. Radulović 2007: 12–13.
[65] Cf. Lindquist 2006: 28.
[66] Ibid., 28–29.
[67] Ibid., 28.
[68] Ibid., 29.
[69] Ibid., 38.
[70] Ibid., 38.
[71] Cf. Radić und Vukomanović 2014: 202. Here I mean the Serbian Orthodox Church primarily.

narodno pravoslavlje (folk orthodoxy), in order to define syncretic elements within the Christian Orthodox religion.[72]

Urban healers in Southeast Europe self-designate traditions that relate directly to their magical activity. At the same time, clients can hear or read about a particular *baba* or *vidovita žena* (clairvoyant woman), because of their successful treatments and prophecies, based on the perceptions of others. As such, the reputation of sorcerers and how they name themselves indicates their skills. Modern healers prefer to call themselves *vidovnjak* (clairvoyant), *prorok* (Prophet), *ekstrasens* (lucid person), *psihoenergoterapeut* (therapist for psycho energy), *bioenergetičar* (specialist for bioenergy), *beli mag* (white magician), or *iscelitelj* (spiritual healer).[73]

Some of these self-designations can refer to the methods of conventional medicine with which their practice competes.[74] At the same time, the association with traditional rural practices remains crucial for them, as elements of specialized knowledge exists in both popular and traditional magic. Modern or popular healers do not however rely on their reputation alone. In addition to advertisements in newspapers, journals, or on billboards, business cards are handed out, while some of these healers appear regularly on television.[75] Other sorcerers have waiting rooms or take client reservations by phone.[76]

The relationship that urban witches have with the Orthodox Church may differ from that of traditional women healers. Although the latter may call upon saints or patron saints for help during their rituals, many of them avoid participating in Church activities, as the Church has a negative attitude of toward their practices.[77]

---

[72] Cf. Sinani 2010: 19. Both terms *narodna religija* and *narodno pravoslavlje* are based on Dušan Bandić's research on the revitalization of the Orthodox religion in post-socialist Serbia.
[73] Cf. Radulović 2007: 261. The terms are all-masculine but have a feminine equivalent as well.
[74] Cf. Jasarević 2012: 935.
[75] Ibid., 926, see also Lindquist 2006: 24–25.
[76] Cf. Vivod 2009: 240–241.
[77] Cf. Kulišić et al. 1998: 25.

In contrast, modern practitioners do not seem to be in conflict with the Church over their exercise of religion and magical activity. Being a member of the Serbian Orthodox Church is experienced as part of their national identity and can influence the way modern magic is performed. In respect of their faith, some popular healers even refuse to practice magic during weekends.[78]

Modern sorcerers tend to explain disorder as a divine intervention or the result of someone's ill wishing.[79] In this context, saints and not spirits, are seen as 'the creatures, from the other side' who send 'warnings' [...] in the form of illness to individuals who do not respect taboos."[80] By using Church paraphernalia, magic surrounds itself with a sacred, institutional aura, and the practitioners gain by being able to invoke in the authority that the church has in Serbia. Furthermore, this fusion of traditional methods and elements of the Orthodox faith can help enhance a sorcerer's reputation.[81]

The use of the Church's instruments and symbolism can also show the intention of modern practitioners to enhance their legitimacy in a primarily Christian context.[82] While Serbian clergy has largely been tolerant when it came to magical practices and practitioners, the Bulgarian Orthodox Church also did not seem to have a set position on issues like magic, the occult, or healing outside the church. Having had fewer debates on issues related to the occult, the Bulgarian Orthodox Church did react vehemently in 2002, when they condemned the Harry Potter books, in fear that they might reduce readers' ability to defend themselves against black magic or could raise their interest in malevolent sorcery.[83]

---

[78] Cf. Vivod 2009: 240.
[79] Ibid., 239–240.
[80] Ibid., 239.
[81] Cf. Lindquist 2006: 39.
[82] Ibid., 29.
[83] Cf. Ramet 2005: 274.

Conclusion

Popular magic reflects the revitalization of institutional religion in post-socialist countries and the dependence of marginalized magical practices on the dominant belief system. Further, gender dichotomies in Southeastern Europe have never been completely abolished, despite traditional patriarchal values, the fact that maternity, and the family have played in people' lives.[84] As a result of the economic crisis of the 1990s and the subsequent social changes, women became more economically dependent on their husbands and families.[85] The economic crisis led more women to withdraw into private life and caused further ideological exclusion from the public sphere.[86] Consequently, repatriarchalization is closely linked to the process of desecularization and the collapse of state communism in the Western Balkans.[87]

However, women healers in Southeast Europe were able to gain some independence through their magical activities. Lidija Radulović found this to also be the case in the 19th century, when the *baba* status gave women informal authority within their communities and families.[88]

In comparison to most traditional, rural magic, practices linked to Western esotericism focus on people's individual freedom. The main difference here from Western esotericism emerges from the context in which it occurs. In short, syncretism is still part of Southeast Europe's everyday life. Even the methods or techniques of modern or popular sorcerers differ only slightly from those of traditional sorcery. Urban magic cannot simply break away from its traditional precursors, because its authenticity and legitimacy are at stake.

The most "modern" element in popular magic is the apparent self-expression and autonomy of practitioners, which remains crucial to their marketing and their practices. Even though alternative religious movements have flourished in urban areas, today they are not just an urban phenomenon. Largely due to the media, alternative beliefs, and practices

---

[84] Cf. Gudac-Dodić 2007: 161.
[85] Cf. Andjelković 1998: 238.
[86] Ibid., 241.
[87] Cf. Bracewell 1996: 214.
[88] Cf. Radulović 2009: 237.

spread quickly throughout society and this has helped change attitudes toward traditional magic. True to the motto: "The stars may affect no one, but astrology affects everyone."[89]

As the transformation of sorcery in post-socialism clearly shows, magic and belief do not only vary from one culture to another but can also change within the same cultural context from one political regime to another.[90] Unlike syncretism, a theoretical model which presumes and enforces a certain degree of coherence, the way people deal with magical practices in their daily lives allows for a number of incongruences linked to their social circumstances. In this sense, magic can reflect current tensions and trends, as Bruce Kapferer noted:

> Sorcery must be taken seriously. It must neither be addressed as a mad and mysterious mystical tour leading to wonders only dreamed of, nor be tamed to the rigors of a solid anthropological common sense that already knows what things are about.[91]

What used to be mostly a secretive act with almost conspirative overtones in the early 1990s suddenly became part of public events. The recent mediatization of the occult has also taken place in other post-socialist countries as well, such as Russia, where modern healers advertised in magazines or appeared on the radio and the television.[92] Today traditional and popular magic exist in parallel within Serbia and other countries of Southeast Europe. However, they all gain their legitimacy by situating their roots in the folk tradition(s) of magic, that is, ethno-medical Balkan practices. According to Bronislaw Malinowski, magic can only work in a way that is specified by tradition and local mythology.[93] "Magic moves in the glory of the past tradition, but it creates its atmosphere of ever-nascent myth."[94] It is this narrative of continuity and cultural authenticity from which sorcerers generate their credibility and that legitimatizes all forms of magic and magical practitioners. In contrast, Western Neo-

---

[89] Truzzi 1972: 20.
[90] Cf. Stratton 2007: 11–12.
[91] Kapferer 1997: 303.
[92] Cf. Lindquist 2006: 35.
[93] Cf. Malinowski 1978 [1925]: 92.
[94] Ibid., 99. My translation.

paganism links itself to prehistory and archaic culture, and legitimizes itself mainly through attempts to revitalize and "restore" old beliefs and practices. Here are some questions that could be asked now: How might the relations of witches and the Orthodox Church's establishment change in the future? To what extent might an economic boom in the region affect the market of the current healing pluralism?

Bibliography

Branka Andjelković, "Reflections on Nationalism and Its Impact on Women in Serbia," in Marylin Rueschemeyer (ed.). *Women in the Politics of Postcommunist Eastern Europe*, 235–248 (New York: M.E. Sharpe, Inc., 1998).

Dušan Bandić, *Carstvo zemaljsko i carstvo nebesko. Ogledi o narodnoj religiji* (Belgrade: Biblioteka XX veka, 1997).

Silvana Bolčić, "O 'svakodnevici' razorenog društva Srbije početkom devedesetih iz sociološke perspektive," in Mirjana Prošić-Dvornić (ed.). *Kulture u tranziciji*, 139–147 (Belgrade: Plato, 1994).

Wendy Bracewell, "Women in Transition to Democracy in South-Eastern Europe," in Mient Jan Faber (ed.). *The Balkans. A Religious Backyard of Europe*, 213–220(Ravenna: Longo Editore, 1996).

Ulf Brunnbauer, "From Equality Without Democracy to Democracy Without Equality? Women and Transition in Southeast Europe," in *SEER—South-East Europe Review for Labour and Social Affairs*, vol. 3 (2002), pp. 151–168. Accessed August 20, 2015. http://www.ceeol.com

Jelena Čvorović, "Magija bez magičnog: novi pristup," in *Glasnik Etnografskog instituta SANU*, vol. 54 (2006), pp. 173–187.

Zorica Divac, "Vračanje u severoistočnoj Srbiji," in Dragana Radojičić (ed.). *Tradicionalno i savremeno u kulturi Srba*, 111–122 (Belgrade: Etnografski institut SANU, 2003).

Dieter Eikemeier, "Schamanismus," in Christoph Auffarth, Jutta Bernard and Hubert Mohr (eds.). *Metzler Lexikon Religion*, 240–248(Stuttgart/Weimar: Verlag J.B. Metzler, 2000).

Vera Gudac-Dodić, "Žena u socijalizmu: Sfere privatnosti," in Zoran Hamović (ed.). *Privatni život Srba u dvadesetom veku*, 165–203 (Belgrad: Clio, 2007).

Larisa Jasarević, 2012. "Pouring Out Post-Socialit Fears: Practical Metaphysics of a Therapy at a Distance," in *Comparative Studies in Society and History*, vol. 54 (2012), pp. 914–941.

Bojan Jovanović, *Duh paganskog nasleđa u srpskoj tradicionalnoj kulturi* (Novi Sad: Sve-Tovi, 2000).

Bruce Kapferer, *The Feast of the Sorcerer. Practices of Consciousness and Power* (Chicago and London: The University of Chicago Press, 1997).

Barbara Kerewsky-Halpern and John Miles Foley. "The Power of the Word: Healing Charms as an Oral Genre," in *The Journal of American Folklore*, vol. 91 (1978), pp. 903–924.

Barbara Kerewsky-Halpern, "Trust, Talk and Touch in Balkan Folk Healing," in *Society, Science and Medicine*, vol. 21 (1985), pp. 319–325.

Barbara Kerewsky-Halpern, "The Complementarity of Women's Ritual Roles in a Patriarchal Society," in Norbert Reiter (ed.). *Die Stellung der Frau auf dem Balkan. Beiträge zur Tagung vom 3.-7. September 1985 in Berlin*, 123–133 (Wiesbaden: Otto Harrassowitz, 1987).

Peter Mario Kreuter, "The Role of Women in Southeast European Vampire Belief," in Amila Buturović and Irvin Cemil Schick (eds.). *Women in the Ottoman Balkans. Gender, Culture and History*, 231–241(London/New York: I.B. Tauris, 2007).

Špiro Kulišić, Petar Ž. Petrović and Nikola Pantelić, *Srpski mitološki rečnik* (Belgrade: Etnografski Institut SANU, 1998).

Galina Lindquist, *Conjuring Hope: Magic and Healing in Contemporary Russia* (New York: Berghahn Books, 2006).

Bronislaw Malinowski, "Die Kunst der Magie und die Macht des Glaubens," in Leander Petzoldt (ed.). *Magie und Religion. Beiträge zu einer Theorie der Magie*, 84–106 (Darmstadt: Wiss. Buchges., 1978 [1925]).

Žarana Papić, "Women in Serbia: Post-Communist, War, and Nationalist Mutations," in Sabrina P. Ramet and Branka Magaš (eds.). *Gender Politics in the Western Balkans*, 153–170 (Pennsylvania: The Pennsylvania State University Press, 1999).

Ljubinko Radenković, *Narodna bajanja kod južnih Slovena* (Belgrade: Vojna Štamparija, 1996).

Radmila Radić and Milan Vukomanović, "Religion and Democracy in Serbia since 1989: The Case of the Serbian Orthodox Church," in Sabrina Ramet (ed.). *Religion and Politics in Post-Socialist Central and Southeatsern Europe. Challanges Since 1989*, 180–211 (Hampshire: Palgrave Macmillan, 2014).

Lidija Radulović, "Tranziciona budućnost: politička upotreba proročanstva u Srbiji devedesetih," in Vladimir Ribić (ed.). *Antropologija post-socijalizma. Zbornik radova*, 258–280 (Belgrade: Etnološka biblioteka, 2007).

Lidija Radulović, *Okultizam ovde i sada. Magija, religija i pomodni kultovi u Beogradu* (Belgrade: Srpski genealoški centar, 2007).

Lidija Radulović, "Zašto su veštice žene ili zašto su žene veštice? Tumačenja u svetlu različitih perspektiva," in Tersila Gato (ed.). *Veštice. Ispovesti i tajne. Ispovesti "Sotoninih sluškinja" u snažnom i potresnom zapisniku o potkazivanjima, mučenjima, suđenjima i pogubljenjima*, 270–294 Kanu (Belgrade: Clio, 2008).

Lidija Radulović, *Pol / rod i Religija. Konstrukcija roda u narodnoj religiji Srba* (Belgrade: Čigoja štampa, 2009).

Sabrina Ramet, "The Politics of the Serbian Orthodox Church," in Sabrina Ramet and Vjeran Pavlaković (eds.). *Serbia Since 1989. Politics and Society Under Milošević and After*, 255–285 (Seattle: University of Washington Press, 2005).

Gabriella Schubert, "Die Frau in der Volksheilkunde auf dem Balkan," in Norbert Reiter (ed.). *Die Stellung der Frau auf dem Balkan. Beiträge zur Tagung vom 3.-7. September 1985 in Berlin*, 219–233 (Wiesbaden: Otto Harrassowitz, 1987).

Danijel Sinani, *Narodna religija: odabrana poglavlja* (Belgrade: Srpski genealoški centar, 2010).

Kimberly B. Stratton, *Naming the Witch. Magic, Ideology, and Stereotype in the Ancient World* (New York: Columbia University Press, 2007).

Marcello Truzzi, "The Occult Revival as Popular Culture: Some Random Observations on the Old and the Nouveau Witch," in *The Sociological Quaterly. Journal of the Midwest Sociological Society*, vol. 13 (1972), pp. 16–36.

Maria Vivod, "The Charms of Biljana, a Bajalica (Conjurer) in Budisava, Serbia," in Jonathan Roper (ed.). *Charms, Charmers and Charming. International Research on Verbal Magic*, 238–245 (Hampshire: Palgrave Macmillan, 2009).

Health Magic in Russian New Age

Anna Ozhiganova

Abstract

The term "Russian New Age" refers to the esoteric groups that have emerged in Russia since the 1990s. While ideologically and typologically associated with Western New Age, they appeal in varying degrees to Russian Neo-pagans. These groups propose a variety of alternative healing practices based on a seemingly mystical understanding of health and human nature. This understanding rests on three principles: integrity (of soul and body, of Universe and human beings), naturalness, and spirituality. The idea of "natural parenthood," which supports nonmedical childbirth, rejecting vaccination, extended periods of breast-feeding, vegetarianism and, in some cases, raw diets, occupies a special place in these alternative concepts of health.

This chapter investigates the practices of some New Age groups working in contemporary Russia. One particularly popular movement is called "Anastasia/Ringing Cedars of Russia." It was founded by Vladimir Merge, author of a book series about a mysterious woman called Anastasia, a witch, a clairvoyant, and a healer who possesses secret spiritual knowledge.

Keywords: New Age, Neo-paganism, magic, esotericism, alternative healing, natural parenthood, Anastasia/Ringing Cedars of Russia movement, PravoVedi community

Health, magic, and religion

In his book *Magic, Science and Religion*, Bronislav Malinowski analyzes the role of magic in modern societies, criticizing theories that claim magic is out of date. Malinowski was convinced that people turned to magic when they saw that the gaps in knowledge and practice focusing on rationality were either "not enough" or not effective:

> Nowhere is the duality of natural and supernatural causes divided by a line so thin and intricate, yet, if carefully followed up, so well marked, decisive, and instructive, as in the two most fateful forces of human destiny: health and death.[1]

Nowadays, despite the considerable progress of allopathic medicine, magic still has an important place, where rituals and religious experiences intertwine. Medical anthropologists note that even "scientific" techno-medical acts are sustained by ritual and can have ritual effects.

> Biomedicine is rational and technical. It would, however, be a mistake to conclude that it does not leave room for symbols and magic (with the accompanying emotions).[2]

Similarly, New Religious Movements (NRM) form unconventional healing systems based on an "alternative" concept of health. This is not accidental, as the NRM put forward as its most important task achieving the "moral-anthropological perfectionism,".[3] The members of NRM consider that through their beliefs and practices they can achieve full recovery from diseases and even gain eternal life. For example, the "Transcendental Meditation" (TM) movement promises its clients "perfect health" and believes this to be the main goal of religious practice. The healing systems used in NRM, borrow elements from Eastern and alternative medicine (Indian yoga, Chi Kung, etc.), concepts from European occultism, as well as current techniques in modern psychotherapy (Holotropic breathing, Rebirthing, Rolfing) and bioenergetics. All these systems have in common a desire to create a holistic human being, and to deny the Western dichotomy between "body" and "soul."

Creating alternative systems here means, above all, a criticism of biomedicine. In fact, these movements find themselves in a dual position—opposing allopathic medicine, while existing within a modern consumer society where allopathic medicine has an importance place. Moreover, NRM is generated by the same growing societal need for self-care, much like biomedicine.

---

[1] Malinowski 1948: 14.
[2] Geest 2005: 141.
[3] Balagushkin 1999: 35.

Today in the marketplace, he body is simply the "finest consumer objects" as Jean Baudrillard notes:

> Its "discovery," which for many centuries represented a critique of the sacred, a call for greater freedom, truth and emancipation—in short a battling for humanity, against God—today occurs as an act of *resacralization*. The cult of the body no longer stands in contradiction to the cult of the soul: it is the successor to that cult and heir to its ideological function.[4]

Thus the social functions of the body and soul change when the doctor becomes a "confessor," a "source of absolution," and medicine is no longer a therapeutic function but it "is consumed as 'virtual' mana."[5]

Despite their countercultural aspirations, members of alternative communities share the same understanding of happiness as modern popular culture, and health occupies an important place in it. Just as financial success among the Protestant ethic is seen as a measure of God's chosen people, New Age movements see health as the result of successful spiritual lives.

Studying the ways modern individuals perceive health and various health practices (health optics) can help shed light on the characteristics of modern religiosity and magic. As Talcott Parsons remarks:

> The health situation is a classic combination of uncertainty and strong emotional interests, which produces strain, and is [thus] very frequently a prominent focus of magic.[6]

In Russia today, the various magical health practices established recently have not been marginalized; on the contrary, they are very popular among different social groups. The fear of hospitals and invasive medical procedures; the distrust in physicians and technocratic approaches; and the plain lack of access to allopathic healthcare, all factor into the widespread belief that the magic and the "natural" can be useful. This attitude refers to homeopathy, traditional medicine, all kinds of alternative healing

---

[4] Baudrillard 1998: 136.
[5] Ibid.
[6] Parsons 1951: 468.

and self-treatment, as well as avoiding any harm brought by "artificial" healing methods (primarily biomedicine).

Galina Lindquist, in her study of magic and healing in post-Soviet Russia, has identified some reasons for magic's extraordinary popularity. Lindquist focused her analysis on traditional folk healers, paranormal studies and bioenergetic healing, as well as looked at the co-existence of different healing and medical systems. She discusses the concept of "aphasia" (speech and language disorders) proposed by Sergei Oushakine to describe a special "magical" state of mind of post-Soviet citizens. Aphasia is characterized by a loss of identity, while the individual develops a "cognitive vacuum," which reflects societal uncertainty.[7] Lindquist argues that in this situation, "magic provides an alternative, albeit homegrown and transitory [means] to the disappearing fields [of cultural production] thus giving hope to the self to be reassembled and redefined."[8] Health magic practices in Russia can be characterized as the emergence of a wide range of practices, which are available to everyone for spiritual and physical self-treatment and self-improvement. This also allows everyone the chance to become healers themselves.

In the scholarly study of modern religion and magic, a few key concepts can be difficult: "New Age," "neo-paganism," "magic," and "esotericism" are terms which receive different meanings when functioning in a Christian Orthodox country. It is generally accepted that research on New Age movements has provided the context in which the NRM[9] have been studied, even though some practices, beliefs, and movements may not ideologically and discursively function the way we envision them. For example in Russia Neo-paganism is seen as part of the New Age movement.

Tanya Luhrmann notes in her study of urban magic in London:

---

[7] Oushakine 2000: 1004.
[8] Lindquist 2006: 20.
[9] Hanegraaft 1996.

> In whatever form magicians practice magic, they situate it within what is proclaimed as the "New Age." However, it must also be said that neo-paganism often has its own distinctive flavor which sets it apart from other New Age trends.[10]

Neo-paganism may be regarded as a religious movement centered on the practice of magic, in the sense that these traditions and communities focus on certain ritual practices, which informs their worldview. We can call Neo-pagan communities "alternative" due to their countercultural declarations and their claim to provide some alternative to modernity and its lifestyle.

However, the words "magician" or "magic" are rarely used by the members of Russian New Age, who prefer terms as "spirituality" and "esotericism." According to Wouter Hanegraaft, one contemporary definition of "esotericism" in New Age communities illustrates instead a focus on an "innerly experienced spirituality."[11]

Russian New Age communities

I use the term "Russian New Age" to refer to the groups and movements that have emerged in Russia since the 1990s, are discursively associated with the Western New Age movement, but also appeal to (and reflect) to varying degrees Russian or Slavic Neo-paganism. Russian Neo-paganism rests almost entirely on other non-Russian traditions, due to the lack of reliable local sources. As Hanegraaft remarks:

> Neo-pagans are avid readers and it is in the scholarly literature, and its semi-scholarly spin-off, that they have found and continue to find much of the information that enables them to revive or reinvent the world of magic.[12]

"Book of Veles" (also "*Isenbeck's Planks*") is a very good example of a literary forgery made in the 1940s–1950s, purporting to be a text of ancient Slavic religion.[13] Book of Veles is the most famous example of such

---

[10] Luhrmann 1989: 7.
[11] Hanegraaft 1996.
[12] Ibid., 84.
[13] Serguei 2011.

semi-scholarly fabrications. Nevertheless, it being a forgery does not prevent numerous groups of Slavic Neo-pagans using it as their sacred text.

Most Russian New Age groups are relatively small. Such an example isthe little-known community of "PravoVedi," located near the town Kolomna whose leader Ma-Lena, a healer and a priest, has created an original ceremonial ritual, and composed spiritual songs and tales.

One of the most popular Russian New Age communities is the "Anastasia/Ringing Cedars of Russia" movement, founded by Vladimir Merge. Hundreds of Merge's/Anastasia's followers are living in so-called "ancestral" (*rodovye*) settlements in Russia and around the world (Europe, the United States, and Turkey). The Anastasia movement was started by people who read Merge's book series "Ringing Cedars of Russia." His series included ten books published between 1996 and 2010 and became instant bestsellers. Merge's writings have been translated into twenty languages and sold some 11 million copies.

I collected field data in the Merge's/Anastasia's settlement of "Blagodat'" ("Grace") in Yaroslavl region in 2010 and interviewed other representatives of the movement (Moscow, 2010–2011). The movement's ideology can be characterized as Russian New Age drawing from various elements: Slavic Neo-paganism, nondenominational Christianity, and modern esoteric teachings. Anastasia's desire to create the ideal society and the ideal human is characteristic of New Age movements. For Anastasia, this was achieved through acquiring "patrimony," in the form of a plot of land at least one hectare, where families would settle in accordance with the teachings of Anastasia.

The creation of their own "patrimony" was seen by the Anastasia followers as radical but at the same way, a solution to modern society's problems:

> That is a solution! Solution, beautiful, perfect, which makes a promise and has the ability to answer nearly all the questions of modern life. This solution solves all contradictions, solves them easily, painlessly, without any violence.[14]

---

[14] Safronov 2007.

HEALTH MAGIC IN RUSSIAN NEW AGE   181

Moving onto the "patrimony" meant living in natural environment and thus encouraging good health for the Anastasia's followers. Currently 1,625 persons (721 families) live in these patrimonies. An additional 5,992 persons (3,620 families) are at different stages of building their future patrimonies.[15] Over the past ten years, the number of "landlords" (or "pomeshhik," as the owners of "patrimonies" call themselves) has not increased very much. Most of these tribal settlements, some 57% of them, have yet to be established, so they mainly belong to the province of urban utopian dreamers.

Anastasia's followers are united by a common worldview, regardless of whether they were already in their "family estate" or not. Anastasia's followers also engage in a variety of common health practices. In their daily life, the settlers are inspired by the image of Anastasia and seek to follow her medical and spiritual advice. In Merge's books, Anastasia lives alone in the Siberian taiga, always walks barefoot, wearing close to no clothes, keeps no stock of food, and even does not have a permanent home. Thus, according to Megre, she is "an integral part of nature."[16]

Moreover, Anastasia claims to represent the ancient traditions of the Slavic pagans—Vedrussia. Therefore, she has many different supernatural powers: with the help of a magical beam she can see into the distance, read thoughts, travel into the future and the past, heal and even revive people from death.[17]

The Russian New Age movement is predominantly made up of small groups of people. Among them is the little-known community "PravoVedi," located near the ancient town of Kolomna (about 100 km from Moscow). The community leader, Ma-Lena (*Mother Lena*, her original name is Elena Martynova) takes on the roles of priest and healer, has created a ceremonial complex, composes songs and tales. Her community has its calendar, which Ma-Lena devised.

The community worships "Eternal Time" as a deity. This god is called "Rod" ("Kin") and the community temple is dedicated to him. While

---

[15] Statistics. Website of the "Anastasia" Movement (http://www.poselenia.ru/worldblock)
[16] Megre 1996: 23.
[17] Megre 2002: 21.

claiming to have recreated the ancient Slavic religious system, members of this community generally invent and reinvent religious traditions based on pseudoscientific research on the ancient Slavic culture and New Age.

The community is closed to most outsiders and one can visit only with Ma-Lena's permission. Nevertheless, this community is widely known among the followers of different New Age and Neo-pagan traditions. In total, there are about fifty people (including children) in the community. Ma-Lena's female relatives constitute the core of the community—her older sisters with their adult daughters and their families, her daughters with their husbands and children, and her three sons.

Since 2005, the community has lived by Ma-Lena's calendar, which has a variety of holidays and ceremonies. The year consists of thirteen month: twelve months of thirty days each and additional four days a year, which together represent a thirteenth month, called "Pillar" ("Stolp"). Dates fall on the same days of the week, each year, according to this calendar. Community members do not use winter and daylight saving time, because they consider this custom to be harmful to their health.

Ma-Lena calls her calendar "fixed," because it contains no time gap, by which she means all months have thirty-one days. She believes that months with less than thirty-one days are harmful: "These days, as the inserted spokes in the wheel, violate the uniform motion of time."[18] Supplementary days are only added to her calendar where it "comes naturally—at the beginning and end" of the year. Also, as in all Neo-pagan communities, PravoVedi's calendar marks the major ritual events of the year: March 21 is the vernal equinox, June 22 is the summer solstice, September 22 is the autumnal equinox, December 22 is the winter solstice, and January 1 is *ChisloKoloGOd* ("Number Wheel Year," which means turn of the year, New Year).

When asked, "What religion do you practice?" Ma-Lena replied: "We serve Eternal time." This means that they have "returned" to "eternal," that is traditional customs, for example they try to raise their children in accordance with the ideas of the traditional Russian peasant way of

---

[18] Field data. Pravovedi. 2011.

life. Their clothes are also a stylization of the traditional Russian costume: *sarafan* and *kokoshnik* for women, and a Russian shirt and wide trousers for men. Families living in the community live in painted wooden houses built according to Ma-Lena's vision, and perform "songs-tales" (*pesni-skazy*), composed by Ma-Lena, during the ceremonies.

Ma-Lena claims that her reconstructions are not strictly "scientific," yet acknowledges that, together with other members of her community, she "gets information from space," by which she means she engages in spiritualism. In reality, her main source is the information space of Russian Neo-paganism: its texts, websites, and forums. Lena explains the community's name, "PravoVedi," this way: "Pravo" is a Law, "Vedi" means "to know." We aren't "Pravedi" nor "Pravovedi" neither "Vedi."[19]

"We are the People (NaRod) living here and now."[20] By saying this, she places the community in the context of Russian Neo-paganism since the conception of "Nav', Prav', and Jav'" as "three sides of existence," where Prav' is a world of light gods, Nav' is a world of dark gods, and Jav' is a terrestrial world of human beings. This cosmology is present in the Book of Veles, the basis of much Russian Neo-pagan philosophy.[21]

Ma-Lena started her spiritual journey more than twenty years ago. She says she was diagnosed with cancer and asked a mysterious healer from Siberia for help and he was able to help her. Later they married and lived alone in the forest, "under lock," as Ma-Lena says, for eight years, during which she gave birth to three sons. During this time, they "received from the Universe much esoteric information": "We experienced all it on ourselves, all that ancestral memory has dictated to us, and then provide this knowledge to our kinsfolk."[22]

When she came out of seclusion, Ma-Lena began working to unite all her relatives into one community. She believes that family bonds

---

[19] These words have additional meanings lost in translation. "Pravo" means not only "law" but also "to be right"; "Pravedi" (or "Pravednik") means a "saint"; "Pravoved" means a "lawyer." Word "Vedi" goes back to the Indo-European root, meaning "to know."
[20] Martynova 2008.
[21] Smorzhevska and Shizhenskiy 2010: 129–137.
[22] Field data. Pravovedi. 2011.

should be more important than all other social ties—moreover, she argues, as they worship ancestral values in the community: we are trying to recover what remained in our memory from the past, not any religion, but "The Spirit of Kin (Rod)."[23]

Ma-Lena's husband mysteriously disappeared, but she believes that maybe one day he will come back and bring new healing practices to the community. Ma-Lena herself is widely known as a healer: her patients come to her from inside and outside the community. Ma-Lena widely uses a miraculous substance named "Ha" which is a type of plant resin. Members of the community wear the resin in homemade amulets; they also use it during childbirth and to treat diseases.

Ma-Lena can also create "living water" from well water when it is combined with her "positive energy." As a kind of wellness ritual, they fix one time for getting tea everyday (at five o'clock in the evening). They believe this practice is important and that it is extremely important to drink this tea with salty food only. During this tea, Ma-Lena tells community members about her new visions, and offers answers to their questions. She might tell stories about the patients she healed or talk about the healing properties of the teas. In fact all the community's ceremonies are thought to have healing effects: dances produce positive energy, collective chants of Ma-Lena songs can have therapeutic effects.

All families in the community have four to six children. All of the women have given birth without medical assistance. The child's father assists at childbirth, ties the umbilical cord, and washes the child. None of the residents use the services of medical doctors, choosing instead to treat all illnesses with community resources. They do not vaccinate children as they ideologically oppose vaccination. Ma-Lena says that getting rid of bad habits, such as smoking and consumption of alcohol, and having a strong, healthy family, by which she means monogamous and heterosexual, keeps the members of the community in good health. She believes everything should be in harmony: time, space, and family life.

---

[23] Martynova 2010: 61.

"Harmonious households and veneration of indigenous traditions can serve as a universal cure."[24]

Health practices and magic

Russian New Age groups use a variety of alternative healing practices based on specific magical understandings of health and human nature, characteristic of New Age philosophy and ideology. The three ideological pillars of Russian New Age movements are integrity (of soul and body, of Universe and human being), naturalness, and spirituality. The idea of "natural parenting," that is, nonmedical childbirth,[25] the rejection of vaccinations, breast-feeding for extended periods of time, strengthening the body (by ice swimming, cold water showers, and "snow baths"),[26] vegetarianism and, in some cases, a raw food diet all occupy a place in New Age belief.

The pursuit of health in the broad sense—ranging from wellness to healing chronic diseases and achieving immortality—becomes a leitmotif of spiritual quests for New Age members. Almost every conversation with "Anastasia" movement members begins and ends with the remark that, ultimately "all we're doing (in the patrimony) makes us healthier." They always talk about the various diseases, which they were able to recover from thanks to their new lifestyles. Much of New Age ideology and practice reflect a commitment to a healthy lifestyle, healthy eating, natural childbirth, and medical self-treatment. The same can be found in New Age websites, where religious and esoteric practices are discussed primarily as ways to stay and/or become healthy.

The pursuit of good health is a common theme among these groups, even in groups seemingly far removed from Slavic Neo-pagan-

---

[24] Field data. Pravovedi. 2011.
[25] The practice of "natural childbirth" is based on the ideas of Igor Charkovsky, who worked out the conception of "babies-dolphins," supernatural beings with a large brain volume and supernatural abilities. Ozhiganova 2015: 272. 262–286.
[26] Strengthening by cold is the main part of the teaching of Russian mystic Porfirii Ivanov (1898–1983), founder of "Ivanovites" movement. Ivanov taught that hardening the body provides health, healing of all diseases, and even immortality. Knorre 2006.

ism. Rodnovers, one such group, uses ethnographic and folkloric research data to reproduce incantations and spells for the group. Another movement, named the Ancestral Bonfire of Native Pravoslavian Faith complex based its healing system "Life" (*Zhiva*) on the practice of Sacred Silence and other Slavic practices. Ritual dance here is seen as personifying the movement of the Sun. The Sun further has become not only an ideological emblem of modern paganism but is also regarded as a connected to numerous healthy practices.[27]

An important aspect of alternative communities is their desire to preserve nature intact, so it is no accident that they often call their communities "ecovillages." These communities tend to favor "ecohealth," together with "natural" and "traditional" methods of health preservation, and see them as opposed to biomedicine. However, this "environmentalism" is much closer to the modern idea of "healthy lifestyle" rather than being a commitment to any particular worldview, even if they discursively construct anything that is modern, technocratic, or biomedical—as absolutely "harmful." The concept of "ancient Slavic medicine" that these groups embrace focuses on "ancient" healing and wellness practices and on thinking that all good things come from nature and one's ancestors.

Both the leaders and members of the community are aware that all these New Age methods and rituals are both very simple and very powerful at the same time. They do not, for example, require particular manifestations of faith or necessarily require any radical changes in everyday life. One does not need to make heroic efforts, as the groups believe positive things happen naturally. They also stress that the ancient traditions are "so powerful," that they "so deeply penetrate the consciousness," that one's beliefs or culture do not matter when it comes to the efficacy of these traditions. Magic can affect individuals regardless of prior beliefs.

The most popular alternative health practices include diet (vegetarianism, raw food), herbalism, Russian banya (sauna), aromatherapy, various types of massage, and kinesiology. All of them are seen as connected to "ancient Russian medicine." Alternative methods of obstetrics

---

[27] Smorzhevska and Shizhenskiy 2010.

and child development (natural childbirth, water birth, early learning to swim, strengthening, and so forth) are believed to be "traditionally Russian," and are actively used in almost all these social groups. Russian New Age groups have also developed a number of wellness techniques: "Beloyar," "Liubki," and "Zhiva" are the most popular among them.

Stanislav Zhukov a psychotherapist, a healer and the creator of the "Beloyar" system (from Russian "*white fire*"; also "The principles of natural development of the personality") argues that the magical Neo-Pagan ideology combines the ancient knowledge of Slavs and the teachings of important Russian psychologists (Leo Vygotsky, Vladimir Bekhterev, Ivan Sechenov, and Alexander Luria).

The "Belojar" system includes three stages: therapeutic, plastic, and the level of "a martial arts master." At the first stage, practitioners do some physical and breathing exercises and get rid of all diseases; on the second stage, they learn the practice of "natural movement" and the "ancient Slavic massage technique"; and in the third stage they engage in Russian national dance and martial arts. The authors of the "Belojar" system believe it can solve important problems, both personal and social: the achievement of good health and resolution of all personal problems, the restoration of strong family, and the improvement of "the genetic fund of Russia."[28]

Similarly, the founders of the "Liubki" training system (from Russian "*admire*") are seen as part of an "ancient Slavic practice of body work," and "the heritage of skomorokh (wandering minstrel-cum-clown) tradition." They argue that "Liubki" can be regarded as (but not limited to) a set of therapeutic body exercises. The system includes four parts: "Healing Liubki" that works with the body, curing it from illness and pain; "Martial Liubki," that is martial arts, working with consciousness; "Philosophical Liubki" developing a world view; and "Funny Liubki" a festival and game.

"Slavic Zhiva" (from Russian *zhivoi* means "life"; also "Zhiva" School of Integrity) was developed by Igor Pushechnikov, based on his personal experience of studying Eastern and Slavic martial arts and

---

[28] Website of "Beloyar" Movement (http://www.beloyar.ru/)

health systems. "Slavic Zhiva" claims to use ancient Slavic knowledge on health practices and military training, preserved, according to the author, by the Russian Cossacks. The mission of the Zhiva School is "Heal yourself, heal the planet," where healing is understood as a return to the state of "Natural Integrity." From an "esoteric" point of view, "Zhiva," a goddess of life, is opposed to Mare, the goddess of death, Zhiva animated Nature, while Mara took away Zhiva's power inducing all kinds of distortion and illusion.[29]

Each of these systems claims to originate from the "ancient Slavic tradition" and calls itself "Slavic yoga." Members of the "Anastasia" communities also actively engage in these practices and organize open workshops and competitions for all levels.

Magic of nature

In accordance with Anastasia's teachings, one does not need to do anything extraordinary to achieve good health, just break mundane life cycles, live in nature, and take advantage of nature's gifts. To be healthy, one needs only clean water, clean food, clean thoughts, and feelings. Anastasia's followers repeat her words:

> You need no drugs, no special tricks and techniques. Walk, stroll, breathe the life-giving air of the planet, turn towards the world, rejoice in what you share with its other inhabitants, drink a small handful of water from a spring, making your way to sun and light, and now you're on your way to recovery.[30]

Anastasia proposes to revise scientific concepts of nutrition:

> You have to eat as you breathe, not paying any attention to food, not taking your mind off what is important. The Creator placed this problem on others, so that a man could live like a man, fulfilling its destination.[31]

Anastasia herself eats only grass, nuts, and mushrooms. She does not cultivate, produce, and stock anything herself because different forest animals, such as squirrels, bring her food. However, she advises that her

---

[29] Website of "Zhiva" Movement (http://zhiva.name/)
[30] Safronov 2007: 23.
[31] Megre 1996: 23.

followers grow everything they need themselves. This should be done primarily in order to improve their health:

> These fruits can effectively build resistance for the human body against any disease, much better than the first-class man-made drugs among now existing and prospective.[32]

Anastasia explains that this is very important because during the process of maturation the plant collects all information about the person who planted it, and this will saturate the seedlings with the necessary ingredients to cure the illnesses of this person. Anastasia maintains that the fruit grown this way will be able to cure of all diseases, stop aging, increase one's mental abilities, and provide peace of mind.

Many members of the movement follow Anastasia's call to vegetarianism and to embrace a raw food diet. For example, in the settlement "Svetodar," Tula region, people would say:

> We are involved in organic farming; everything is done in harmony with nature. Animals are our friends. We do not eat friends. All of us are vegetarians. Many take up a raw food diet.[33]

Lectures and seminars on raw food and master classes on preparing raw food have become a compulsory event for the members of the "Anastasia" movement. As well almost all inhabitants of the "Grace" settlement are vegetarians, with several families of raw foodies.

Vegetarian raw food culture is considered to be the best diet by the Anastasia followers, and one opposed to the so-called "blyudoman" culture—people who eat cooked meals (even vegetarians). Some Anastasia followers would like to only have raw foodies live in their settlements. According to Anastasia:

> Food is one of the basic, fundamental issues in the transition to a new level of awareness. We firmly believe that people can be physically and spiritually healthy, by solely feeding on the species that Nature intended for him to eat, food that he

---

[32] Ibid., 52.
[33] "Svetodar" Settlement, Website of the "Anastasia" Movement (http://www.poselenia.ru/node/3020).

grew himself. It was decided to organize a settlement of raw foodies. Today we have [been] delivered from this powerful addiction to drugs such as boiled food.

Anastasia teachings further claim that people do not need housing or clothes, because the human body, when wrapped in clothes, loses its ability to adapt to the environmental. Anastasia herself sleeps on the grass in the taiga. When the weather turns cold, she lives in a bear's den. Anastasia also goes to rest as soon as it gets dark and wakes up at dawn. Anastasia, as Megre, writes:

> The first thing she does when she wakes up is rejoice [at the] rising sun, at new shoots appearing on tree branches, new sprouts coming out of the ground. She touches them, strokes them. Then she runs to small trees, pats them on the trunk. Something like pollen or dew sprinkles her from the trembling tree limbs. Then she lies down on the grass and stretches blissfully and exercises for some minutes. Her body covered with something like moistening cream.[34]

Anastasia has inspired her followers to "bathe in the dew," which has become one of their current health practices, as well as "sleeping under the stars." In their everyday life, members of the movement attempt to emulate what Anastasia has done in the books of Megre. Anastasia's starts off by teaching the followers that they need to plant a cedar tree because it has unique properties:

> Even in a small piece of cedar tree, there is more gracious power than in all power stations in the world put together.[35]

For Anastasia, patrimony is not just an uncultivated piece of land but something that requires special energy, to create a "Space of Love." that for Anastasia recalls the Siberian taiga where the plants, animals, and people live together in peace, forming a kind of brotherhood, or "a unique ecosystem," as Megre writes. All the inhabitants of such a place are sentient creatures and all can understand each other's language.

One can create a "Space of Love" only in their own "patrimony" where their family members live in love and harmony with nature. In the teachings of Anastasia, plants help people to create this "Space of Love."

---

[34] Megre 1996: 25.
[35] Ibid., 4–5.

The practice of natural childbirth is also closely linked to the concept of "Space of Love": Anastasia's followers believe that only in "patrimony" parents can conceive, give birth, and bring up a healthy, perfect baby.

Magic concept of health

The concept of health, as understood by Russian New Age communities, is not only anti-allopathic; it is a form of therapeutic nihilism. In short, for the members of the Anastasia movement, there should be nothing "artificial" used in the process of healing: no medical interventions, no pharmaceutical products. Everyone is believed to have the ability to recover from disease on their own, if they lead healthy "natural" lives and heal using natural remedies. In Russian New Age communities, people can be their own healers, invent their healing methods, test them for themselves, and share these experiences with others. This process creates healing in Anastasia communities. These -treatment practices serve to strengthen the community and further instill confidence in community members, so that they enjoy healthy lives, without using biomedicine.

In order to justify the use of these alternative-healing practices, leaders and members of alternative communities usually claim they are using "ancient traditions" or relying on the "experience of ancestors." One such example is the "mosquito-therapy." In one of Megre's books, Anastasia comforts the author, who has been bitten by mosquitoes. Anastasia says that every bug is designed for our benefit. This scene legitimized the "mosquito-therapy" practice among Anastasia's followers.

An article called "Mosquito-therapy was published on Anastasia's Kazan website. The authors ask their readers to "think logically" and agree that, if apitherapy and hirudotherapy are efficient programs, and that if even snake venom can be used as medicine, then mosquito bites may also have a therapeutic effect:

> When a mosquito sits on you next time, do not rush to kill it—it could hold a divine cure. Just take a breath and relax the area where the bite hurts, send positive energy that way, and the energy will pass through the affected area and promote

healing. And remember to thank the mosquitos for this free, professional and effective acupuncture course.³⁶

The article was widely disseminated on the Internet, under the name "Mosquito-therapy in the Slavic tradition and appeared on many neo-pagan websites." Its preface reads "Since ancient times, our ancestors knew that non-malarial mosquitoes have the ability to treat people, heal serious ailments, much like acupuncture." Adherents to this practice attested that for many years, their mosquito bites have had a positive effect on their health. Such discussions encouraged the members of New Age communities to create and test the potential of a wide variety of healing practices derived from this and other "invented" traditions. Many members of these communities also market healing services, organize lectures, seminars, and exhibitions.

Health itself is not the final goal of alternative communities, but it is closely connected to their Utopian dream of creating a perfect humanity and a new, just, harmonious society. The main idea behind this concept of health is "integrity," in the sense that a person has to be perceived as a unity of his physical, spiritual, and social qualities. They believe that every person initially has different abilities; the members of alternative communities term them "supernatural," but are actually just "natural," "given by Nature."

In *Ancestral Book*, the sixth book of the series "Ringing Cedars," Anastasia reveals to Megre that children born and brought up in the "Space of Love" will not be disabled spiritually. According to Anastasia, these children will "give us back Paradise, originally owned by us."³⁷ Neo-pagans believe that it is thanks to these children who possess clairvoyance, telepathy, teleportation, and other such abilities, that the transformation of the world will occur: all weapons will be destroyed, national borders removed, states will cease to exist, and all the people will live in their "ancestral homes," in harmony with nature and each other.

---

[36] Mosquito-therapy or once more about healing forces of nature. Website of "Anastasia" movement of Kasan region "Tartaria." (http://www.tartaria.ru/Chelovek/Zdorovie/Komaroterapia.aspx)
[37] Megre 2002.

In short, this magic-medical ideology and rhetoric, which relies on the alternative concept of illness and health, has become progressively more important in Russia. From this perspective, illness is essentially a projection of emotional, mental, existential problems, and therefore, a necessary stage of recovery, requires magic rebirth and the reinvention of the self. Members of Neo-pagan groups believe in the possibility of achieving a fundamentally new quality of health: not simply the absence of diseases, which helps maintain a perfect, unfaltering mind and body.

According to this disease model, New Age practitioners cannot in principle get ill. I have heard variations of this from members of many of the alternative communities: "Esotericians do not get sick. Whatever has happened to them is only "cleaning" or "karma." This concept of integral healing rests on the inherent God-given virtues of each individual. Thus, each person has the capacity for self-treatment and does not need clinics, doctors, or drugs to be well. Even if this kind of "autonomy" remains an elusive dream, their refusal to use medical services becomes an expression of their countercultural aims, It is a way of gaining independence from state and market institutions.

Thus the perceptions on health and healing an alternative community's members hold can play a key role in understanding modern magic and religiosity. For them, there is no Durkheimian division between ritual and everyday life. There is no division here between magicians and adepts, healers and clients, since everybody can practice the healing rituals and cure themselves and their relatives. Moreover, each person can invent their own health and religious practices and can share them with whomever they choose. From this point of view, Russian New Age, as well as Neo-shamanism,[38] seems to be individual religions. As a result, these New Age communities to a sort of social networks mediated by individuals who active participants of the health and healing services.

---

[38] Brunton 2003.

Bibliography

Julia Andreeva, "'Places of Power', 'spirits of dolmens' and 'primary source knowledge': Archaeological Sites and New Age Movement "Anastasia," In *Ethnographic Review*, vol. 5 (2014), pp. 73–87.

Jean Baudrillard, *The Consumer Society: Myths and Structure* (London: Sage, 1998).

Evgeny Balagushkin and Aum Shinrikyo, *Religion of the Peoples of Contemporary Russia* (Moscow: Encyclopedic Dictionary, 1999).

Brunton Bill, "The Reawakening of Shamanism in the West," in *Shamanism*, vol. 16, no. 2 (2003).

Hanegraaft Wouter, *New Age Religion and Western Culture. Esotericism in the Mirror of Secular Culture* (Lieden, NY: Koeln: Briil, 1996).

Knorre Boris, The system of Porfirii Ivanov: Cult and Movement. Burdo, S. Filatov (red.). *Religious Life in Today Russia. Experience of Systematic Description* (Moscow: University Book, Logos, 2006. Vol.4.).

Lindquist Galina, *Conjuring Hope: Magic and Healing in Contemporary Russia* (New York; Oxford: Bergham Books, 2006).

"Liubki" as a Russian National Wrestling. http://slavculture.ru/slav-kult/562-lyubki.html

Tanya Luhrmann, *Persuasions of the Witch's Craft Ritual Magic in Contemporary England* (Cambridge: Harvard University Press, 1989).

Bronislav Malinowski, *Magic, Science and Religion* (Glencoe IL: The Free Press, 1948).

Elena Martynova, *Conversations 2008* (Moscow: n.p., 2008).

Elena Martynova, *Conversations 2010* (Moscow: n.p., 2010),

Vladimir Megre, *Anastasia* (Petersburg: Dilia, unknown).

Vladimir Megre, *Ancestral* (Petersburg: Dilia, 2002).

Mosquito-Therapy or Once More About Healing Forces of Nature. Web-site of "Anastasia" Movement of Kasan Region "Tartaria". http://www.tartaria.ru/Chelovek/Zdorovie/Komaroterapia.aspx

Anna Ozhiganova, "The Children of New Age: A Utopian Project of 'Anastasia' Movement," in *State, Religion and Church in Russia and Woldwide*, vol. 2, no. 33 (2015), pp. 262–286.

Serguei Oushakine, "In the State of Post-Soviet Aphasia: Symbolic Development in Contemporary Russia," in *Europe-Asia Studies*, vol. 52, no. 6 (2000), pp. 991–1016.

Serguei Oushakine *Falsification of Historical Sources and the Construction of Ethnocratic Myths* (Moscow: IA RAS, 2011).

Field data. Pravovedi. 2011.

Oleg Safronov, *Patrimony: A Step Towards Dream* (Moscow: Agricultural Laboratory Press, 2007).

Oksana Smorzhevska and Roman Shizhenskiy, *Modern Paganism in the Religious and Cultural Life: Historical Essays* (N. Novgorod: NGPUPubl., 2010).

Statistics. Website of the "Anastasia" Movement. http://www.poselenia.ru/worldblock

"Svetodar" Settlement, Website of the "Anastasia" Movement. http://www.poselenia.ru/node/3020

Sjaak Van der Geest, "'Sacraments' in the Hospital: Exploring the Magic and Religion of Recovery," in *Anthropology and Medicine*, vol. 12, no. 2 (August 2005), pp. 135–150.

Website of "Beloyar" Movement. http://www.beloyar.ru/

List of Contributors

Tatiana Bužeková, (PhD) obtained her doctorate at the Institute of Ethnology of the Slovak Academy of Sciences. At present she works as an Associate Professor at the Department of Ethnology and Museology, Faculty of Arts of the Comenius University. She has done ethnographic research on contemporary witchcraft beliefs in Slovakian villages and neoshamanic practices in Bratislava. Currently she is doing research on ageing in rural spaces. She teaches courses on theory and methodology, rituals, gender studies, symbolic anthropology, and medical anthropology. She published two books and numerous articles on Slovak folk beliefs related to misfortune, explained in terms of memory functioning, emotions, and social cognition. Contact: dmtania@gmail.com

Alexandra Coțofană is a PhD candidate in sociocultural anthropology at Indiana University Bloomington, with a doctoral minor in Religious Studies. Topically, her interests focus on definitions of the secular, secondary economies, ontologies and modernities of others.

For her dissertation Alexandra analyzes ontologies of the secular by looking at the effects of dictatorial regimes on spiritual practices and postsocialist divides within the Christian Orthodox cosmology. She explores changes in the relation of religion and magic within Romanian Christian Orthodoxy, with a strong focus on politicians working with witchcraft. Contact: siacotof@umail.iu.edu

Ekaterina Grishaeva (PhD) holds a doctorate in philosophy from the Ural Federal University, Yekaterinburg, Russia. As a doctoral student she specialized in orthodox theology, mainly in neopatristic synthesis. Since 2011 she is a lecturer at the Department of Philosophy at the Ural Federal University. In 2014 she was a junior fellow in the Institute for Human Science, Vienna Orthodox Christianity and Politics in Post-Soviet Culture as Depicted in Russian blogs. In 2015-2016 she worked as an Erasmus postdoctoral fellow for the project *The criticism of European*

model of development in Russian neoconservative discourse of traditional values, at the Jagiellonian University, Institute of Political Science and International Relationship. In 2015-2017 she was head of a research team on the project on Orthodox believers' identities in Russia, funded by Russian Foundation of Humanitarian Science.
Contact: ekaterina.grishaeva@teol.uu.se

Dzvenyslava Hanus (PhD) received her doctorate in History from the M. Rylsky Institute for Art, Folklore Studies and Ethnology of National Academy of Sciences of Ukraine (M. Rylskyi IAFSE). She studied history and ethnology at Ivan Franko Lviv National University, Department of Ethnology, and she completed a postgraduate course at M. Rylskyi IAFSE. In her thesis she considered main beliefs and rituals of the population of Ukrainian-Polish borderland, performed from the birth of the infant until the age of one. At present she works as a research fellow in Ukrainian Ethnological Centre of M. Rylskyi IAFSE. Here she studies ethno-cultural aspects of the Western Ukrainian borderland, Ukrainian oral history and medical anthropology. Contact: dzvin4ik@ukr.net

Tatyana Khoruzhenko (PhD) is a faculty member of the philological department of the Ural Federal University. She delivers lectures in modern Russian folklore for the students of master program. The sphere of her interest is Russian fantasy, folklore elements in modern literature, newslore and internetlore. Contact: tkhoruzhenko@mail.ru

Patrick Michelson, (PhD) is an Assistant Professor in the Department of Religious Studies at Indiana University Bloomington. He is an intellectual historian of Russian Orthodox thought and, more broadly, modern Christian thought on the European Continent. His principal work explores the many intersections among Russian Orthodox theology, the discursive and ideological traditions of Russia's educated society, church-state relations in a multi-confessional empire, and the creation of normative categories during the Church's Synodal period (1721–1917). Contact: plmichel@indiana.edu

James M. Nyce (PhD) is Professor Emeritus of Anthropology, Ball State University, IN, USA and docent at Linköping University, Sweden. He is also affiliated professor at Lund University and an affiliated researcher at the Karolinska Institute. Nyce has done fieldwork in Romania since 2004.
Contact: jnyce@rocketmail.com

Anna Ozhiganova (PhD) is an anthropologist, a researcher at the Institute of Ethnology and Anthropology Russian Academy of Sciences, a member of the Association of Medical Anthropologists (AMA). Her research interests concerns the intersections of religion, health, alternative medicine and alternative social movements. Her publications include "New religiosity in contemporary Russia: doctrines, organizations, practices" (Moscow, 2006), co-authored with Jury Filippov; "Children of New Age: a utopian project of 'Anastasia' movement" in State, Religion and Church in Russia and Worldwide, №2 (33), 2015: 262-286; "The birth of a new human: the utopian project of the natural birth movement" in Constructing the childish (philology, history, anthropology), (eds.. V. Bezrogov, M. Balina et al.) (Moscow-Petersburg, 2011: 444-460); "Battle for school: modernizers and clericals" in Debates on Politics and Culture, № 2 (106), 2016: 92-105. Contact: anna-ozhiganova@yandex.ru

Sarah Rafajlović (PhD) holds a doctorate in anthropology from the Ludwig-Maximilians-University Munich, Germany. Her dissertation „Babaveštica: Women, magic and the occult in (post)socialist Serbia" focuses on magic, syncretism and the cultural construction of the witch-figure in the Western Balkans. During her research she worked with the Department of Ethnology and Anthropology at the University in Belgrade and with the Ethnographic Museum in Belgrade. Her main research interests concern the religious revitalization and retraditionalization in the Post-Yugoslav space, as well as changes in gender relations.
Contact: Sarah.Rafailovic@gmx.de

Victor Shnirelman (PhD) is a Russian historian, cultural anthropologist and a member of Academia Europaea (since 1998). He is a senior researcher of N. N. Miklukho-Maklai Institute of Ethnology and Anthropology at the Russian Academy of Sciences and an author of over 450 works, including over 30 monographs on cultural memory, politics of the past, racism, nationalism, Neo-paganism, eschatology in Russia, and archaeology. Shnirelman's main fields include the ideologies of nationalism in Russia and CIS, ethnocentrism and xenophobia. Contact: shnirv@mail.ru

Shumkova Valeria is PhD student at the Institute of Social and Political Science, the Ural Federal University, Yekaterinburg, Russia. Contact: wolzogen@gmail.com

SOVIET AND POST-SOVIET POLITICS AND SOCIETY

Edited by Dr. Andreas Umland

ISSN 1614-3515

1   Андреас Умланд (ред.)
    Воплощение Европейской
    конвенции по правам человека в
    России
    Философские, юридические и
    эмпирические исследования
    ISBN 3-89821-387-0

2   Christian Wipperfürth
    Russland – ein vertrauenswürdiger
    Partner?
    Grundlagen, Hintergründe und Praxis
    gegenwärtiger russischer Außenpolitik
    Mit einem Vorwort von Heinz Timmermann
    ISBN 3-89821-401-X

3   Manja Hussner
    Die Übernahme internationalen Rechts
    in die russische und deutsche
    Rechtsordnung
    Eine vergleichende Analyse zur
    Völkerrechtsfreundlichkeit der Verfassungen
    der Russländischen Föderation und der
    Bundesrepublik Deutschland
    Mit einem Vorwort von Rainer Arnold
    ISBN 3-89821-438-9

4   Matthew Tejada
    Bulgaria's Democratic Consolidation
    and the Kozloduy Nuclear Power Plant
    (KNPP)
    The Unattainability of Closure
    With a foreword by Richard J. Crampton
    ISBN 3-89821-439-7

5   Марк Григорьевич Меерович
    Квадратные метры, определяющие
    сознание
    Государственная жилищная политика в
    СССР. 1921 – 1941 гг
    ISBN 3-89821-474-5

6   Andrei P. Tsygankov, Pavel
    A. Tsygankov (Eds.)
    New Directions in Russian
    International Studies
    ISBN 3-89821-422-2

7   Марк Григорьевич Меерович
    Как власть народ к труду приучала
    Жилище в СССР – средство управления
    людьми. 1917 – 1941 гг.
    С предисловием Елены Осокиной
    ISBN 3-89821-495-8

8   David J. Galbreath
    Nation-Building and Minority Politics
    in Post-Socialist States
    Interests, Influence and Identities in Estonia
    and Latvia
    With a foreword by David J. Smith
    ISBN 3-89821-467-2

9   Алексей Юрьевич Безугольный
    Народы Кавказа в Вооруженных
    силах СССР в годы Великой
    Отечественной войны 1941-1945 гг.
    С предисловием Николая Бугая
    ISBN 3-89821-475-3

10 Вячеслав Лихачев и Владимир
    Прибыловский (ред.)
    Русское Национальное Единство,
    1990-2000. В 2-х томах
    ISBN 3-89821-523-7

11 Николай Бугай (ред.)
    Народы стран Балтии в условиях
    сталинизма (1940-е – 1950-е годы)
    Документированная история
    ISBN 3-89821-525-3

12 Ingmar Bredies (Hrsg.)
    Zur Anatomie der Orange Revolution
    in der Ukraine
    Wechsel des Elitenregimes oder Triumph des
    Parlamentarismus?
    ISBN 3-89821-524-5

13 Anastasia V. Mitrofanova
    The Politicization of Russian
    Orthodoxy
    Actors and Ideas
    With a foreword by William C. Gay
    ISBN 3-89821-481-8

14   Nathan D. Larson
     Alexander Solzhenitsyn and the
     Russo-Jewish Question
     ISBN 3-89821-483-4

15   Guido Houben
     Kulturpolitik und Ethnizität
     Staatliche Kunstförderung im Russland der
     neunziger Jahre
     Mit einem Vorwort von Gert Weisskirchen
     ISBN 3-89821-542-3

16   Leonid Luks
     Der russische „Sonderweg"?
     Aufsätze zur neuesten Geschichte Russlands
     im europäischen Kontext
     ISBN 3-89821-496-6

17   Евгений Мороз
     История «Мёртвой воды» – от
     страшной сказки к большой
     политике
     Политическое неоязычество в
     постсоветской России
     ISBN 3-89821-551-2

18   Александр Верховский и Галина
     Кожевникова (ред.)
     Этническая и религиозная
     интолерантность в российских СМИ
     Результаты мониторинга 2001-2004 гг.
     ISBN 3-89821-569-5

19   Christian Ganzer
     Sowjetisches Erbe und ukrainische
     Nation
     Das Museum der Geschichte des Zaporoger
     Kosakentums auf der Insel Chortycja
     Mit einem Vorwort von Frank Golczewski
     ISBN 3-89821-504-0

20   Эльза-Баир Гучинова
     Помнить нельзя забыть
     Антропология депортационной травмы
     калмыков
     С предисловием Кэролайн Хамфри
     ISBN 3-89821-506-7

21   Юлия Лидерман
     Мотивы «проверки» и «испытания»
     в постсоветской культуре
     Советское прошлое в российском
     кинематографе 1990-х годов
     С предисловием Евгения Марголита
     ISBN 3-89821-511-3

22   Tanya Lokshina, Ray Thomas, Mary
     Mayer (Eds.)
     The Imposition of a Fake Political
     Settlement in the Northern Caucasus
     The 2003 Chechen Presidential Election
     ISBN 3-89821-436-2

23   Timothy McCajor Hall, Rosie Read
     (Eds.)
     Changes in the Heart of Europe
     Recent Ethnographies of Czechs, Slovaks,
     Roma, and Sorbs
     With an afterword by Zdeněk Salzmann
     ISBN 3-89821-606-3

24   Christian Autengruber
     Die politischen Parteien in Bulgarien
     und Rumänien
     Eine vergleichende Analyse seit Beginn der
     90er Jahre
     Mit einem Vorwort von Dorothée de Nève
     ISBN 3-89821-476-1

25   Annette Freyberg-Inan with Radu
     Cristescu
     The Ghosts in Our Classrooms, or:
     John Dewey Meets Ceauşescu
     The Promise and the Failures of Civic
     Education in Romania
     ISBN 3-89821-416-8

26   John B. Dunlop
     The 2002 Dubrovka and 2004 Beslan
     Hostage Crises
     A Critique of Russian Counter-Terrorism
     With a foreword by Donald N. Jensen
     ISBN 3-89821-608-X

27   Peter Koller
     Das touristische Potenzial von
     Kam''janec–Podil's'kyj
     Eine fremdenverkehrsgeographische
     Untersuchung der Zukunftsperspektiven und
     Maßnahmenplanung zur
     Destinationsentwicklung des „ukrainischen
     Rothenburg"
     Mit einem Vorwort von Kristiane Klemm
     ISBN 3-89821-640-3

28   Françoise Daucé, Elisabeth Sieca-
     Kozlowski (Eds.)
     Dedovshchina in the Post-Soviet
     Military
     Hazing of Russian Army Conscripts in a
     Comparative Perspective
     With a foreword by Dale Herspring
     ISBN 3-89821-616-0

29 Florian Strasser
    Zivilgesellschaftliche Einflüsse auf die
    Orange Revolution
    Die gewaltlose Massenbewegung und die
    ukrainische Wahlkrise 2004
    Mit einem Vorwort von Egbert Jahn
    ISBN 3-89821-648-9

30 Rebecca S. Katz
    The Georgian Regime Crisis of 2003-
    2004
    A Case Study in Post-Soviet Media
    Representation of Politics, Crime and
    Corruption
    ISBN 3-89821-413-3

31 Vladimir Kantor
    Willkür oder Freiheit
    Beiträge zur russischen Geschichtsphilosophie
    Ediert von Dagmar Herrmann sowie mit
    einem Vorwort versehen von Leonid Luks
    ISBN 3-89821-589-X

32 Laura A. Victoir
    The Russian Land Estate Today
    A Case Study of Cultural Politics in Post-
    Soviet Russia
    With a foreword by Priscilla Roosevelt
    ISBN 3-89821-426-5

33 Ivan Katchanovski
    Cleft Countries
    Regional Political Divisions and Cultures in
    Post-Soviet Ukraine and Moldova
    With a foreword by Francis Fukuyama
    ISBN 3-89821-558-X

34 Florian Mühlfried
    Postsowjetische Feiern
    Das Georgische Bankett im Wandel
    Mit einem Vorwort von Kevin Tuite
    ISBN 3-89821-601-2

35 Roger Griffin, Werner Loh, Andreas
    Umland (Eds.)
    Fascism Past and Present, West and
    East
    An International Debate on Concepts and
    Cases in the Comparative Study of the
    Extreme Right
    With an afterword by Walter Laqueur
    ISBN 3-89821-674-8

36 Sebastian Schlegel
    Der „Weiße Archipel"
    Sowjetische Atomstädte 1945-1991
    Mit einem Geleitwort von Thomas Bohn
    ISBN 3-89821-679-9

37 Vyacheslav Likhachev
    Political Anti-Semitism in Post-Soviet
    Russia
    Actors and Ideas in 1991-2003
    Edited and translated from Russian by Eugene
    Veklerov
    ISBN 3-89821-529-6

38 Josette Baer (Ed.)
    Preparing Liberty in Central Europe
    Political Texts from the Spring of Nations
    1848 to the Spring of Prague 1968
    With a foreword by Zdeněk V. David
    ISBN 3-89821-546-6

39 Михаил Лукьянов
    Российский консерватизм и
    реформа, 1907-1914
    С предисловием Марка Д. Стейнберга
    ISBN 3-89821-503-2

40 Nicola Melloni
    Market Without Economy
    The 1998 Russian Financial Crisis
    With a foreword by Eiji Furukawa
    ISBN 3-89821-407-9

41 Dmitrij Chmelnizki
    Die Architektur Stalins
    Bd. 1: Studien zu Ideologie und Stil
    Bd. 2: Bilddokumentation
    Mit einem Vorwort von Bruno Flierl
    ISBN 3-89821-515-6

42 Katja Yafimava
    Post-Soviet Russian-Belarussian
    Relationships
    The Role of Gas Transit Pipelines
    With a foreword by Jonathan P. Stern
    ISBN 3-89821-655-1

43 Boris Chavkin
    Verflechtungen der deutschen und
    russischen Zeitgeschichte
    Aufsätze und Archivfunde zu den
    Beziehungen Deutschlands und der
    Sowjetunion von 1917 bis 1991
    Ediert von Markus Edlinger sowie mit einem
    Vorwort versehen von Leonid Luks
    ISBN 3-89821-756-6

44 *Anastasija Grynenko in
    Zusammenarbeit mit Claudia Dathe*
    Die Terminologie des Gerichtswesens
    der Ukraine und Deutschlands im
    Vergleich
    Eine übersetzungswissenschaftliche Analyse
    juristischer Fachbegriffe im Deutschen,
    Ukrainischen und Russischen
    Mit einem Vorwort von Ulrich Hartmann
    ISBN 3-89821-691-8

45 *Anton Burkov*
    The Impact of the European
    Convention on Human Rights on
    Russian Law
    Legislation and Application in 1996-2006
    With a foreword by Françoise Hampson
    ISBN 978-3-89821-639-5

46 *Stina Torjesen, Indra Overland (Eds.)*
    International Election Observers in
    Post-Soviet Azerbaijan
    Geopolitical Pawns or Agents of Change?
    ISBN 978-3-89821-743-9

47 *Taras Kuzio*
    Ukraine – Crimea – Russia
    Triangle of Conflict
    ISBN 978-3-89821-761-3

48 *Claudia Šabić*
    "Ich erinnere mich nicht, aber L'viv!"
    Zur Funktion kultureller Faktoren für die
    Institutionalisierung und Entwicklung einer
    ukrainischen Region
    Mit einem Vorwort von Melanie Tatur
    ISBN 978-3-89821-752-1

49 *Marlies Bilz*
    Tatarstan in der Transformation
    Nationaler Diskurs und Politische Praxis
    1988-1994
    Mit einem Vorwort von Frank Golczewski
    ISBN 978-3-89821-722-4

50 *Марлен Ларюэль (ред.)*
    Современные интерпретации
    русского национализма
    ISBN 978-3-89821-795-8

51 *Sonja Schüler*
    Die ethnische Dimension der Armut
    Roma im postsozialistischen Rumänien
    Mit einem Vorwort von Anton Sterbling
    ISBN 978-3-89821-776-7

52 *Галина Кожевникова*
    Радикальный национализм в России
    и противодействие ему
    Сборник докладов Центра «Сова» за 2004-
    2007 гг.
    С предисловием Александра Верховского
    ISBN 978-3-89821-721-7

53 *Галина Кожевникова и Владимир
    Прибыловский*
    Российская власть в биографиях I
    Высшие должностные лица РФ в 2004 г.
    ISBN 978-3-89821-796-5

54 *Галина Кожевникова и Владимир
    Прибыловский*
    Российская власть в биографиях II
    Члены Правительства РФ в 2004 г.
    ISBN 978-3-89821-797-2

55 *Галина Кожевникова и Владимир
    Прибыловский*
    Российская власть в биографиях III
    Руководители федеральных служб и
    агентств РФ в 2004 г.
    ISBN 978-3-89821-798-9

56 *Ileana Petroniu*
    Privatisierung in
    Transformationsökonomien
    Determinanten der Restrukturierungs-
    Bereitschaft am Beispiel Polens, Rumäniens
    und der Ukraine
    Mit einem Vorwort von Rainer W. Schäfer
    ISBN 978-3-89821-790-3

57 *Christian Wipperfürth*
    Russland und seine GUS-Nachbarn
    Hintergründe, aktuelle Entwicklungen und
    Konflikte in einer ressourcenreichen Region
    ISBN 978-3-89821-801-6

58 *Togzhan Kassenova*
    From Antagonism to Partnership
    The Uneasy Path of the U.S.-Russian
    Cooperative Threat Reduction
    With a foreword by Christoph Bluth
    ISBN 978-3-89821-707-1

59 *Alexander Höllwerth*
    Das sakrale eurasische Imperium des
    Aleksandr Dugin
    Eine Diskursanalyse zum postsowjetischen
    russischen Rechtsextremismus
    Mit einem Vorwort von Dirk Uffelmann
    ISBN 978-3-89821-813-7

60   Олег Рябов
     «Россия-Матушка»
     Национализм, гендер и война в России XX века
     С предисловием Елены Гощило
     ISBN 978-3-89821-487-2

61   *Ivan Maistrenko*
     Borot'bism
     A Chapter in the History of the Ukrainian Revolution
     With a new introduction by Chris Ford
     Translated by George S. N. Luckyj with the assistance of Ivan L. Rudnytsky
     ISBN 978-3-89821-697-5

62   *Maryna Romanets*
     Anamorphosic Texts and Reconfigured Visions
     Improvised Traditions in Contemporary Ukrainian and Irish Literature
     ISBN 978-3-89821-576-3

63   *Paul D'Anieri and Taras Kuzio (Eds.)*
     Aspects of the Orange Revolution I
     Democratization and Elections in Post-Communist Ukraine
     ISBN 978-3-89821-698-2

64   *Bohdan Harasymiw in collaboration with Oleh S. Ilnytzkyj (Eds.)*
     Aspects of the Orange Revolution II
     Information and Manipulation Strategies in the 2004 Ukrainian Presidential Elections
     ISBN 978-3-89821-699-9

65   *Ingmar Bredies, Andreas Umland and Valentin Yakushik (Eds.)*
     Aspects of the Orange Revolution III
     The Context and Dynamics of the 2004 Ukrainian Presidential Elections
     ISBN 978-3-89821-803-0

66   *Ingmar Bredies, Andreas Umland and Valentin Yakushik (Eds.)*
     Aspects of the Orange Revolution IV
     Foreign Assistance and Civic Action in the 2004 Ukrainian Presidential Elections
     ISBN 978-3-89821-808-5

67   *Ingmar Bredies, Andreas Umland and Valentin Yakushik (Eds.)*
     Aspects of the Orange Revolution V
     Institutional Observation Reports on the 2004 Ukrainian Presidential Elections
     ISBN 978-3-89821-809-2

68   *Taras Kuzio (Ed.)*
     Aspects of the Orange Revolution VI
     Post-Communist Democratic Revolutions in Comparative Perspective
     ISBN 978-3-89821-820-7

69   *Tim Bohse*
     Autoritarismus statt Selbstverwaltung
     Die Transformation der kommunalen Politik in der Stadt Kaliningrad 1990-2005
     Mit einem Geleitwort von Stefan Troebst
     ISBN 978-3-89821-782-8

70   *David Rupp*
     Die Rußländische Föderation und die russischsprachige Minderheit in Lettland
     Eine Fallstudie zur Anwaltspolitik Moskaus gegenüber den russophonen Minderheiten im „Nahen Ausland" von 1991 bis 2002
     Mit einem Vorwort von Helmut Wagner
     ISBN 978-3-89821-778-1

71   *Taras Kuzio*
     Theoretical and Comparative Perspectives on Nationalism
     New Directions in Cross-Cultural and Post-Communist Studies
     With a foreword by Paul Robert Magocsi
     ISBN 978-3-89821-815-3

72   *Christine Teichmann*
     Die Hochschultransformation im heutigen Osteuropa
     Kontinuität und Wandel bei der Entwicklung des postkommunistischen Universitätswesens
     Mit einem Vorwort von Oskar Anweiler
     ISBN 978-3-89821-842-9

73   *Julia Kusznir*
     Der politische Einfluss von Wirtschaftseliten in russischen Regionen
     Eine Analyse am Beispiel der Erdöl- und Erdgasindustrie, 1992-2005
     Mit einem Vorwort von Wolfgang Eichwede
     ISBN 978-3-89821-821-4

74   *Alena Vysotskaya*
     Russland, Belarus und die EU-Osterweiterung
     Zur Minderheitenfrage und zum Problem der Freizügigkeit des Personenverkehrs
     Mit einem Vorwort von Katlijn Malfliet
     ISBN 978-3-89821-822-1

75 Heiko Pleines (Hrsg.)
    Corporate Governance in post-
    sozialistischen Volkswirtschaften
    ISBN 978-3-89821-766-8

76 Stefan Ihrig
    Wer sind die Moldawier?
    Rumänismus versus Moldowanismus in
    Historiographie und Schulbüchern der
    Republik Moldova, 1991-2006
    Mit einem Vorwort von Holm Sundhaussen
    ISBN 978-3-89821-466-7

77 Galina Kozhevnikova in collaboration
    with Alexander Verkhovsky and
    Eugene Veklerov
    Ultra-Nationalism and Hate Crimes in
    Contemporary Russia
    The 2004-2006 Annual Reports of Moscow's
    SOVA Center
    With a foreword by Stephen D. Shenfield
    ISBN 978-3-89821-868-9

78 Florian Küchler
    The Role of the European Union in
    Moldova's Transnistria Conflict
    With a foreword by Christopher Hill
    ISBN 978-3-89821-850-4

79 Bernd Rechel
    The Long Way Back to Europe
    Minority Protection in Bulgaria
    With a foreword by Richard Crampton
    ISBN 978-3-89821-863-4

80 Peter W. Rodgers
    Nation, Region and History in Post-
    Communist Transitions
    Identity Politics in Ukraine, 1991-2006
    With a foreword by Vera Tolz
    ISBN 978-3-89821-903-7

81 Stephanie Solywoda
    The Life and Work of
    Semen L. Frank
    A Study of Russian Religious Philosophy
    With a foreword by Philip Walters
    ISBN 978-3-89821-457-5

82 Vera Sokolova
    Cultural Politics of Ethnicity
    Discourses on Roma in Communist
    Czechoslovakia
    ISBN 978-3-89821-864-1

83 Natalya Shevchik Ketenci
    Kazakhstani Enterprises in Transition
    The Role of Historical Regional Development
    in Kazakhstan's Post-Soviet Economic
    Transformation
    ISBN 978-3-89821-831-3

84 Martin Malek, Anna Schor-
    Tschudnowskaja (Hrsg.)
    Europa im Tschetschenienkrieg
    Zwischen politischer Ohnmacht und
    Gleichgültigkeit
    Mit einem Vorwort von Lipchan Basajewa
    ISBN 978-3-89821-676-0

85 Stefan Meister
    Das postsowjetische Universitätswesen
    zwischen nationalem und
    internationalem Wandel
    Die Entwicklung der regionalen Hochschule
    in Russland als Gradmesser der
    Systemtransformation
    Mit einem Vorwort von Joan DeBardeleben
    ISBN 978-3-89821-891-7

86 Konstantin Sheiko in collaboration
    with Stephen Brown
    Nationalist Imaginings of the
    Russian Past
    Anatolii Fomenko and the Rise of Alternative
    History in Post-Communist Russia
    With a foreword by Donald Ostrowski
    ISBN 978-3-89821-915-0

87 Sabine Jenni
    Wie stark ist das „Einige Russland"?
    Zur Parteibindung der Eliten und zum
    Wahlerfolg der Machtpartei
    im Dezember 2007
    Mit einem Vorwort von Klaus Armingeon
    ISBN 978-3-89821-961-7

88 Thomas Borén
    Meeting-Places of Transformation
    Urban Identity, Spatial Representations and
    Local Politics in Post-Soviet St Petersburg
    ISBN 978-3-89821-739-2

89 Aygul Ashirova
    Stalinismus und Stalin-Kult in
    Zentralasien
    Turkmenistan 1924-1953
    Mit einem Vorwort von Leonid Luks
    ISBN 978-3-89821-987-7

90	*Leonid Luks* Freiheit oder imperiale Größe? Essays zu einem russischen Dilemma ISBN 978-3-8382-0011-8	97	*Kamran Musayev* Die postsowjetische Transformation im Baltikum und Südkaukasus Eine vergleichende Untersuchung der politischen Entwicklung Lettlands und
91	*Christopher Gilley* The 'Change of Signposts' in the Ukrainian Emigration A Contribution to the History of Sovietophilism in the 1920s With a foreword by Frank Golczewski ISBN 978-3-89821-965-5		Aserbaidschans 1985-2009 Mit einem Vorwort von Leonid Luks Ediert von Sandro Henschel ISBN 978-3-8382-0103-0
		98	*Tatiana Zhurzhenko* Borderlands into Bordered Lands Geopolitics of Identity in Post-Soviet Ukraine With a foreword by Dieter Segert ISBN 978-3-8382-0042-2
92	*Philipp Casula, Jeronim Perovic (Eds.)* Identities and Politics During the Putin Presidency The Discursive Foundations of Russia's Stability With a foreword by Heiko Haumann ISBN 978-3-8382-0015-6	99	*Кирилл Галушко, Лидия Смола (ред.)* Пределы падения – варианты украинского будущего Аналитико-прогностические исследования ISBN 978-3-8382-0148-1
93	*Marcel Viëtor* Europa und die Frage nach seinen Grenzen im Osten Zur Konstruktion ‚europäischer Identität' in Geschichte und Gegenwart Mit einem Vorwort von Albrecht Lehmann ISBN 978-3-8382-0045-3	100	*Michael Minkenberg (ed.)* Historical Legacies and the Radical Right in Post-Cold War Central and Eastern Europe With an afterword by Sabrina P. Ramet ISBN 978-3-8382-0124-5
94	*Ben Hellman, Andrei Rogachevskii* Filming the Unfilmable Casper Wrede's 'One Day in the Life of Ivan Denisovich' Second, Revised and Expanded Edition ISBN 978-3-8382-0044-6	101	*David-Emil Wickström* Rocking St. Petersburg Transcultural Flows and Identity Politics in the St. Petersburg Popular Music Scene With a foreword by Yngvar B. Steinholt Second, Revised and Expanded Edition ISBN 978-3-8382-0100-9
95	*Eva Fuchslocher* Vaterland, Sprache, Glaube Orthodoxie und Nationenbildung am Beispiel Georgiens Mit einem Vorwort von Christina von Braun ISBN 978-3-89821-884-9	102	*Eva Zabka* Eine neue „Zeit der Wirren"? Der spät- und postsowjetische Systemwandel 1985-2000 im Spiegel russischer gesellschaftspolitischer Diskurse Mit einem Vorwort von Margareta Mommsen ISBN 978-3-8382-0161-0
96	*Vladimir Kantor* Das Westlertum und der Weg Russlands Zur Entwicklung der russischen Literatur und Philosophie Ediert von Dagmar Herrmann Mit einem Beitrag von Nikolaus Lobkowicz ISBN 978-3-8382-0102-3	103	*Ulrike Ziemer* Ethnic Belonging, Gender and Cultural Practices Youth Identitites in Contemporary Russia With a foreword by Anoop Nayak ISBN 978-3-8382-0152-8

104 Ksenia Chepikova
     ‚Einiges Russland' - eine zweite
     KPdSU?
     Aspekte der Identitätskonstruktion einer
     postsowjetischen „Partei der Macht"
     Mit einem Vorwort von Torsten Oppelland
     ISBN 978-3-8382-0311-9

105 Леонид Люкс
     Западничество или евразийство?
     Демократия или идеократия?
     Сборник статей об исторических дилеммах
     России
     С предисловием Владимира Кантора
     ISBN 978-3-8382-0211-2

106 Anna Dost
     Das russische Verfassungsrecht auf dem
     Weg zum Föderalismus und zurück
     Zum Konflikt von Rechtsnormen und
     -wirklichkeit in der Russländischen Föderation
     von 1991 bis 2009
     Mit einem Vorwort von Alexander Blankenagel
     ISBN 978-3-8382-0292-1

107 Philipp Herzog
     Sozialistische Völkerfreundschaft,
     nationaler Widerstand oder harmloser
     Zeitvertreib?
     Zur politischen Funktion der Volkskunst
     im sowjetischen Estland
     Mit einem Vorwort von Andreas Kappeler
     ISBN 978-3-8382-0216-7

108 Marlène Laruelle (ed.)
     Russian Nationalism, Foreign Policy,
     and Identity Debates in Putin's Russia
     New Ideological Patterns after the Orange
     Revolution
     ISBN 978-3-8382-0325-6

109 Michail Logvinov
     Russlands Kampf gegen den
     internationalen Terrorismus
     Eine kritische Bestandsaufnahme des
     Bekämpfungsansatzes
     Mit einem Geleitwort von
     Hans-Henning Schröder
     und einem Vorwort von Eckhard Jesse
     ISBN 978-3-8382-0329-4

110 John B. Dunlop
     The Moscow Bombings
     of September 1999
     Examinations of Russian Terrorist Attacks
     at the Onset of Vladimir Putin's Rule
     Second, Revised and Expanded Edition
     ISBN 978-3-8382-0388-1

111 Андрей А. Ковалёв
     Свидетельство из-за кулис
     российской политики I
     Можно ли делать добро из зла?
     (Воспоминания и размышления о
     последних советских и первых
     послесоветских годах)
     With a foreword by Peter Reddaway
     ISBN 978-3-8382-0302-7

112 Андрей А. Ковалёв
     Свидетельство из-за кулис
     российской политики II
     Угроза для себя и окружающих
     (Наблюдения и предостережения
     относительно происходящего после 2000 г.)
     ISBN 978-3-8382-0303-4

113 Bernd Kappenberg
     Zeichen setzen für Europa
     Der Gebrauch europäischer lateinischer
     Sonderzeichen in der deutschen Öffentlichkeit
     Mit einem Vorwort von Peter Schlobinski
     ISBN 978-3-89821-749-1

114 Ivo Mijnssen
     The Quest for an Ideal Youth in
     Putin's Russia I
     Back to Our Future! History, Modernity, and
     Patriotism according to *Nashi*, 2005-2013
     With a foreword by Jeronim Perović
     Second, Revised and Expanded Edition
     ISBN 978-3-8382-0368-3

115 Jussi Lassila
     The Quest for an Ideal Youth in
     Putin's Russia II
     The Search for Distinctive Conformism in the
     Political Communication of *Nashi*, 2005-2009
     With a foreword by Kirill Postoutenko
     Second, Revised and Expanded Edition
     ISBN 978-3-8382-0415-4

116 Valerio Trabandt
     Neue Nachbarn, gute Nachbarschaft?
     Die EU als internationaler Akteur am Beispiel
     ihrer Demokratieförderung in Belarus und der
     Ukraine 2004-2009
     Mit einem Vorwort von Jutta Joachim
     ISBN 978-3-8382-0437-6

117 Fabian Pfeiffer
Estlands Außen- und Sicherheitspolitik I
Der estnische Atlantizismus nach der
wiedererlangten Unabhängigkeit 1991-2004
Mit einem Vorwort von Helmut Hubel
ISBN 978-3-8382-0127-6

118 Jana Podßuweit
Estlands Außen- und Sicherheitspolitik II
Handlungsoptionen eines Kleinstaates im
Rahmen seiner EU-Mitgliedschaft (2004-2008)
Mit einem Vorwort von Helmut Hubel
ISBN 978-3-8382-0440-6

119 Karin Pointner
Estlands Außen- und Sicherheitspolitik III
Eine gedächtnispolitische Analyse estnischer
Entwicklungskooperation 2006-2010
Mit einem Vorwort von Karin Liebhart
ISBN 978-3-8382-0435-2

120 Ruslana Vovk
Die Offenheit der ukrainischen
Verfassung für das Völkerrecht und
die europäische Integration
Mit einem Vorwort von Alexander Blankenagel
ISBN 978-3-8382-0481-9

121 Mykhaylo Banakh
Die Relevanz der Zivilgesellschaft
bei den postkommunistischen
Transformationsprozessen in mittel-
und osteuropäischen Ländern
Das Beispiel der spät- und postsowjetischen
Ukraine 1986-2009
Mit einem Vorwort von Gerhard Simon
ISBN 978-3-8382-0499-4

122 Michael Moser
Language Policy and the Discourse on
Languages in Ukraine under President
Viktor Yanukovych (25 February
2010–28 October 2012)
ISBN 978-3-8382-0497-0 (Paperback edition)
ISBN 978-3-8382-0507-6 (Hardcover edition)

123 Nicole Krome
Russischer Netzwerkkapitalismus
Restrukturierungsprozesse in der
Russischen Föderation am Beispiel des
Luftfahrtunternehmens "Aviastar"
Mit einem Vorwort von Petra Stykow
ISBN 978-3-8382-0534-2

124 David R. Marples
'Our Glorious Past'
Lukashenka's Belarus and
the Great Patriotic War
ISBN 978-3-8382-0574-8 (Paperback edition)
ISBN 978-3-8382-0675-2 (Hardcover edition)

125 Ulf Walther
Russlands "neuer Adel"
Die Macht des Geheimdienstes von
Gorbatschow bis Putin
Mit einem Vorwort von Hans-Georg Wieck
ISBN 978-3-8382-0584-7

126 Simon Geissbühler (Hrsg.)
Kiew – Revolution 3.0
Der Euromaidan 2013/14 und die
Zukunftsperspektiven der Ukraine
ISBN 978-3-8382-0581-6 (Paperback edition)
ISBN 978-3-8382-0681-3 (Hardcover edition)

127 Andrey Makarychev
Russia and the EU
in a Multipolar World
Discourses, Identities, Norms
With a foreword by Klaus Segbers
ISBN 978-3-8382-0629-5

128 Roland Scharff
Kasachstan als postsowjetischer
Wohlfahrtsstaat
Die Transformation des sozialen
Schutzsystems
Mit einem Vorwort von Joachim Ahrens
ISBN 978-3-8382-0622-6

129 Katja Grupp
Bild Lücke Deutschland
Kaliningrader Studierende sprechen über
Deutschland
Mit einem Vorwort von Martin Schulz
ISBN 978-3-8382-0552-6

130 Konstantin Sheiko, Stephen Brown
History as Therapy
Alternative History and Nationalist
Imaginings in Russia, 1991-2014
ISBN 978-3-8382-0665-3

131 Elisa Kriza
Alexander Solzhenitsyn: Cold War
Icon, Gulag Author, Russian
Nationalist?
A Study of the Western Reception of his
Literary Writings, Historical Interpretations,
and Political Ideas
With a foreword by Andrei Rogatchevski
ISBN 978-3-8382-0589-2 (Paperback edition)
ISBN 978-3-8382-0690-5 (Hardcover edition)

132   Serghei Golunov
       The Elephant in the Room
       Corruption and Cheating in Russian
       Universities
       ISBN 978-3-8382-0570-0

133   Manja Hussner, Rainer Arnold (Hgg.)
       Verfassungsgerichtsbarkeit in
       Zentralasien I
       Sammlung von Verfassungstexten
       ISBN 978-3-8382-0595-3

134   Nikolay Mitrokhin
       Die "Russische Partei"
       Die Bewegung der russischen Nationalisten in
       der UdSSR 1953-1985
       Aus dem Russischen übertragen von einem
       Übersetzerteam unter der Leitung von Larisa Schippel
       ISBN 978-3-8382-0024-8

135   Manja Hussner, Rainer Arnold (Hgg.)
       Verfassungsgerichtsbarkeit in
       Zentralasien II
       Sammlung von Verfassungstexten
       ISBN 978-3-8382-0597-7

136   Manfred Zeller
       Das sowjetische Fieber
       Fußballfans im poststalinistischen
       Vielvölkerreich
       Mit einem Vorwort von Nikolaus Katzer
       ISBN 978-3-8382-0757-5

137   Kristin Schreiter
       Stellung und Entwicklungspotential
       zivilgesellschaftlicher Gruppen in
       Russland
       Menschenrechtsorganisationen im Vergleich
       ISBN 978-3-8382-0673-8

138   David R. Marples, Frederick V. Mills
       (eds.)
       Ukraine's Euromaidan
       Analyses of a Civil Revolution
       ISBN 978-3-8382-0660-8

139   Bernd Kappenberg
       Setting Signs for Europe
       Why Diacritics Matter for
       European Integration
       With a foreword by Peter Schlobinski
       ISBN 978-3-8382-0663-9

140   René Lenz
       Internationalisierung, Kooperation
       und Transfer
       Externe bildungspolitische Akteure in der
       Russischen Föderation
       Mit einem Vorwort von Frank Ettrich
       ISBN 978-3-8382-0751-3

141   Juri Plusnin, Yana Zausaeva, Natalia
       Zhidkevich, Artemy Pozanenko
       Wandering Workers
       Mores, Behavior, Way of Life, and Political
       Status of Domestic Russian Labor Migrants
       Translated by Julia Kazantseva
       ISBN 978-3-8382-0653-0

142   David J. Smith (eds.)
       Latvia – A Work in Progress?
       100 Years of State- and Nation-Building
       ISBN 978-3-8382-0648-6

143   Инна Чувычкина (ред.)
       Экспортные нефте- и газопроводы
       на постсоветском пространстве
       Анализ трубопроводной политики в свете
       теории международных отношений
       ISBN 978-3-8382-0822-0

144   Johann Zajaczkowski
       Russland – eine pragmatische
       Großmacht?
       Eine rollentheoretische Untersuchung
       russischer Außenpolitik am Beispiel der
       Zusammenarbeit mit den USA nach 9/11 und
       des Georgienkrieges von 2008
       Mit einem Vorwort von Siegfried Schieder
       ISBN 978-3-8382-0837-4

145   Boris Popivanov
       Changing Images of the Left in
       Bulgaria
       The Challenge of Post-Communism in the
       Early 21st Century
       ISBN 978-3-8382-0667-2

146   Lenka Krátká
       A History of the Czechoslovak Ocean
       Shipping Company 1948-1989
       How a Small, Landlocked Country Ran
       Maritime Business During the Cold War
       ISBN 978-3-8382-0666-0

147   Alexander Sergunin
       Explaining Russian Foreign Policy
       Behavior
       Theory and Practice
       ISBN 978-3-8382-0752-0

148 Darya Malyutina
Migrant Friendships in
a Super-Diverse City
Russian-Speakers and their Social
Relationships in London in the 21st Century
With a foreword by Claire Dwyer
ISBN 978-3-8382-0652-3

149 Alexander Sergunin, Valery Konyshev
Russia in the Arctic
Hard or Soft Power?
ISBN 978-3-8382-0753-7

150 John J. Maresca
Helsinki Revisited
A Key U.S. Negotiator's Memoirs
on the Development of the CSCE into the OSCE
With a foreword by Hafiz Pashayev
ISBN 978-3-8382-0852-7

151 Jardar Østbø
The New Third Rome
Readings of a Russian Nationalist Myth
With a foreword by Pål Kolstø
ISBN 978-3-8382-0870-1

152 Simon Kordonsky
Socio-Economic Foundations of the
Russian Post-Soviet Regime
The Resource-Based Economy and Estate-Based Social Structure of Contemporary Russia
With a foreword by Svetlana Barsukova
ISBN 978-3-8382-0775-9

153 Duncan Leitch
Assisting Reform in Post-Communist
Ukraine 2000–2012
The Illusions of Donors and the Disillusion of Beneficiaries
With a foreword by Kataryna Wolczuk
ISBN 978-3-8382-0844-2

154 Abel Polese
Limits of a Post-Soviet State
How Informality Replaces, Renegotiates, and Reshapes Governance in Contemporary Ukraine
With a foreword by Colin Williams
ISBN 978-3-8382-0845-9

155 Mikhail Suslov (ed.)
Digital Orthodoxy in the Post-Soviet World
The Russian Orthodox Church and Web 2.0
With a foreword by Father Cyril Hovorun
ISBN 978-3-8382-0871-8

156 Leonid Luks
Zwei „Sonderwege"? Russisch-deutsche Parallelen und Kontraste (1917-2014)
Vergleichende Essays
ISBN 978-3-8382-0823-7

157 Vladimir V. Karacharovskiy, Ovsey I. Shkaratan, Gordey A. Yastrebov
Towards a New Russian Work Culture
Can Western Companies and Expatriates Change Russian Society?
With a foreword by Elena N. Danilova
Translated by Julia Kazantseva
ISBN 978-3-8382-0902-9

158 Edmund Griffiths
Aleksandr Prokhanov and Post-Soviet Esotericism
ISBN 978-3-8382-0903-6

159 Timm Beichelt, Susann Worschech (eds.)
Transnational Ukraine?
Networks and Ties that Influence(d) Contemporary Ukraine
ISBN 978-3-8382-0944-9

160 Mieste Hotopp-Riecke
Die Tataren der Krim zwischen Assimilation und Selbstbehauptung
Der Aufbau des krimtatarischen Bildungswesens nach Deportation und Heimkehr (1990-2005)
Mit einem Vorwort von Swetlana Czerwonnaja
ISBN 978-3-89821-940-2

161 Olga Bertelsen (ed.)
Revolution and War in Contemporary Ukraine
The Challenge of Change
ISBN 978-3-8382-1016-2

162 Natalya Ryabinska
Ukraine's Post-Communist Mass Media
Between Capture and Commercialization
With a foreword by Marta Dyczok
ISBN 978-3-8382-1011-7

163 Alexandra Cotofana,
 James M. Nyce (eds.)
 Religion and Magic in Socialist and
 Post-Socialist Contexts I
 Historic and Ethnographic Case Studies of
 Orthodoxy, Heterodoxy, and Alternative
 Spirituality
 With a foreword by Patrick L. Michelson
 ISBN 978-3-8382-0989-0

164 Nozima Akhrarkhodjaeva
 The Instrumentalisation of Mass
 Media in Electoral Authoritarian
 Regimes
 Evidence from Russia's Presidential Election
 Campaigns of 2000 and 2008
 ISBN 978-3-8382-1013-1

165 Yulia Krasheninnikova
 Informal Healthcare in Contemporary
 Russia
 Sociographic Essays on the Post-Soviet
 Infrastructure for Alternative Healing
 Practices
 ISBN 978-3-8382-0970-8

166 Peter Kaiser
 Das Schachbrett der Macht
 Die Handlungsspielräume eines sowjetischen
 Funktionärs unter Stalin am Beispiel des
 Generalsekretärs des Komsomol
 Aleksandr Kosarev (1929-1938)
 Mit einem Vorwort von Dietmar Neutatz
 ISBN 978-3-8382-1052-0

167 Oksana Kim
 The Effects and Implications of
 Kazakhstan's Adoption of
 International Financial Reporting
 Standards
 A Resource Dependence Perspective
 With a foreword by Svetlana Vlady
 ISBN 978-3-8382-0987-6

168 Anna Sanina
 Patriotic Education in
 Contemporary Russia
 Sociological Studies in the Making of the
 Post-Soviet Citizen
 ISBN 978-3-8382-0993-7

ibidem.eu